Heaven on Earth

HEAVEN ON EARTH

A Handbook for Parents of Young Children

Sharifa Oppenheimer

Photography by Stephanie Gross

SteinerBooks

© Sharifa Oppenheimer 2006

Published by
SteinerBooks
610 Main Street
Great Barrington, MA 01230
www.steinerbooks.org

All photos for the book were taken of children attending The Rose Garden, the author's Waldorf-based Early Chilhood Home-Program, in Virginia's Blue Ridge Mountains.

COVER PHOTO: Rob Gendler
BOOK DESIGN: William (Jens) Jensen

LIBRARY OF CONGRESS CATALOGING-IN-PUBLICATION DATA

Oppenheimer, Sharifa.
   Heaven on earth : a handbook for parents of young children / Sharifa Oppenheimer ; photography by Stephanie Gross.
      p. cm.
   Includes bibliographical references.
   ISBN 0-88010-566-6 (alk. paper)
   1. Child rearing. 2. Parenting. 3. Child development. 4. Experiential learning. 5. Early childhood education—Parent participation. I. Title.

HQ769.O643 2006
649'.5—DC22

2006010737

ISBN-13: 978-0-88010-566-8

10   9   8   7   6   5   4   3

For Loren, Ethan and Noah, my children.

And for the children of the world.

Our children are, in the words of Kahlil Gibran, the gift of Life's longing for Itself. They run toward Life, arms open, and Life loves Itself through their small bodies. Pressing themselves into the sand, sifting dirt, watching an inchworm measure a branch, reaching toward the black cat, who evades, then looks at them through inscrutable green eyes... it is their biological imperative to reach toward Life, and we, their caregivers, must structure the way in which Life reaches back, the way they are touched in return.

They need to be touched by grass, flowers, sunshine, birdsong. They need a pile of dirt, and earthworms, clay for mud pies and dirt balls for target practice. They need sticks and bare feet, stubbed toes, too. They need songs, stories, paints, costumes. And games that go on without end.

These children are Life reaching out to discover Itself. What they touch must be *vibrantly* alive, that in growing they may learn to respect, to nurture, to cherish and protect. This is our task; it is urgent they thrive.

They are Hope itself, here, now, forever.

CONTENTS

ACKNOWLEDGEMENTS

I WANT TO BEGIN by thanking my superb family for all the delight, challenge and fun, for the laughter and tears we have shared through a lifetime. For the threads of our lives, woven into this basket of Love. I also want to thank the many families I have worked with throughout the years. It is because of the parents' generosity in giving me, day after day, their fine children, that this book can be. I would like to recognize with gratitude my colleagues in Waldorf Education. It is the dedication, inspiration and hard work of these excellent friends that you the reader, find here. We have been explorers together; I have simply chronicled the journey.

Now, thanks to very particular people:

To Diane Nelson, for saying "Go for it!" and opening the door.

To Sam and Cyndy Caughron, for the labor of love, in shaping and managing Open Hands.

To all the many friends and donors who, through Open Hands, made the writing possible.

To Jack Hutchinson, for tolerating and educating my technical ignorance.

To Eve Supica for honing my fledgling computer skills, for always being there, no matter how rudimentary the question.

To Art Bulger and Sarah Tremaine, for the great and good gift of an entire summer!

To Ralph Earle, for showing me the bare bones of editing.

To Sue Lim, for help with research.

To the Charlottesville Waldorf School and Rose Garden families who read the manuscript and gave essential feedback.

To the Waldorf Early Childhood Association of North America (WECAN) for help with appendix and bibliographic information.

To Alyssa Bonilla, for being the bridge to SteinerBooks.

To Gene Gollogly, my publisher, for seeing the potential in a seed.

To the staff of SteinerBooks, for bringing this seed to fruition.

To Sarah Gallogly, my editor, for pruning, with a subtle and meticulous hand, that the fruit should be of the finest.

To Stephanie Gross, my photographer, for inspired vision and the photographic skill to embody this vision.

To Dr. Ed Murphy, University of Virginia Astronomy Department, for sleuth work into photos of the universe.

To Rob Gendler for his galaxy image on the cover.

To William (Jens) Jensen for his eye and for his elegance and simplicity of design.

Finally, and always, to The Great Mystery, to the amazing flow of magic, the miracles large and small, that made this book, my life and all Life possible.

How to Use This Book

THIS BOOK IS designed as a springboard for your own creativity. It is
not a rule book for parenting, rather an inspiration and a model. The
margins are wide. There you will find salient points from the text, pulled
out for easy reference. I made it this way with you, busy parents, in mind.
Some evening, when the baby is crying and the five-year-old won't put on her
pajamas, you'll think, "What did that book say about bedtime?" It's easier
and quicker to find what you are looking for in the margin. You will also
find recipes, ideas, tips and secrets in the margins. The margins are yours, so
add your own thoughts, too.

In the Chapter Notes, I have given you specific information about various books, resources and ideas that are particular to the subject of each
chapter. In the Appendix, you will find a general list of resources including
ordering information. And in the Bibliography, there is a beginning reading
list for parents.

One of the fundamental premises of this book is that our brains function
in such a way that learning takes place through sensory experience, through
activity. This remains true throughout our lifetime. Here is an experiment
you can try if you like; it is something you can *do*, to "lock in" your own
learning process. Make your learning "interactive" by investing in a blank
book, a journal. Get something as simple as a spiral notebook, or a beautiful
hardbound one, if you prefer. Divide it into nine sections, to correlate to the
nine chapters in this book.

Let's look, now, chapter by chapter, at the interwoven pattern we can create together, between your book and mine.

Chapter One, "How Our Young Children Learn," gives a sketch of the
biology of learning. Recent brain research has opened many windows of
understanding for us. This is infinitely fascinating to me—perhaps to you,
too. You will also discover the dire effect the media has on learning—a critical understanding that will empower your decision to turn off the TV and

play together as a family. You may decide to include in your journal a "travel log" of your family's journey from media-land to the world of the creative imagination. If the science of this becomes too tedious, you can skip to the following chapters. There you will be shown how to *participate in the science of learning*, with your child by your side, in the kitchen, outdoors, or in the tub.

In Chapter Two, "The World of Rhythm," you will find a wealth of ideas about how to enhance your family's home life. In this chapter I encourage you to bring your daily and weekly activities into a rhythmic pattern. If you are keeping a journal, you may wish to note which daily tasks you want your child to share with you, both now and as your child grows. You can also draw your family's daily schedule, making it colorful and inviting, or create beautifully decorated charts of weekly meals and chores. Think about making a "master plan" of everyone's week, day by day, color-coding it for practicality as well as beauty. These are only a few ideas. Your journal can become the book *you* write about parenting!

In Chapter Three, "Celebrating Festivals Together," you will find not only thoughts about the importance of family festivals, but also how-to suggestions. We will discuss the necessity of "building" a festival through preparatory activities, songs, stories and festive foods. We then look, step by step, at the creation of an autumn, winter and spring festival, as well as a simple birthday party. You may want to keep in your journal a year-by-year description of the festivals your family celebrates. If you have ideas that are too advanced for your children's age, make a note for future reference. If you try a particular recipe and it's a winner, remind yourself that you want it to appear every year. Or record a special moment that you know you'll want to remember. We conclude the chapter with a look at the nature of time, the necessity of festive "nodal" points, and the imperative of presence in the moment.

In Chapter Four, "Indoor Play," you will find a discussion on the essential nature of creative play. We will look at the developmental schemata, or stages of play, from infancy through age six or seven, the age of grade-school readiness. We'll also discuss the critical necessity of "educating the senses," and find specific ways to approach this work. You may wish to note in your journal your own ideas to bring into your child's experience of "sense-education." You'll find step-by-step suggestions for creating an open-ended creative indoor playspace, as well as necessary furnishings, equipment and toys. Sketch your ideal playspace in your journal, and make your wish list of playthings. You'll also find a section on making toys yourself, using the "foolproof" doll pattern in the appendix. You will learn how to encourage your children in open-ended imaginative play, and will want to chronicle, for posterity, some of the remarkable games your children create. Worried about violent play? Look for a discussion and a long list of nonviolent yet exciting games of adventure and intrigue.

Chapter Five, "Outdoor Play," is filled with fun ideas for creating magical, challenging outdoor playspaces. We'll look at the elements of a balanced outdoor playspace, including grass, hills, sand and water. We'll discuss how and where to gather natural building materials that will offer years of fort-building potential for your child. You will learn how to create adult-built play structures from bamboo and saplings. Your journal is the perfect place to sketch fun playhouses you'd like to craft, or keep track of the natural building materials your child loves and where you have collected them. The conversation on the garden as playspace is full of gardening ideas as well as ways to bring child's play between the rows! It is always pleasurable to keep a garden journal: you can make notes of vegetative growth and your child's growing sense of the natural world as well. After exploring insect life, backyard wildlife, and enhancing the soundscape, we end with a discussion about bringing our family's life into the great outdoors, including art under the trees, backyard campouts and winter picnics.

Chapter Six, "The Wonder of Stories," is an adventure you'll want to record. We'll look at the developmental needs of infants through early grade-schoolers. You will be given developmental guidelines, as well as encouraged to try your hand at "homemade" stories. Your journal may not be adequate for all the stories you'll generate! Rhyming stories for the toddlers and tiny ones, nature stories for the threes and fours, fairy tales for the fives and sixes—and adventure stories will last for many years after that. You will be shown the powerful use of story to guide your child through the inevitable bumps and bruises life involves. If you tap into the ever-flowing fountain of stories that lives inside *you*, you'll need a separate story journal. Wouldn't that be a keepsake to hand down? We'll also look at books to enrich the imagination.

In Chapter Seven, you'll find artistic experiences that are rewarding, age-appropriate and soul-nourishing. There are step-by-step instructions for wet-on-wet watercolor painting, as well as many ideas for modeling materials. You will also find instructions for a craft to complement each of the festivals described in Chapter Three. Your journal is a good place to make notes of these festive crafts and to plan a sequence of experiences for your child. Wool, and its luscious touchability, is discussed at length. You'll learn how to felt your own wool, and find suggestions for projects that use the felt.

There are so many questions parents have brought to me over the years, and Chapter Eight, "Other Topics Parents Wonder About," addresses some of the most often asked. On subjects as diverse as clothing battles and nightmares, from choosing a child-care setting to talking about death, this chapter offers beginning answers to these difficult questions. Make a note of other questions in your journal, and see the back page for ways to contact me if you'd like to share your thoughts.

Chapter Nine takes all of the insight and ideas from the previous chapters and weaves it together into a fabric—your Family Culture. You can create a family culture that incorporates the wisdom, creativity and busy, purposeful activity, both indoors and out, described in this book. It is this warm, lively and loving atmosphere in your home that creates the foundation of your children's lives. It also creates the foundation of discipline. The meaning of the words "discipline" and "disciple" is the same: to follow with love. You can create a home environment that encourages your child to follow with love... but what happens when he doesn't? You will be shown, step by step, a simple, non-emotional method of steering him, again, in the right direction. Remember, the purpose of discipline is to call on the child's highest, to call forth his best self, not to make him suffer. Using the five-pointed star design, sketch in your journal the shining light of *your own family's culture*. What are the "legs" of your family's star—what rhythms have you established and how do you work and play together? What are the "arms"—how have you created your children's playspaces, and what artistic experiences do you offer? And what is the "head" of your star—how do you manage discipline? It may be helpful to draw the star now, at the outset of this adventure, to help envision what your dreams are. Then revisit this exercise occasionally, as your family grows.

My hope is that you will treasure this book for many years. I hope its pages will become soft with use and smudged from being in the kitchen with you, or out in the garden, or beside the tub. I hope it will urge you toward writing your own book, the chronicle of your family's journey together. These two books, yours and mine, will become woven together, and we will have created something remarkable. But my greatest hope is that you and your splendid family will have fashioned a thing of great beauty ... Heaven on Earth.

Chapter 1

HOW OUR YOUNG CHILDREN LEARN

*H*ow do our young children learn? This is a relatively new question in human history. For millennia we have simply lived the answer in Nature's exquisitely devised blueprint. Now, though, we have ever more subtle scientific instruments whereby we can measure learning, and also creative minds eager to begin the exploration of the vastly interconnected answer. An in-depth look at this ancient, elegant and forward-thrusting continuum of evolution—the human capacity to learn—is a life's work. We can thank the many scientists, educators, visionaries and others who have given their lives to understanding the workings of the human mind-body-environment connection. Slowly their light is seeping into our collective understanding.

To simplify their findings, we can say that young children learn

a) through sensory experience
b) through both energetic and fine movement, and
c) through imitating everything they see modeled in their environment.

If this is enough information for you, and you would like to get on with the business of what to do, here and now, with your preschool child, then turn to the following chapters. There you will learn

1. how to design environments that foster a broad, diverse sensory experience for your child,
2. how to encourage movement that is purposeful, finely focused and vigorous, and
3. how to provide Nature's imperative, adequate modeling, which works in tandem with the young child's natural gift of imitation.

How do children learn?

Through sensory experience

Through both large and small motor movement

Through imitating everything in the environment

Is this enough information for you?

Turn to the following chapters to learn:

How to create environments full of sensory experience

How to encourage healthy movement

How to optimally use the principle of imitation

If, on the other hand, you would like a thumbnail sketch of the biology of learning, then read on!

A Five-Minute Tour of the Developing Human Brain

The primary way young children gather information from their environment is through sensory input—touching, tasting, pushing, smelling, seeing and so forth. The way they make this information *meaningful* is largely through emotionally responsive movement, i.e., they move toward the cat if they have a positive emotion about it, or away if they have a negative one. Through *balanced sensory input and free exploratory movement,* young children make meaning of life—they learn. This principle remains true even for adults, because it becomes a foundation for abstract thought. The entire human body is a brilliantly tuned instrument designed to gather information at levels far more subtle than the conscious mind. This sensory information is gathered, a personal emotional connection is registered, and a responding movement occurs.[1] In recent years there has been an outpouring of new brain research, all of which supports the ancient notion that learning is a lifelong event involving the body, emotions and mind. The bulk of this book will deal with helping you, the parent, make choices and create environments that foster a broad sensory education as well as a skillful continuum of movement for your child.

Unlike most other creatures with whom we share this earth, we human beings are born "unfinished." We are given the astounding gift of our human brain, which remains "unfinished" even into old age. Our capacity to learn ever more complex systems is a product of the brain's ability to continually remodel itself until the day we die. A bear will never decide she's just not in the mood to hibernate this year, but a human being can decide nearly anything at all, and then proceed to create that reality.

But sensory experience and movement are not all children need in order to learn. Working in conjunction with these two essentials is a third: the child's innate ability to imitate, and the need for a human model. *It takes human modeling to create a human being.* In the New York Longitudinal Study, 133 people were followed from infancy to adulthood. Three factors in the early learning

---

First trimester of pregnancy

The oldest, reptilian part of brain is formed.

Seat of all sensory input

Function is survival and defense

Categorizes sense input as friend or foe

Preverbal

Function is immediate, in the present tense

Growth is shaped by the sounds of the mother's voice

Second trimester of pregnancy

The mammalian, or limbic, brain is formed.

Seat of emotion; the emotional-cognitive brain

Realm of emotional IQ, or "body-knowing"

Emotional knowledge is essential for survival

Realm of memory function and relationship to the past

Regulates hormones for nurturance, species survival

environment were required to produce competency in adulthood. First, a rich sensory environment was necessary, both indoors and out; second, free exploratory movement was vital; and third, *a parent was available for interaction when questions arose*.[2] As Joseph Chilton Pearce tells us, "The first imperative of nature is simple as rain, and as natural: no model, no development."[3]

To understand how modeling and imitation work, we need to take a tour through the development of the embryonic brain in utero. Our human brain is a beautiful example of the slow, meticulous way Mother Nature builds toward higher states of being.

In the first trimester of pregnancy, the oldest part of our brain, often called the reptilian brain, is formed. All sensory input and sensory learning are routed through the reptilian brain, which contributes toward our species' survival by categorizing all stimuli as either "friend" or "foe." Astonishingly, this system is "grown" through the embryonic responses to the tones of the mother's voice.[4] Each phoneme, a language's smallest distinctive audible unit, elicits a unique and specific muscular response from the fetus. This *movement in response to the sounds modeled* lays down neural pathways, or conduits of information, in the baby's developing brain. Through this ballet in the embryonic waters, the brain is forming the foundation of all future learning. At birth, these movements are still visible and easily observed, as the baby's arms and legs wave and dance. Although they rapidly become too small to be seen, these movements in response to sound can still be detected by instruments throughout life.[5]

In the second trimester, the mammalian or limbic brain is formed. The mammalian brain is the seat of emotion, or the emotional-cognitive brain. In our western worldview, we tend to separate emotion from rational thought, believing that we can engage our mind without involving our emotions. Neuroscience, however, is showing us the inherent intelligence in the "body-knowing" that is emotion. All relational learning, especially memory, which depends on emotional flagging of information, is founded in the limbic brain. Emotional knowledge provides the cognitive thought process with information that is essential for survival.[6] Emotional knowledge also stimulates cascades of hormones that foster our mammalian instinct to nurture. In turn, the pregnant mother's emotional state, and the hormones she releases in consequence, dramatically influence the development and functioning of the

---

THIRD TRIMESTER OF PREGNANCY

The neocortex develops.

Seat of verbal-intellectual capacities

Ever-responsive information network

Calls functions of reptilian and mammalian brain into its service

Carries new ability: to imagine the future

THE NECESSITY FOR THE HUMAN MODEL

The mother's emotional state during pregnancy impacts fetal brain development.

If she is healthy, happy, well cared for, and relatively stress-free, the whole brain can develop to its highest potential.

If she is in danger, anxiety-ridden, uncared-for, and emotionally distraught, the stress hormones released prepare her for flight or fight.

The constant presence of these hormones "wires" the fetal brain to be used for defense.

The baby is conditioned to respond to stimuli through the lower, defensive brain center.

Higher functions receive less stimulation.

limbic, emotional brain in the second trimester and the continued growth of the neocortex in the third trimester. [7]

Nature builds on the old forms, progressing from the most primitive, survival-oriented capability of the reptilian brain in the first trimester to the connecting, relating ability of the limbic brain in the second trimester and finally to the highest imaginable verbal-intellectual capacities of the

neocortex. We know of no limits to the ever-responsive information network of the neocortex, and it is thought that we use only a fraction of its capacities. Whereas the reptilian brain registers only the present tense, and the mammalian brain registers both present and past (hence its connection to memory), this third brain gives us the gift of envisioning a future. It is primarily the experiences of the emotional brain that determine whether we step toward the future with curiosity and trust, or go reluctantly, in fear. Both of our old brains, reptilian and mammalian, can be called into the service of the high brain, the thinking capacity of the neocortex.

The mother's emotional state has great impact on whether this occurs or not. As the emotional/hormonal model, the human mother is the pivot. Here is how it works, in a rough outline: If the mother is well cared for and happy, the hormones released will foster the continued evolution of development and "use" of the whole brain. The emotional brain and the neocortex will continue to form, and the elaborate wiring that helps them to work together with the reptilian brain as a whole will become fully developed.

If, on the other hand, the mother is unsafe, undernourished, anxiety-ridden or under great stress, *her* limbic brain sends out stress hormones that call the old reptilian brain into play. Remember, its job is to discern friend from foe, and to prepare us for battle or flight. She becomes caught in the repeating cycle of fear, fight or flight. Her hormones set patterns for neural pathways in the developing fetus's brain that "wire" the unborn child for this automatic defense response, diminishing the functioning of the high brain. It is not that the higher areas of the brain are not developed, but that the "wiring pattern" is habituated to the older "defense model" of the lower brain.[8] The "life energy" then goes into protection and defense, rather than being free to move toward intellectual curiosity and exploration.

We all know what this feels like. Do you remember the anxiety you felt as a child, walking into a classroom toward a test you were not well prepared for? And do you remember being so stressed you simply couldn't think, even if you knew the answers? The urgency of the emotion and the body responses eclipsed the more refined powers of thought. For some children, walking into *any* challenging, adult-critiqued situation creates the same feelings: stomachache, short and shallow breaths, tight shoulders. These body sensations are caused by adrenaline and other stress-related neurotransmitters[9] that serve the old brain in its primal desire to outrun the tiger. The tiger may be long gone in today's human societies, but we still live with the "protective devices" so well designed by Mother Nature a long time ago.

THIS IS JUST THE BEGINNING OF IMITATION AND MODELING

The necessity for a human model continues after birth, and involves the comparatively newest part of our brain. This is the development of the prefrontal cortex, which lies immediately behind the ridge of our brow. Until as recently as thirty years ago, this area was called "the silent area"[10] because its function was largely unknown. Today, neuroscientists have a variety of viewpoints concerning its function, but some researchers have attributed to the prefrontal cortex our higher virtues of compassion, empathy and understanding; MacLean called this part of the brain the "angel lobes."[11] This last and perhaps finest part of the brain begins its major growth after birth, and continues this primary growth spurt for about the following nine months. Again, the emotional state of the mother or caregiver and the quality of nurturing that the infant receives can affect the prefrontals at a cellular level.[12] Prefrontal growth and development is dependent upon the infant's environment, as determined by the human model, the parents.

Let us assume we have a happy mother, well nourished and safe. She has given birth to a baby whose brain has been wired to reach its highest

> THE NEED FOR THE HUMAN MODEL CONTINUES AFTER BIRTH
>
> *The last, and finest, part of the brain develops.*
>
> *The pre-frontal cortex, or angel lobes, does not have a major growth spurt until after birth, in the first nine months.*
>
> *The prefrontal cortex is the seat of compassion, empathy, understanding.*
>
> *This growth is specifically environment-dependent.*
>
> *Parents determine the capacity for these higher qualities to grow.*

functioning. Now what do we do to help foster lifelong learning and zest for life? Again and again throughout this book you will hear me say, *"Let Nature be our guide."* So let's see how Nature intends our new arrival to continue learning.

We know that movement in response to the vibrations of the mother's voice does not stop at birth but continues into infancy, laying down neural pathways in the brain and strengthening the sensory-motor response system, making a strong foundation for all sensory learning. And we know that the main avenue of discovery for the first several years of a child's life is through sensory stimulation. For maximum sensory stimulation, it is critical that the child be kept "in arms" in the first weeks or months. All indigenous cultures have known this truth and kept their babies close. They have designed various devices that attach babies to the mother's body, giving her free range of motion and allowing her to continue to go about her work, or they have handed the baby into another pair of arms in their large extended families or tribal groups.

The sensory information digested during the "in arms" period is critical to all future learning. For example, the human face, which is the only object a newborn baby can actually see, becomes the pattern upon which all future sight is built.[13] All visual learning is in reference to the familiar face; then, slowly over the course of the first year, as visual patterns are built and expanded and the visual system develops, the face becomes unnecessary as a reference. During the baby's first few weeks, however, the parent's face needs to be close to the baby, six to twelve inches away, for most of the child's waking hours. Nature has provided well for this necessity, offering a whole cascade of maternal hormones that keep us peering wonderingly into this brand new being's eyes!

Only part of the vast quantity of sensory information taken in during these first weeks is visual. The vestibular sense, or the experience of the body in movement, gravity and balance, and the proprioceptive sense, or the experience of body position and body parts, are also beginning to develop as the baby is held.[14] All the jostling, swinging, walking, the pressure of bodies in contact, help to form these subtle but critical senses. Children who do not develop these have difficulty in later developmental stages. This can show up as a lack of awareness of the physical body and its boundary. They may bump into people or things, to get a "feel" for their boundary, or, conversely, may show a stiff lack of coordination. They may also crave fast spinning movement or show the opposite extreme, an apprehension about movement and being touched, a fear of feeling.[15]

So, *wear your baby*! Front, back or sideways, it doesn't matter, just do it! I attached a set of tiny chimes to the frame of my baby backpack, so we made music as we moved! Baby front packs and backpacks are great not only for an outdoor stroll, but also for use inside the house. Wear your baby as you wash dishes, fold laundry, go up and down stairs, make the bed… everywhere! Besides, as a new mother concerned about "getting your figure back," you'll never have to go to the gym, carrying this precious and ever-increasing load!

You may wonder, as a new mother, "How will I ever take a shower, or pay the bills?" This is where the next activity critical to baby's future learning comes into play: creeping.

The baby is laid on the carpet on his back and allowed to simply *be*, to move, explore, experience frustration, perhaps to cry, to eventually problem-solve toward rolling over, to wiggle toward a toy as he stretches his capacities. The communication between the core (trunk) muscles and the brain continues to develop these senses of touch and proprioception, and to strengthen the vestibular system. Eventually the baby develops the core strength and the coordination to push up and creep, inching along in what is often called "the army crawl." To be on the tummy, moving, stretching and rolling, is empowering to the baby; this allows him an *active* exploration of life. He is "in touch" with his own body and the world; he is learning the relationship between the two. He experiences movement as filled with purpose. And this purposefulness will radiate through his whole being. Perhaps we know a few young people or adults who radiate a sense of purpose and knowing their place in the world. This confidence begins as the baby is held in arms and also laid on the floor, to creep purposefully toward his future.

After creeping, another essential step to insure baby's continued brain development is crawling. The importance of crawling cannot be stressed enough! Crawling, because of the cross-lateral use of arms and legs, patterns the cross-lateral communication of the different hemispheres of the brain. It activates both hemispheres in a balanced way, and the corpus callosum, or the part of the brain that orchestrates the processes between the hemispheres, becomes more fully developed. Crawling involves not only the coordinated use of both arms and legs, but also eyes, ears, hands and feet.[16] Children who miss the crucial crawling stage may show learning difficulties later on.[17]

I worry for children who are held passively at a forty-five-degree angle in the new baby carriers that do triple duty. These devices act as a baby seat that can be set on the counter or desk and rocked when Baby cries (instead of picking him up), as a baby carrier for going to and from the car or in and out of the store, and can be strapped into a car for travel. Every minute of Baby's new life is an opportunity for essential learning. When he is passively watching life from a supine position, he is not in immediate physical contact with the rhythm and pressure of another human body, or wriggling or crawling along his exploratory way. This is critical time lost for brain development.

Now for a word about walking. The baby needs to be allowed to stand up in her own time, in her own way, and to walk at her own pace. Mother Nature did not design those round plastic "walkers," and there are reasons to avoid them. Core muscles are not well exercised, because the device supports the baby's weight, rather than her own growing strength. For the same reason, the walker does not allow the baby to practice the all-important skill of balance. Finally, there is the tendon guard reflex.[18] This reflex involves the tightening and shortening of the calf muscles and was designed to prepare us for flight in times of danger. It is meant to function only for short periods, to help us outrun danger, but babies who are put in walkers can develop shortened calf muscles by constantly flexing their toes in order to propel themselves along. Neurophysiologist and educator Carla Hannaford, and colleague Paul Dennison, in their work with autistic and speech-impaired children, have seen a link between shortened calf muscles and difficulty with speech.[19]

Nature has set a plan in motion, over the course of millennia, that has satisfied all the needs of the developing infant's brain: the need for touch, pressure, movement, the need for the closeness of the face, the need for nutrition, and the need for heart contact with the mother. In utero the baby's heart beats in rhythm with the mother's, responding to the electrical, hormonal, neural and sound patterns of her heart. After birth, the baby's heart rhythm needs to become stabilized over the course of the first year by being held

MOTHER NATURE
KNOWS BEST!

The ancient way we have met all these needs for proper brain development is through breast-feeding! La Leche League is a great resource.

close to the mother's heart.[20] In one fell swoop, Nature has provided gener-ously—for *when we nurse our babies, all of these needs are met.*

There are many books devoted to the benefits of breast-feeding, and the La Leche League is a tremendous resource for pregnant and newly nursing mothers. Be sure to see the Chapter Notes for information on the multidi-mensional benefits of breast-feeding.

As you can see, human beings grow according to very specific devel-opmental patterns. We are discovering the powerful necessity of each of these stages as they unfold, step by step, to foster our child's ever-growing capacities. If your child has missed any of these critical stages, and you are seeing subtle or not-so-subtle developmental difficulties or delays, help is available! A brilliant system of activating, patterning and rewiring the brain for optimal functioning has been developed. Look in the Chapter Notes for information about the Brain Gym system.[21] Using simple and fun body movements, Brain Gym systematically goes about undoing the damage of our modern, "movement-deprived" lifestyle. The human brain is an open-ended system that has a nearly limitless capacity to repair itself! Brain Gym is also powerful for adults, so be sure to look into it.

HAS YOUR CHILD MISSED ANY OF THESE STAGES?

Look for information about Brain Gym—a series of simple, fun movements to retrain the brain!

SENSORY EXPERIENCE, MOVEMENT, AND IMITATION ARE STILL CRITICAL

In the last few pages, we have seen many ways in which sensory input, move-ment and the imprinting of a human model are critical to embryonic and infant brain development, and therefore critical to early learning. These prin-ciples remain vital throughout the child's early years. Sensory experience and movement remain essential to learning into adolescence and even into adulthood. Movement and a sensory involvement with life are prescribed as both prevention and treatment for stress, depression and most disease, for all ages.

Let's look specifically at the role imitation, or the relationship with the model, plays in the life of the toddler, preschool and kindergarten child. This time we will examine the process not from a biological standpoint, but from that of "felt experience."

THE ROLE OF IMITATION REMAINS CRITICAL!

How do we work with imitation?

Be the best person one can be, for her to imitate.

Arrange our home with imitation in mind

• *Simple*

• *Uncluttered*

• *Machine-noise-free*

• *Touchable*

• *Explorable*

If we want her to do something, do it ourselves, as well.

She will imitate hurrying, too, so go slowly!

I often think of the young child's capacity for imitation as *nutritional*. The way the child imitates is akin to the way she digests the food we offer. She simply takes it in, and depending on the nutritional value of the meal, she is well fed or undernourished. By creating indoor and outdoor environments that nourish your child's lifelong learning, and by establishing healthy life rhythms that will nourish your child's sleep times, mealtimes, work and play times, and so forth, you will lay essential foundations for learning.

We can also use this understanding of imitation in the way we approach daily activities. A simple rule is this: if we want the child to do something, then we must do it ourselves, in order to offer him someone to imitate. If you say, "Come brush your teeth," have your toothbrush in hand, too. Or, if it's time for breakfast, be sure you, also, are having a portion. If you wish your child were more active outdoors, put on your jacket, get out the rake and get going yourself.

The young child does not watch us carefully, and then in a studied way choose to imitate, for instance, the tone of our voice as we talk to the cat. Rather, the young child, who is so new to life, simply *lives into* our actions and makes them her own. We, her parents, are the template of what it is to be human. In the same way that the mother's face is the template upon which all visual learning is based, we are the pattern for what it is to be human. The young child has not yet developed the capacity to recognize her separateness yet. She experiences herself as merged with the environment, and when we understand this, we can consciously arrange ourselves as the emotional environment, and our home as the physical environment, in such a way that she is imitating the best we have to offer.

In each of the many small tasks we do with our child, remember that we are showing him not "our" way, or the regional way. From his perspective, we are offering the secrets of the universe, showing him The Way. So, let's do each thing with as much consciousness as we can bring to the task. Think of the ancient Zen master, who rakes the sand garden or pours tea with a simple economy of movement and grace.

Often when I talk to parents about the profundity of the role of imitation, I see a small wave of panic run through them. "How on earth can we measure up, and show them what it is to be human? We're just regular people." It will be a long time before your children recognize that you are "just regular." The only way I ever learned to carry the weight of my children's admiration, their need and expectation, was to know deep in my bones that I would never, ever be perfect, or even close. But I also knew that Love *is* perfect, and also perfectly reliable. So, with all the imperfections that occur in a day, I always relied on Love, knowing in the end all my transgressions (against my own ideal, by the way, not theirs!) were washed clean by Love's great generosity. So you can relax and enjoy the rest of our discussion about imitation.

Hurrying and Imitation

What about hurrying? This is the disease of our time, and we are all exposed to it in varying degrees. We must each find our own way to inoculate ourselves against it. For if we hurry our family's lives along, our young child will incorporate this hurrying into his own body. Hurrying causes stress, and the American Medical Association tells us that over ninety percent of illness is stress-related.[22] So practice breathing slowly, observe yourself as you model a task for your child, make mental notes, and try to bring more awareness to it the next time. Because your child imitates *everything*, she will imitate your comfort, ease and joy in movement. She will also imitate your deep intention to do it better next time!

Speaking with Imitation in Mind

Another way you can use your understanding about imitation is in the way you speak to your child. Young children imitate so perfectly because they are not, as yet, separated from that which they imitate. So when you talk to your child, a magic wand you can wave is the use of the golden "we." Your child still belongs to the awareness of "we," and is not yet an "I." You will be amazed at the power of addressing your child in exactly the place where he exists. It is often easy to address a baby as "we"—for instance, "Now let's change our diaper." As the child moves out of the baby stage, and seems to us so much more an individual, this can become more difficult. We must realize that for about the first five or six years (yes, that long!) he is still a "we" at heart. Whenever you have a "command," such as, "Come for dinner!" try to place it in the great "we," and see how this can smooth the road. Though this may seem like a fine point, I think of it as a very slender wand that produces great magic.

We can also employ the principle of imitation in answering our children's questions. The child still has a feeling of being "at one" with the world. For her, this world is full of mystery. It is our adult awareness of separateness that gives us the ability to "understand" the world in a conceptual manner. We understand the world by thinking about it. The child understands the world by moving through it, experiencing it bodily. The *meaning* exists in the interface between the child's body and the thing itself. So when our child comes to us with one of her astonishing questions, let's practice answering, not in concepts, but in pictures and images she can "feel her way into."

A perfect example of this happened in my classroom. A very little boy of three years came to me, one autumn morning, with this question: "Do pumpkins grow on the moon?" In my utter delight, and while my mind did flips to find an image with which to reply, I stalled. My assistant came to my rescue and said, "Pumpkins are round, just like the moon!" He was completely satisfied and danced away, singing, "The pumpkins and the moon! The pumpkins and the moon!" All he was asking for was confirmation of his own joy. By not closing the door, by refraining from talking about oxygen, water and sunlight, my assistant allowed him to revel in roundness.

TIP

Speak with imitation in mind: Use the golden "we."

WHAT ABOUT
CHILDREN'S QUESTIONS?

Answer with imitation in mind:

• *Remember that he experiences himself "at one," part of the great mystery.*

• *He learns through bodily explorations; answer in images he can "feel his way into."*

• *Save scientific explanations for later.*

• *Affirm his curiosity and joy.*

• *Assure him that you wonder about things, too.*

• *Be ready for his reply: a window into his soul!*

My youngest son asked many times, when he was just three, where the water from the toilet went. I would always say, "See, it goes round and round before it goes down." He then would offer me a window into his growing imagination through stories of underground water worlds and the creatures that lived there. Often, if we hold back from "answering" a question like this, if we just offer an image that affirms their observations, we will then be treated to an inside view of the child's soul.

A great reply to carry in your back pocket is, "Hmmm... I wonder about that, too." When we say this, we give our child permission to hold open a door to wonder, to recognize that she, even into adulthood, can participate in the great Mystery.

In our ability to conceptualize, and in our very western training of the mind, we believe we have the "answers," and are often glad to give scientific explanations to our children. But the new science, the new physics, points us back to our roots, back to the great unitive Mystery.[23] Let us allow our children to live in this natural wonder and freedom.

STRESS AND LEARNING FOR THE YOUNG CHILD

Earlier we discussed the effect of the pregnant mother's stress on the developing embryo. Let's look now at more specifics of stress. During stress, adrenaline, cortisol and other neurotransmitters prepare the body for danger, helping us to run, or turn and fight. It is in the lower brain and the brain stem that this activity begins, spreading from there to our entire body. Studies have shown that the release of adrenaline, through a complex biochemical event, negatively impacts our ability to focus and control our thought.[24] This is because the body-mind complex has routed the focus toward the periphery, readying us muscularly, visually and vascularly for threat. In other words, the life energy is being spent on protection, not focused thought. Cortisol increases blood sugar levels to face the oncoming ordeal, and constricts the blood vessels at the surface of the body (to reduce wound bleeding), which increases blood pressure to the core of the body. Ever wonder why, under stress, you feel like you are in a pressure cooker? It is no wonder that increased cortisol is correlated with decreased learning and memory, as well as attention problems.[25]

STRESS AND LEARNING

During stress, adrenaline, cortisol and other neurotransmitters prepare the body for danger: this is the reptilian brain at work.

- *Adrenaline negatively impacts our ability to focus and control thought.*

- *Cortisol is correlated with decreased learning and memory, as well as attention problems.*

AN OPTIMAL ENVIRONMENT FOR BRAIN DEVELOPMENT

As adults, we can retrain "old brain responses" through the use of higher reasoning. But how do we help our little children?

- *Plenty of water to drink*
- *Adequate protein*
- *Regular home rhythms*
- *Plenty of time for play*
- *Plenty of time for movement*
- *Plenty of time for stories*
- *Plenty of time for conversation*

We know that stress is a health risk, and many physicians today urge patients to work toward stress reduction through exercise, nutrition, recreation and so forth. What we are just discovering now is how detrimental stress is to learning.[26] The first studies on the effects of stress were conducted with men in the work force, because they were exhibiting physical symptoms. As women began to join the work force, they began exhibiting the same symptoms. Now we see that this malady has also reached our children. We see stress in the schools, with test scores dropping and behavior deteriorating. What is going on, and what can we do about it?

Stress is a bodily response to perceived danger.[27] Each of us is unique, and so we will perceive situations differently. We no longer live in a world in which "stress" is confined to the roar of the tiger or the danger of the hunt. What one person may interpret as "friend," another may experience as "foe." As adults, *we can learn to retrain our reptilian brain-induced body reactions through the conscious use of the frontal lobes, through conscious choice.* We can discuss the problem or verbally express our emotion; we can learn to breathe slowly while under stress; we can take up a meditation practice.

But how do we keep our young children, who do not yet have full use of their frontal lobes, stress-free? Stress-free living supports dynamic brain development, and a well-developed brain supports stress-free living. Like so many things in life, we can move into an upward spiral of abundance, or a downward spiral of depletion. Where do we begin?

Poor Brain Functioning Produces Stress

Optimal brain functioning supports the child's ability to perceive and interact with her world in a positive, optimistic way.[28] This builds strong self-esteem. Strong self-esteem is a primary protector from stress. When a child's brain function is weakened, her interactions lack skill and coordination, which can negatively impact her sense of self. Here are a number of common factors in early childhood that, if attended to well, will support vigorous brain development, and thereby help to protect our child from the experience of stress.

As you read the following, you'll want to get out your journal and make notes. Plan concrete actions: make water available at child level, put a sign on the mirror reminding you to "PLAY"; perhaps when your digital watch chimes at the hour be sure you and your child are in movement, and so forth. The sections below will flesh out these beginning ideas, so let's begin now!

To Support Vigorous Brain Functioning

Drink adequate water: Brain functioning is primarily an electrical activity. Water conducts electricity. The brain, and in fact the whole body, is comprised primarily of water, and in fact, our entire bodies are. Be sure your child drinks plenty of water each day, to avoid stress.[29] Herbal teas can "count," but not milk or fruit juices, and certainly not sugary sodas. About one third of an ounce per pound of body weight is usually recommended. Caffeine is a diuretic and, rather than increasing body fluid, actually depletes the body of its necessary moisture. Chocolate and many soft drinks contain caffeine. Keep a source of water in a low place that is accessible for your children. If you put a pitcher and a small cup on a low table, they can also practice eye-hand coordination and experiment with weight, volume, and displacement of liquids!

Eat adequate protein: Proteins and fats are the building blocks of the whole body, but especially the brain.[30] Pregnant women and children—especially before the age of five, but throughout the whole of childhood—need extra protein for the essential work of building a well-developed brain. Children with learning difficulties often have inadequate protein intake. Think of cheese, nuts, a hard-boiled egg and milk when snack time arrives. Be cautious of offering store-bought yogurt, which is often overly flavored and sugared. Sugar is counterproductive to optimal brain development.[31]

You can make nutritious yogurt at home! In a quart jar, place three cups room-temperature milk, one-half cup dry milk, (to thicken it), a spoonful of honey, a spoonful of acidophilus from the health food store, and one-half cup plain unflavored yogurt in a quart jar. Shake it well and wrap a heating pad around it. Set the pad on high for four hours, then on medium for twenty-four to thirty-six hours. Voila! Flavor it with fruit, and your family will be in heaven. If it seems thin, serve it as a smoothie and add more dry milk next time. If your heating pad runs hot, and you end up with a soft

---

PROTEIN SUPPORTS
BRAIN FUNCTIONING

Make your own yogurt!

• *Put milk, dry milk, honey, acidophilus and plain yogurt in a quart jar. Shake well.*

• *Wrap in a heating pad, and wait 24-36 hours—Yum!*

cheese, add garlic and scallions, serve on crackers, and experiment with the temperature setting next time.

Establish regular home rhythms: All learning takes place as a slowly building process. All of us, but especially our young children, learn by moving from what is familiar toward the new. The experience of the new is built on the foundation of the familiar. Offering our child a regular, rhythmic home life sets in place an optimal learning environment. We can look at this not as a rigid adherence to time, but rather as a gentle flow of energy. Think of moving from one activity of the day to the next in the same way morning imperceptibly climbs toward noon. The chapter on "The World of Rhythm" offers you simple, joyous ways to plan your days and weeks. "Celebrating Festivals Together" helps bring a rhythmic pattern to the years.

Offer plenty of time to play: Play is crucial to children's cognitive development. It is through play that the child takes sense experience and organizes it into mental and emotional patterns.[32] As the child grows and matures, these patterns become ever more complex. The three-year-old will play "making dinner" at the toy stove. You may be offered the same bowl of soup over and over again. Here we see the development of motor skills, eye-hand coordination and the budding of care and nurturance, to mention only a few abilities. The five-year-old's game becomes more elaborate. She and her sister may have spent the last hour in the "hospital" bandaging all the stuffed animals' wounds with baby powder and toilet paper, and now, acting as not only the vet but also the restaurant owner, she stands at the toy stove making pizza for all her patients. Having built the pizza delivery truck of chairs and pillows, Sister is ready, and off she zooms. The learning that takes place in a well-developed imaginative scenario like this is astonishing. Eye-hand coordination, both large and small motor skills, balance, movement, motor planning, social cooperation, emotional self-monitoring, speech, hearing and language development, as well as the remarkably elastic conceptual skills of imagination and thought, are all employed in the world of make-believe. See the chapter on Indoor Play to learn more about the necessity for play in childhood, as well as how to create optimal play spaces.

Much of modern preschool children's time is now taken up by either structured activities, such as "enrichment classes," or passive activities like media exposure. *The prime imperative for the young child is movement through play.* It is our responsibility to make as much time available for imagination-rich play as possible.

Offer plenty of time to move: We have seen how essential movement is to brain development, and therefore to every aspect of the child's life. You will want to choose, from the many ideas offered in this book, where you would like to begin to enrich your child's movement and play environments. Choose just one idea, implement it, experience the magic, incorporate it into your family life, and then choose the next! Let's look now at just a few movement activities that will foster balanced brain development. Get your journal ready:

OUTDOORS:

- Bouncing on a "hippety-hop ball," the kind that is straddled, with a handle. You can stake a tarp down for bouncing, to avoid punctures.
- Plenty of sand and water play. Put the water at a distance from the sand to encourage running, balance (try carrying a bowl full of water!), strength and cooperative play. Bowls and spoons for mixing.
- Plenty of mud play. Mud is very different from sand, and every child I know prefers mud to sand, or likes to mix the two.
- Swinging— on swings, gliders (the kind of swing that two children ride together, back to back), hammocks, rope swings.
- Imaginative play in natural structures—hay-bale houses, bamboo-pole tipis, butterfly-bush houses and such.
- Outdoor building projects. Have lots of building materials available, like board ends, firewood, stumps, sticks, pine cones, bricks, stones, garden pots, pieces of slate, lengths of bamboo, rope and so forth.
- Using tools. Go to the Salvation Army to get cheap tools. Look for small, lightweight ones—hammers, wrenches, pliers, paintbrushes— that will fit your child's hands. Screwdrivers are usually too sharp.
- Seesaw play. It's great for balance, strength, overall coordination, a hands-on experience of weights and balances, social cooperation.
- Pushing and pulling. Get a wagon and add building materials!
- Interacting with bugs and insects. Get a small screened "bug house."
- Roly-poly time. Roll in the grass, or on a small hill. Bear-hug down the hill.

INDOORS:

- Artistic experience. Watercolor, play dough, finger paint, clay, scissors with old magazines and glue, tissue paper art, pastels. Your library is full of idea books.

- Water play. At the kitchen sink, in the bathtub, at a "tea party," helping to scrub bathroom and kitchen, washing the doll's clothes.
- Sand play in the kitchen. See the chapter on Indoor Play for ideas about an indoor sandbox. Add small figures, vehicles and animals for imaginative play. Some child psychologists use a sand tray for therapeutic purposes because this kind of play allows the child to "play through" the emotions.
- Imaginative play. In the chapter on Indoor Play you will learn how to create an open-ended playspace to foster your young child's imagination—for child's play is transformed into thought.
- Cook together. Chop, mix, stir, beat, knead, fold, grate. Excellent for honing fine motor coordination and helping with visual focus.
- Clean together. Sweep, dust, wash, scrub, polish, fluff. Each activity sharpens different senses and activates different parts of the brain.
- Rough and tumble. Children love to roughhouse with their parents, who are utterly challenging, impervious to pain, and entirely safe. Be careful of tickling, though, because it can constrict the breath. With my younger son, all I had to do was *look* like I was going to tickle him to send him into gales of laughter. A fun game is Steamroller: put him in a "pillow sandwich" and then roll your body across him, inside his pillows.
- Dress-ups. Keep the best of your next Salvation Army load for the dress-up corner. Old hats, gloves, shoes, ties and shawls are all heavenly.
- Rocking. Have a large rocker for yourself and a small one for your child, so you can rock together in one chair, rock together in your own chairs, or your child can work at rocking in your big chair. Rockers can also be turned upside down at playtime, and used for... well, anything!
- Roly-poly time. After lunch, before your pre-nap outdoor play, have your child log-roll on the living room carpet. *You* can take a couple of rolls, too. It is an amazing experience, and you'll understand why your child loves it.
- Bear hugs. This is whole-body stimulation, with a firm squeeze from head to toe. It involves all the senses, is excellent "brain food" and feels great for both of you. "Hug sandwiches" are the best.
- Baths. Warm and bubbly, with water toys, pouring and squeezing.

Offer plenty of time for stories: The use of language promotes the development of the left neocortex, involving the sensory, auditory, visual, motor speech and other areas.[33] Listening is fundamental to language, and hearing stories strengthens this ability. Language is a primary avenue through which we express our unique self, and therefore is crucial for self-esteem. When modeling the use of language through stories, you will want to choose material that is age-appropriate. See the chapter on the Wonder of Stories to understand the developmental needs as your child grows.

Offer plenty of time for conversation: Have conversations with your child throughout the day. Be aware and use full sentences. This allows the child to hear and then imitate full ideas. Incomplete speech patterns lead to incomplete thought patterns. See the chapter on Home Rhythms for a fuller discussion about conversation at the dinner table.

When we attend to each of these areas, we provide our child with a balanced "diet" of sense experience, and offer an excellent foundation for cognitive functioning. This in turn helps our child experience positive interactions as she grows, which establishes strong self-esteem. Strong self-esteem will help shield our child from the various stresses life entails.

THE MEDIA AND LEARNING FOR THE YOUNG CHILD

There are many ways in which the media, whether TV, movies, video games or computers, negatively impact the young child's development. We will touch briefly on the media's impact on the child's all-important movement, the capacity to imitate, social development, language development, and development of the imagination. See the bibliography for books that delve more deeply into this critical subject. We will also discuss alternatives to media experiences.

Ninety-eight percent of American homes have at least one television, and the average television is on for over seven hours a day.[34] The average American child spends forty hours a week watching various forms of visual electronic media, more time than in any other waking activity, including playing.[35] A six-month-old infant spends an average of one and a half hours a day watching TV, and the average preschooler spends more than four hours daily in front of a screen.[36]

With this much time spent immobile, *what is happening to the child's powerful imperative of movement?* Some parents believe that monitoring the content of their child's viewing is all that is needed to avoid damage. Let's consider this. As we know, movement in response to sensory input lays down neural networks in the brain. Less movement means less neural networking. Less neural networking means less communication between the different regions of the brain. Less communication means a lack of sensory integration. Less sensory integration means less adaptability in learning new skills.[37] In *Television and the Aggressive Child*, Huesmann and Eron write, "Children of lower intellectual achievement generally watch more television more violent television…and behave more aggressively."[38] Time spent before a screen is time lost to movement and healthy development.

And what kind of model does the media provide for movement in our children? The physical gestures we typically see in the media are often overly dramatized, since in order for movement to translate to the screen, subtlety is often sacrificed. Movements are also frequently hurried, voices are loud, and responses are quick. Regularly, in talking to parents, I have said, "You will never see a video program of someone watching through the window as the rain falls." And yet, how soothing it is to focus and refocus first on the distant rain against the background of trees, and then on the tiny rivulets created on the glass. For a child there is tremendous imaginative potential in a scene as simple as this. This powerful experience can never translate to electronic media. Will the child's sense of subtlety be blunted by the over-dramatization electronic media requires?

Language development is critical as a foundation for cognitive learning as well as emotional intelligence. As we mentioned earlier, in order for the child to learn to think complete thoughts, she must hear this demonstrated before her, through language. Much of the language in the media is truncated, and slang is used as a dramatic effect. Often, even in children's programming, a kind of cynical humor is introduced, and allusions that the child does not understand are left hanging in the air. This situation deprives the child not only of exposure to whole language, but also—since children mostly view the media without their parents—of the opportunity to ask a question when she doesn't understand. Unlike conversation, in viewing the media we use the passive skill of listening without the partner skill of actively speaking. Children learn language not only by listening but by actively participating through speech. Overexposure to the media can negatively impact the child's developing language acquisition.

Of course, speech is only one avenue through which meaning is expressed in real life.[39] Parents who are attuned to their children respond in integrated

---

FACTS ON MEDIA
AND LEARNING

In the average home, the television is on for 7 hours a day.

The average child watches 40 hours of electronic media each week. When is there time for

• *Imaginative play?*

• *Both fine and vigorous movement?*

• *Hearing and making up stories?*

• *Learning the fine art of conversation: language acquisition?*

The NAEYC states: "Children of lower intellectual achievement generally watch more television…." I wonder which came first, the chicken or the egg?

Your child will imitate whatever she sees, including what happens in the media.

multiple sensory modes, so all the senses are at work when parents and children interact. During a pregnant pause in a conversation, the child may be aware of subtle facial movements, or the restful rhythm of his own heartbeat. He may hear the ticking of the clock or birdsong out the window. This multisensory awareness offers constant opportunities to glean meaning and perspective. The media, however, depends primarily on the visual, and secondarily on the auditory function, to the exclusion of the other senses. Especially for the young child, this creates a deficit in the sense of movement and "embodiedness." Because the eye responds to movement, there can be few pauses in media programming, and children, following the imitation imperative, mimic the hectic, incoherent pace they observe there.

The young child is geared to experience certain environmental stimuli as stressful.[40] Chief among these are facial displays of alarm, anger or disinterest. The media is full of these: they "sell," whereas quiet joy and focused attention are not money-makers. Other stressful stimuli are excessive noise and lack of coherence. How many media programs for children are characterized by just these qualities, and what are the effects in terms of imitation? Although to an adult viewer the actions on the screen may seem coherent, the young child is just learning, in a multisensory fashion, how human coherence works. When an exchange happens in real life and the child does not understand the coherence, there is an opportunity for inquiry (the familiar "Why?"). As noted above, however, most of the time children view the media without the company of parents, who may use the media as a means to occupy the child's time while they try to get household work done. In this situation, the child's stimulus-response pattern can be affected. When viewing an event on the screen, the child encounters a visual stimulus, but there is no opportunity for an appropriate response. The child cannot reach out and touch, smell, taste or interact with what she sees. Not only that, but with the hurried pace of many television shows suggesting that a life situation can be experienced, worked with and resolved, all in the short time between commercials, there is no time for understanding to grow. Finally, screenplays are written in a very formulaic way, each "movement" following a very patterned course in terms of timing, action and resolution. Life, on the other hand, is full of twists and unexpected events. The young child needs to be allowed to imitate our

---

FACTS ON MEDIA
AND LEARNING (CONT.)

The media focuses on visual and auditory stimulation, to the exclusion of other sensory stimulus, especially the sense of movement.

- *The child's stimulus-response pattern is affected: the child encounters a visual stimulus, but no appropriate response can be made. The child cannot reach out and touch, or interact with what she sees.*

Often children do not understand interactions they see on the screen.

- *Programs are too fast-paced to ask for help.*

- *Parents tend to use the media as a babysitter, so often no adult is present to ask.*

Visual electronic media can produce stress in children.

- *Media violence goes against instinctual species survival.*

- *Excessive noise and lack of coherence, as well as facial displays of anger, alarm and indifference—all common in children's media—produce stress.*

human capacity to adapt to the new, and not be constrained by imitating these prescribed patterns.

When it comes to media violence, imitation is not the only concern. In a study conducted at Stanford University, television viewers' brains responded to movements on the screen as if they were actually real, preparing the nervous system for a physical response.[41] When children, and adults as well, witness television violence, their bodies interpret it as though it is a real occurrence.

We know from our discussions above that when the "fight or flight" mechanisms of the brain are activated, this diminishes the efficacy of the higher cognitive capacities. When preparing for battle, it is nearly impossible to think rationally. Einstein tells us, "It is impossible to simultaneously prepare for and prevent war." When humans see aggressive or threatening behaviors onscreen, and the ancient brain interprets this as reality, this repeated activation of the defense mechanisms reduces the engagement of the young child's higher brain centers. There is less of the necessary "life force" available for the development of these higher functions. The capacity for dialogue and rational thought is fettered.

According to the American Academy of Pediatrics, research has associated exposure to media violence with "a variety of physical and mental health problems for children and adolescents, including aggressive behavior, desensitization to violence, fear, depression, nightmares, and sleep disturbances." In over thirty-five hundred research studies investigating the association between media violence and violent behavior, they claim, all but eighteen have shown a relationship—and some indicate that aggressive behavior associated with media exposure persists for decades. They go on to cite a National Television Violence study that evaluated ten thousand hours of broadcast programming from 1995 to 1997, and found that sixty-one percent contained interpersonal violence, eighty percent of which was portrayed in a glamorized manner. The highest proportion of violence was found in children's programming, with violent incidents increasing year by year.[42]

Remember, the brain interprets movements seen on the screen as actual happenings. This means children who are exposed to media violence believe they live in a world with ever-increasing acts of violence. What kind of human being does this create? And what happens to social behavior?

Because of the enormous role of imitation in mental development, children learn through media violence that aggression is an acceptable way to achieve goals and solve problems. The National Association for the Education of the Young Child voices these concerns about media violence:

- Children may become desensitized to the pain and suffering of others.
- They may be more likely to behave in aggressive ways toward others.
- They may become more fearful of the world around them, perceiving the world as a mean place.[43]

This third scenario is perhaps the most insidious. "Research has revealed," the NAEYC warns, "that violence on television plays an important role in communicating the social order and in leading to perceptions of the world as a mean and dangerous place."[44] Again, we have the old fight-or-flight defense mechanism being called into action, to the detriment of higher cognitive function. It is also worth noting that it is not just violent programs that stimulate aggressive behavior. Frenetic, hectic programming that creates a high level of arousal in children can also create the same effect.[45]

My Personal "Research"

In my own experience as a classroom teacher, children who view too much media are hampered in their capacity to play collaboratively, in their imaginative capacity, in their creativity, in their ability to imitate and in their movement. Over the last thirty years, I've observed that my little TV watchers need to play and replay the actions seen on the screen. As we know, children make meaning by "playing through" the actions they see around them. Because the media is so fast-paced, and often beyond a child's understanding,

---

MEDIA AND VIOLENCE

Remember, children imitate everything!

• *The average 18-year-old has witnessed 200,000 acts of television violence.*

• *The human brain perceives media violence as real, and prepares the body for defense.*

• *3,500 research studies have shown a relationship between television viewing and aggressive behavior.*

• *It is not just media violence that stimulates aggressive behavior. Programs that are frenetic, hectic, and produce high states of arousal do the same.*

• *The child learns, through media exposure, that the world is a "mean and scary place."*

these confusing scenarios lie unresolved in the child. In the classroom, the capacity to play collaboratively is hampered by the pressing need to keep playing through media situations, hoping for resolution. Also, because collaboration is not a venue that plays well on the screen, the child has no model for cooperation in her quest to understand the confusing, often "anti-species survival" (i.e., violent) and emotionally laden material. Instead, her old-brain defense system is activated by these unresolved, stress-producing scenarios. All of this does not bode well for the subtle intricacies that cooperative creative imaginary play requires. The NAEYC says "media children" are "less likely to benefit from creative imaginative play as the natural means to express feelings, overcome anger, and gain self-control."[46]

These children suffer in their imaginative capacity, also. All conceptual thought lies on the foundation of our innate ability to create and remember mental images. Without this "image-making capacity" we would meet each thing new, as though for the first time, every time. The only way we can talk about a horse, for example, is to carry a mental image of the horse within. When the child is young, this work of "image-making" is critical. With use, the brain develops neural networks that strengthen and reinforce this essential human capacity. Each experience augments this growth. When, on the other hand, the child is fed predetermined images of someone else's imagining, opportunities to strengthen their own image-producing facility are diminished. If the average American child is watching forty hours of electronic media each week, what is happening to our collective foundation of intelligence?

I have seen, though, that *when screen time is dramatically reduced, there is a blossoming of imagination in the child*. It is the child's natural, biological inclination to creatively imagine her world. Given a chance, this impulse will reassert itself. Since time immemorial, children have gone outdoors and created phenomenal worlds of intricate detail, all with sticks, bark, stones, water... whatever materials were available. In my classroom, as well as in my home, I have tried to offer these same kinds of open-ended toys and play materials. Children who are too influenced by media lack the imaginative ability to see how these very simple, open-ended creative props can be used. It is difficult for them to imagine how a seashell could possibly be a cell phone; they want a toy cell phone as a prop for their game! However, *if we give* children very little exposure to the media, they will discover many opportunities to creatively express their very own twenty-first-century life. Here is one example.

One of our kindergarten toys is a basket of shiny gold paper cut into various odd pieces, which lends itself to a variety of games. One day, when the children were playing "store," the little store owner had collected all the "gold coins" in payment for his wares, and now hoarded them. The other children felt impoverished and came to me for assistance. I had him bring me the basket, and announced that the bank had now opened, and I would

be glad, as the banker, to share the wealth. The little culprit, knowing his power had been usurped, thought about this quietly. Unwilling to be on par with everyone else, he gave me back his gold coins, picked up a corn cob, stuck it through his belt and said as he sauntered off, "I'll just use my credit card!" A modern application of an ancient toy!

But how can essential human activities, the "dailiness" of life, compete with media images that are larger than life? I worry that such images, which are designed to hold the eye's attention, overwhelm the child's capacity to create his own inner images from the imitation of ordinary scenes of daily life. Often I have found, particularly during circle time, when the child's academic foundations are being prepared through movement, song, story, gesture, rhythm and rhyme, that the "media children" have difficulty following the intricate sequencing, the movement patterns and language use. They miss out on the enormous potential for brain development because their imitative capacity is overwhelmed by media images. How can a song with gestures, about a pony galloping through the autumn fields, pique their imagination, when they have just come from early morning cartoons, filled with all the media's over-exaggeration?

In summary, to quote Brown University's Mary G. Burke, "the concerns about VEM (visual electronic media) are

- They overstimulate the visual system, at the expense of other sensory systems.
- They deprive the child of necessary social interactions that foster self-regulation and contradict the child's innate ability to recognize the significance of facial affect.
- They arouse the child, but in a situation where he lacks the means for appropriate containment of his arousal.
- They blunt his capacity for generating symbols and imaginary problem-solving.
- They interfere with the development of autonomy." [47]

WHAT CAN WE DO?

The good news, as I mentioned earlier, is this: the human brain is capable of enormous self-repair. Factors that diminish media-induced behaviors are: moderation in use, family activities, parents who are attuned to the child and model coherent behavior, and a large repertoire of alternative activities, particularly those that offer the child a sense of mastery. The *Brown University Letter* states, "The cheapest, least invasive and least risky intervention we can prescribe to families is to turn off the TV and play together." [48]

Turn Off the TV and Play Together!

"But, I don't know where to begin!" you may say. You hold in your hand a recipe book for exactly this. Turn the page and you will find ideas ranging from how to get the children to bed on time to the specifics of making a tipi or an indoor sandbox. You will find how to create family celebrations you will all remember for a lifetime, as well as how to arrange the family work day. You will learn how to let Love lead in discipline situations, and how to

---

> ### WHAT TO DO?
>
> *Turn to the following chapters of this book and choose one idea, to begin with.*
>
> *Turn off the TV.*
>
> *Create, plan, play and enjoy your family life together!*

make up the best bedtime stories. This book is a broad, in-depth study of family life. You and your family have a long, long time to work with it!

Relax, be creative and enjoy!

One Last Thought about the Media

You may be thinking, "But how will I have a minute to myself, or even make dinner without the TV? How could I ever talk on the phone?" Let me just tell you my experience, as a mother of three, who worked full time and performed the daily juggling act this involved.

I would never have survived *with* the media in our life! I was far too busy to deal with the whining discontent the media creates in children! *Because I relied entirely on my children's innate capacity to create, imagine, be active, and entertain themselves, they did exactly that.* They never came begging for my attention, wanting to be entertained. How could I, a dull old grown-up, compare to their free-flying imaginative world?

Eventually, my boys did learn the word "bored." I believe they learned it from friends, and saw the power it contained. They tried using it from time to time, to see if it was as effective as it seemed. My standard reply was, "Hmm… you know, when you are bored, this is a good thing! It means there is a little empty space inside, just waiting for an excellent idea, a really great game. Why don't you run along, and come back to tell me when you have the new idea?"

What I am trying to say to you is that this is the easy way! Of course you are concerned for your own well-being, and that you have a few moments of personal space. Cut out the media, give your children open-ended toys and plenty of story as fodder for the imagination, and you will have the time you need! This is the secret to excellent parenting: trust your children's natural capacity to create, be courageous, and leap! You will not regret it.

Chapter 2

THE WORLD OF RHYTHM

RHYTHM IS THE magic word for parents and educators of young children. Young children thrive on a simple, flexible rhythm that carries them through their day, through each week and through the slowly unfolding years of their lives. Rhythm lays a strong foundation, not only in our children's lives but also in our own. We humans have been shaped over the millennia by the rhythmic rotation of the earth, by the diurnal dance of day and night. We have been formed by the rosy shadings of light at dawn, and by nighttime's reply as scarlet and violet descend into velvet black. We have grown and evolved in Earth's slow journey around the sun. Day by day our world shifts imperceptibly, moving inexorably from spring's first blossom toward a world glittering in ice diamonds. Both the rapture and the travails of this cycle have formed our human psyche. Although our modern life is far removed from this earth-based consciousness, still our fundamental shaping has been in a rhythmic pattern. Our children, who live closer to basics than we do, are profoundly affected by the life rhythms we determine for them. Many problems we experience with our children can be addressed by setting a simple daily rhythm that allows their needs to be met in a timely way.

RHYTHMIC ACTIVITIES

Children live in the rhythms of their bodies more than we adults do. We can help bring a sensory experience of rhythm into their lives through daily rhythmic tasks. When we awaken each morning, we can ask their help in stirring the herbal tea, or in setting out bowls and spooning the oatmeal. They can help with their small broom as we sweep after the meal. Because they learn by imitation, it will help the development of their natural "whole-body" awareness if we bring greater consciousness to our own gestures as we

MOVEMENT TIP

Observe your movement as you work with your child. Try to move with a graceful, natural rhythm.

CHILD'S WEEKLY CHORES

Mon: Polish wooden toys (choose a few each week)

Tues: Run carpet sweeper

Wed: Polish dining table

Thurs: Run carpet sweeper (another room)

Fri: Hand wash place mats

"HOME REMEDIES" FOR HURRIED PACE

Rake leaves

Shovel snow

Turn garden soil over

Wash windows

Dust with feather duster

Polish furniture

Sweep with broom

Hand wash cups

go about these daily activities. As we wash the morning dishes, sweep the floor, dust the furniture, let's ask ourselves what our child sees in our gesture. Does he see care in our bodily rhythm as we bend toward the task, or does he see a hurried duty? Does he see our pleasure in the task, or resentment? Because the young child learns by imitation, he will imitate not only our physical gestures, but also our "inner gesture." We can teach our child to enjoy the rhythmic activity of the care of his toys and playthings by our own conscious enjoyment of the care of our home. As we bring our conscious presence to the rhythm of these tasks, we give our child a dual gift: a sense of *purpose* and *presence* in the rhythms of daily life.

Many of our routine tasks have been relegated to the domain of machines: vacuum, washing machine, coffee grinder, orange juicer, bread machine, and more! Let's ask ourselves which of these tasks must be done by machine, and which ones we can still do by hand. The tasks we do with our young child by hand will be the ones they know *by heart* when they are grown. If we feel the dishes must be done by machine, can we save the cups to do by hand? Can we offer our child a basin of warm soapy water and a sense of purposeful work? Once a week, could we wash the place mats from the kitchen table by hand? Vacuuming may be necessary on a weekly basis, but daily we can sweep with a broom, our child following along with a child-size broom. Or we can give our child the task of "sweeping" the carpet with one of the old-fashioned, non-electric carpet sweepers that are still carried in many department stores. This is a task the four-, five- and six-year-olds love! Certainly our lives are busy with all the pressures of career, finances, and so forth, but if we look carefully at the course of each day and comb through the events of the week, we will find small tasks that we can do by hand with our young child.

It may help you remember these "hand tasks" if you organize them on a daily and weekly basis. Some tasks, like washing the cups, need to be done daily. Others, like polishing the wood furniture, and a few of your child's wooden toys as well, can be done on a weekly basis.

By participating in the "hand work" of caring for the home, our child learns, in a rhythmic, physical way, to love and care for the materiality of this earth. When we share with our children these whole-body tasks, we model for them a total, integrated gesture. By imitating us, they learn purposeful movement, or how to use the body in an efficient, graceful way. We can rake leaves, shovel snow, turn the soil in the garden; we can wash windows, dust with a feather duster, polish wooden furniture. This is a great "home remedy" for the effects of media images of erratic, harried and hurried movement. We only have to tune our eyes and our hearts to look for the small, significant opportunities to bring a sense of bodily rhythm into our children's lives.

We can also help them develop a sense of rhythmic, purposeful movement by discovering a physical activity that *we* enjoy, one that gives us a sense of rhythm and well-being. Perhaps you like to walk, or ride a bike—your child will hurry to come along, too! Or perhaps you enjoy wood carving, or sculpting. Your child will love to play for hours with the wood shavings and chips. There are many indoor handwork activities, as well, that invite a child's participation. If you knit, you can give your three- or four-year-old a piece of yarn to play with, and watch the creative mind in action! Or give your five- or six-year-old a piece of yarn and show her how to finger-knit (a series of slipknots). Soon you will have miles of finger-knit cords, waiting to be made into jump ropes or fishing lines, or coiled into hot pads and coasters! Hand-spinning sheep's wool or felting the wool to make winter hats is more involved (see the chapter on Artistic Activities for details), but let your imagination go! What activities would *you* really like to do with your hands that your child could share with you? Remember, children learn by imitation, and we give them a great gift by modeling our deep pleasure in rhythmic physical activities.

DAILY RHYTHMS

We can also bring a sense of rhythm into our child's life by carefully crafting the rhythm of her day. Not only do we want her day to be filled with rhythmic physical activities in which she can join us, but we also want these activities to move throughout her day in a rhythmic fashion. Our child's day actually begins the night before, at bedtime—so let's begin there. Of the many suggestions offered here, choose just one thing to begin with, and give it a try. See what magic ensues—and be sure to get your journal and make notes. A year from now, you will be happy to reread these beginning steps, and to see how far you have come!

ATTITUDE TIP

If you work with love, your child will, too!

CHILD'S DAILY CHORES

Morning
- *Stir breakfast tea*
- *Wash bowl and spoon*

After Nap Time
- *Fold nap blankets*
- *Put them on the shelf*
- *Do a small "weekly" chore**

Evening
- *Sweep kitchen with parent, as dinner cooks*

About Bedtime

AN EVENING ROUTINE

6:00 Eat dinner

6:30 Bath time

6:50 Out of tub, into pajamas

7:00 Bedtime snack

7:10 Brush teeth, lay out clothes

7:15 Story

7:30 Candle time

Hugs and kisses

Lights out

TRIED AND TRUE
BEDTIME SNACK

*Buttered toast with honey, and
warm milk with honey and
cinnamon—works like a charm!*

SNACK TIP

*Join your child in the snack. It
will work wonders for you, too.*

CLOTHING TIP

*Give away all clothes that don't
meet with both your approval and
theirs! Grandma's lovely itchy
wool sweater and the superhero
T-shirt, both.*

When my children were young—and I had three energetic boys—our evenings had a predictable, easy flow of movement. Here is a schedule that worked for our family, and it may be one you'd like to try. Because I wanted to get the boys to bed by 7:30, I started the evening ritual right after dinner, around 6:30. Luckily for me, the bathroom was off the kitchen, so I popped all three of them into the bathtub as soon as the table was cleared. Then, with bubbles and plenty of laughter, they played while I washed dishes. I never worried about the water on the floor, and kept the mop handy for a quick clean-up. Their pleasure before bed and especially my sense of calm were more important than a dry floor. When the dishes were finished, out of the tub and into their pajamas they went.

Then—yes, right after supper—I gave them a bedtime snack, which was always the same thing. Night after night their entire childhood, I made whole wheat toast with honey, and warm milk with cinnamon. The warm milk, honey, and even the starch in the bread are all mild sedatives. Even for adults, warm milk and toast can help on restless nights! Over the years I have given this bedtime snack "formula" to many parents, who are amazed at the consistent result: a happily sleepy child. This bedtime snack was a beloved ritual for my sons, who would begin yawning even as they ate. Then we went on to tooth brushing and laying out clothes for the next day.

Here is a discovery I made that deflated the clothing battle: *throw out or give away everything that does not have both your approval and theirs.* So the lovely itchy little wool sweaters went out, along with the polyester superhero sweatshirts. (There will be more to say about clothing in the chapter on "Other Topics Parents Wonder About.")

After this, we all piled into one bed and heard a story. The story we choose for bedtime will plant seeds, images they will carry into their dream life. Bedtime stories are the most important stories of the day. Infants and babies can be put to bed with finger and toe games, with simple songs and rocking rhymes. Mother Goose is still the classic, and you can add gestures, touching face, fingers, tummies, toes. Watch them giggle! Toddlers want to know about the world inside the house and expanding out into the yard, with its plants, trees, squirrels, birds, insects and family pets. For children up to the age of four, simple stories of the natural world, of familiar places, people and animals, are excellent. They need to hear about the world they live in, with its slowly expanding horizon. Fives, sixes and sevens love the imaginative world of fairy tales, with kings and queens, gnomes and fairies. Eights and upward love adventure stories. Even when my boys could read these adventure stories themselves, they still asked to be read to at bedtime! It is a tremendous gift to lie back, close your eyes, and hear a story told by a beloved voice. You can find a full discussion in the chapter on Stories, but for now just a few words.

The more we adults can cultivate our imagination, take the leap and tell an original story, the better we can model a rich inner world for our children. A story that *you* make up for your child is alive in a way completely different from any other. We needn't be concerned that we don't have a clear story line, or that character development isn't robust. For our young child, simple is better. The golden rule, in most circumstances, is "Simple, Simple, Simple." A simple story might be one that reflects back to the child her own day. For the two- and three-year-old child you can use her own name in the story and mention the things she has done in the day—something like this: "Once upon a time there was a little girl named Madeline. Now, when Madeline woke up each morning the first thing she liked to do was look out her window and watch the birds as they awoke in their nest," or, "she liked very best to have French toast for breakfast. This was her lucky day!" As your child matures, you can continue to tell her stories about her own adventures, only in a more subtle way.

For many years I told my boys a story called The Grandpa Story. It was about an old man and three young boys who lived together in the woods. Slowly the story wound through the seasons, and through various events in my sons' real lives. These stories can begin to live their own lives, and sometimes your child will ask to be told particular scenarios that may address a difficulty he is experiencing. When a story like this becomes established, you may also give hints or advice within the story line. As your child grows, he

REMEMBER

Offer only one story.

Make up your own stories.

Carefully choose books that:

• *Feature a luminous central image in each illustration*

• *Model social behavior*

• *Portray high character*

BEDTIME STORY POINTERS

Infants and babies

• *Finger and toe rhymes*

• *Lullabies and rocking rhymes*

Twos through fours

• *Stories of home, yard and animals*

• *Stories about their own day*

Fives, sixes and sevens

• *Fairy tales*

• *Images of fine human qualities*

Eights and up

• *High adventure*

may choose to help in the telling of the story, or prompt you when you are a little slow. A made-up story is a tremendous gift we can give, and I would encourage all parents to try their hand at this, keeping in mind that high adventure can wait until children are seven or eight years old.

Of course, there are many wonderful children's books. Look for ones in which the illustrations are clear, colorful, and not too busy visually. Each illustration might have one luminous central image that carries the child's imagination through the text of the story. We can choose stories that offer our child images of particular qualities that will be helpful as they go through life. Traditional stories and fairy tales are filled with images of various human qualities. In traditional societies, stories have always been used to model desired social behavior, and to redirect unacceptable behavior. We can do a little research to find which images we would like to offer at particular times. For instance, if your child is experiencing fears, stories that image comfort (for the threes and fours) or courage (for the fives and sixes) could have a subtly powerful effect. The images we offer our children are alive, and will continue to live on in their souls. So let us choose, especially at bedtime, with great care.

Now for a key pointer—offer your children only one story at bedtime. Choose carefully, and if they ask for more, read, tell, or look carefully at the same pictures again, but let the image or theme you have chosen remain singular for them. If they want a little more contact, sing to them or rub their back. The closer we can keep the bedtime ritual to a simple repetition of actions, with little or no variance, the more easily our child will slip into the world of sleep. When we acquiesce to the cries of "I'm hungry" or "Just one more story," it becomes harder for our child to relax and drift off.

After the story, a candle-lighting moment will bring the magic of fire into your child's inner life. Since time immemorial, we humans have drifted off to sleep by the light and warmth of the central fire, in the hearth, the village or the cave. Although our modern lives are far removed from these roots, somewhere in our ancestral memory we are still mesmerized by the life force of an open flame. As adults too, we long for the fire, for vacation evenings in a cabin, gazing into the fireplace, being lulled by the warmth and the tiny crackling sounds as the coals burn low. We can give our child a living image of fire, with a simple moment before sleep. When the story is finished, you can turn off the lamp and light a special "sleep candle," one given perhaps as a gift at a birthday, or chosen together with the child. You can see something precious in his face at this moment—perhaps a feeling you'll want to record in your journal. Then, by the candle's glow, you can say a little prayer or poem for your child. We want to evoke a sense of calm, of quiet joy and protection. Then your child may blow or snuff out the light, and get tucked in for the night.

Of course, we must know the needs of our own child. My youngest son chose this moment, and not a moment sooner, to tell me whatever was most important in his day. Whether it was a small hurt or a philosophical question about life, he needed to say it before he went to sleep. With this in mind, I tried to begin the bedtime ritual leaving enough time for this last significant thing, and still get the lights out close to 7:30. So, if your child needs a little back rub or a special song, plan for it and start early. Our ritual, including bath, dishes, snack, story, candle and prayer, took about one hour, with the last fifteen to twenty minutes actually in bed, with me in the room. If we focus on not deviating from the ritual, bedtime can be an easy, relaxing meander toward sleep.

A question we parents must grapple with is the age at which we expect our child to be able to let us leave the room after the ritual is over, if they are not yet asleep. Your toddler may need you to lie down and snuggle with her till she drifts off, but at a certain point you can begin to sit on the edge of the bed instead, and pat her back a few minutes. There can be a gradual process, moving from holding your child in your lap for the story and snuggling her to sleep (when she is a toddler) to telling the story beside her in bed and patting her to sleep (sometime around age four). By age five you can move toward telling the story from the side of the bed and knitting in the chair beside her as she drifts off, until that magic day when you can tell the story, blow out the candle, give hugs and kisses and walk out of the room. Is your child too young for you to even imagine this day? Remember, as with everything in parenting, it is our calm and certainty that carry the day. More than the details of what we do, it is our inner conviction that our child will deeply take into her soul.

Having put your child lovingly to bed at an early hour, you have now given yourself a little time to enjoy an adult life! There is time for an adult

---

Did You Know?

Television viewing is associated with altered sleep patterns and sleep disorders in children.[1]

Bedtime Blessing

Guardian angels
Whom we love,
Shine on us
From up above.
Now I lay me
Down to sleep,
I pray the Lord
My soul to keep.
In the morning
When I wake,
Show me the path
Of love to take.
Amen.
Blessings on our sleep.

BEDTIME TIP

Say the blessing while the candle is lit. Watch their eyes shine!

EXAMPLE OF WEEKLY BREAKFASTS

Mon: Oatmeal with fresh fruit

Tues: Cream of wheat with dried plums

Wed: Rice with raisins

Thurs: Couscous with sunflower seeds

Fri: Creamy oats (oat bran, cooked) with banana

Sat: French toast

Sun: Pancakes and berries

BREAKFAST TIP

Save the scrumptious, time-consuming foods for weekends!

conversation or simple relaxation. We need to keep in mind that the most important gift we can give our children is a happy, well-rested parent; their well-being depends on ours. An early bedtime not only gives them their much-needed sleep, it can give us a little bit of rejuvenation. We live in a sleep-deprived society, and we may not have had the experience of knowing what a well-rested child, or even our well-rested selves, can be. Many daytime difficulties can be addressed most effectively by giving your child the opportunity to sleep deeply and well. For children under the age of seven, eleven or twelve hours of sleep is optimal. If your child is napping two hours, ten hours at night may be fine. But if your child has given up a nap, she will probably need to go to bed early!

About Morning Time

Having rested well, your child will wake up eager for the day. For a young child, each day is a feast of well-beloved experiences and an adventure through new ones. If we have managed to get to bed at a reasonable hour ourselves, we may echo their eagerness. Most young children want to run into our bedrooms first thing in the morning and snuggle us awake. This is a perfect time, with the freshness of the morning, to be aware of the freshness our children bring into our lives. The soul of the young child lives in *the growing forces*, and like grass, or spring flowers, there is an innate sense of joy, of newness, of hope that clings to them like morning dew. We can breathe in their jubilation, and awake with gratitude.

My children greeted us with hugs and kisses and cries of "We're starving!"—so we leapt into the day. What about breakfast? In today's world of fast food and instant preparation, we can keep in mind that a warm breakfast gives a physical experience of comfort, and simple cooked cereals are usually loved by all children. Oatmeal, cream of wheat, couscous and reheated rice from last night's dinner are all quick, easy and delicious when served with milk and fruit. Herbal fruit teas, served warm with honey, are calming and avoid the trap of too much fruit juice, which fills your child up and leaves no room for the more slowly digesting complex carbohydrates. Remember, it used to be said that oatmeal "sticks to your ribs."

Meals can be simplified by thinking through a "round" of meals for the week. You know as parents that the hardest part of meal preparation is deciding what to cook and taking everyone's preferences into consideration. To streamline this process, you can make a schedule for the week, assigning a particular breakfast to each day. As you think through your weekly schedule, keep in mind warm breakfasts, with a low sugar content, and warm herbal tea. You will know your family's preferences and can see that each meal has something that each person will like. For example, if one of your children doesn't like rice, serve warmed applesauce with it, so she has something to love in the meal. Save pancakes and French toast, which are more time-consuming, for the slower weekend pace.

A beloved ritual with ancient roots as well as modern applications is to take a moment before the meal to experience gratitude. This can be in the form of a traditional blessing, a little song, a moment of silence. What feels best for you will work the best for your children. This moment gives us the opportunity to connect with the larger world, the source from which our food comes, to connect with those with whom we share the meal, and to connect, in this pause from the clatter of life, with ourselves. Your younger children will probably like a song best, and as they grow, they may come to love a moment's silence.

Recently, a friend told me this story. She had an old friend visit overnight one Sunday, in preparation for an early business meeting the next morning. In the morning, her family woke up and proceeded as usual. Their entire family life, they had shared breakfast together, everyone gathering over a meal, before they went into their separate lives for the day. With one daughter away at college, they continued this tradition with their younger daughter, a senior in high school. With their guest, they sat down, shared food, drank tea, and enjoyed each other's company. It was life as usual for them. Later in the day, their guest called to say how moved he had been by this. He said it was the most civilized experience he'd had in a long time, and he found himself affected all day by this caring moment together. In our hectic pace of life we forget the power of the small acts that affirm our love and connection. When we come together in these small human acts, to share a meal, or rake leaves, or plant a flower, we offer each other food for the soul. This nourishes us, certainly.

> MEAL BLESSINGS
>
> *Blessing on the blossom,*
> *Blessing on the fruit,*
> *Blessing on the leaf and stem,*
> *Blessing on the root.*
>
> *Also:*
>
> *Earth who gave to us this food,*
> *Sun who made it ripe and good,*
> *Dearest Earth, and Dearest Sun,*
> *We'll not forget what you have done.*
>
> *(from the Waldorf Schools)*

Of course, we want to serve whole foods, as unpackaged and close to the earth as we can manage. Studies abound showing the higher nutritional value of unprocessed foods. But I don't know of a way we can measure the nutritional value of love, of belonging and connection. We may not be able

to measure the love that is in the food we eat, but we can surely taste it! Do you remember the way your mother's favorite dish tasted? Or the home-made candy from Grandma at Christmas? From a lifetime of mornings spent together at the breakfast table, your child will take away not only good eating habits but a well-nourished soul that will nourish others in the future.

About Daily Activities

Breakfast is finished, now on to the day. Many parents spend a part of the morning either driving to work, driving children to school, or both. If we can arrange to keep our young children out of the car, however, that is best. Later in our parenting, we will find that car time with our children is precious time. When they are older, we have a captive audience for conversation, sharing with them details of our day. But for now, the less car time for our children, the better. If, in spite of your best efforts, you need to put your young child in the car in the morning, see if you can manage to keep the radio off. There are other times of the day to hear the news, and your child does not need these often violent images cluttering up his imagination. You can have car songs that you sing together, or the old traditional car games, such as "I Spy." Sometimes it is lovely to simply be together in silence, also.

If your child attends preschool or kindergarten, see the chapter on "Other Topics Parents Wonder About" for tips on choosing a child-care setting. On the days he doesn't attend and weekends, you can plan an open rhythm of indoor play, outdoor play, snack times, nap times and social times with playmates. In today's society, there is pressure to give our young child "enrichment opportunities" from an exhaustive list of possibilities such as dance lessons, music lessons and baby gymnastics. We need to remember that there is nothing more "enriching" for a young child than exploring his own world of home, filled with natural playthings and the work of caring for a family—housework, laundry, cooking—and exploring his own backyard. Look for the chapters on the magic of Indoor Play, Outdoor Play and Artistic Experience.

Here is a simple schedule that you can think about, and perhaps adapt to your needs:

9:00–10:30 Outdoor play. Begin the day in the fresh air! It sets the tone for the whole day.

10:30 Snack. Think light and simple—fruit, raisins, crackers, etc., and leftover tea.

11:00–12:00 Indoor play, clean up.

12:30 Lunch, wash dishes, run outdoors a little.

1:00–3:00 Nap. Quiet time for older ones.

3:30 Snack. More on the importance of afternoon snack below.

4:00 A perfect time for a walk, or outdoor play.

5:00 Dinner preparation. Include your child!

About Nap Time

Now a word about sleep. How easily children fall into the deep waters of sleep, and how necessary is this easy movement between two worlds. There is the world of our Earth, with its shape, form, intention and purpose. In time they will take this world between two hands to hold, nurture and protect. But we are also made of the other world—the world of light and unity, of mystery and great archetypes. Sleep is the bridge between these worlds, which reside in our own being. When we as a culture trade sleep for productivity, we close a door to the nourishment and wisdom of dreams.

Nap time is a great gift we give our children. It is an opportunity to begin again. Do you remember waking from a nap as a child? It was a brand new day, with fresh energy and new adventures to explore, adventures as simple as a well-loved snack or a game with the family cat. If your child has been busy and active indoors and out, and if you make nap time a ritual affair, with familiar steps, your child can fall into sleep with ease. Here are some ideas for a smooth nap time.

After lunch is cleared away, it is wonderful for your child to have a quick run, jump and tumble outdoors. A half hour of outdoor play gives time for children to begin digestion, and to run some of the wiggling out of their system. Indoors again, they can use the bathroom, wash up a bit, and then off to nap. I cannot strongly enough suggest dark curtains or a dark shade for nap time, so that when they enter the nap room it is dark and inviting. You will want to have their special blanket or soft cuddly toy ready for them, too. Think cozy. A fan, in all weather, is a good idea. It creates some "white noise" that will mask other afternoon noises. It also creates a breeze and encourages your child to stay snuggled under a blanket. The weight of the blanket, and its softness snuggled around their neck and head, creates a sense of burrowing in. You can create the same effect for infants by dressing them in warm, close-fitting clothes and placing them on their backs, in an empty crib, until they are old enough to lift their heads and roll over. When these recommendations have been followed, the instances of SIDS have dropped dramatically.

You can sit beside the bed to read a story as your child drifts off. Choose a simple chapter book without pictures, for instance the Old Mother West

---

A SIMPLE NAP ROUTINE

After lunch:

• *Run outside, play*

• *Potty and wash up*

• *Make nap room dark*

• *Have the "blankie" ready*

• *Fan for white noise*

• *Chapter books (not picture books)*

• *Minimal voice inflection*

• *Sit in rocker, for rhythmic sound*

RESTLESS NAPPERS?

Try any or all of these:

• *Homeopathic rescue remedy (from flowers)*

• *Small lavender pillow*

• *No sweets at lunch*

• *Rest your hand on her back*

• *Hum quietly*

• *Have her lie on her side*

Wind series. This children's classic, first published in 1910, pictures the world when it was brand new, through stories of the many animals and how they came to have their unique characteristics. The Little House on the Prairie series shows frontier life in all its beauty and hardship. And the Brambly Hedge Series (see Chapter Notes) features the lives of a community of mice as they move through the seasons. These books are full of nature images, simple enough to help the younger child drift toward sleep but with just enough story line to keep your older child interested. Remember that the purpose of the story is to lull your child into dreamland, so use a fairly quiet voice with little inflection, and choose books that won't distract from the drifting-off process. Also, if you are sitting in a rocking chair close by, the motion of your chair will create a rhythmic, hypnotic sound, a kind of "shush, shush," that can also be comforting. If you follow a few simple steps with absolute regularity, and make nap time ritualized, your child should drop off to sleep easily and happily.

If you also are tired, this is a moment to lie down, put your feet up and close your eyes. Even twenty minutes of rest can make a huge difference in your afternoon and evening. Try putting your feet a bit higher than your head, perhaps with a pillow under your knees, for a few minutes. You will be amazed! Then roll over to lie on your side. This allows for the thinking mechanism to turn off, and the drifting images of dreams to float in. As parents of young children, we are eager to squeeze work into each available moment of the day, but a twenty-minute siesta will reinvigorate the rest of your afternoon.

NAP TIP

Take a power nap after he's asleep. Twenty minutes will work wonders for you.

About Afternoon Snack

When your child awakens, he will be ready to jump into a brand new afternoon. Because you have given yourself twenty minutes of down time, and have just had an hour to accomplish some work, you also will be ready for fun.

Afternoon snack is an important time and needs special attention. Our biorhythms tend to converge at a low point sometime around 4:00. Planning a hearty, healthy snack can nip afternoon crying jags and tantrums in the bud. My children were always starving at this time, and I decided to ignore the old wisdom that a snack would ruin their dinner. Instead I chose to give them the right amount of the right food, deciding that if they were not very hungry for dinner, I wouldn't worry. So I gave them some protein—a nut butter, or cheese, or hard-boiled egg—and cut-up veggies with a good yogurt-based dip. I tried to stay away from starches, which would tend to fill them up too much. And I stayed far away from the packaged, overly salted, or sugared snacks that are marketed to children. I tried to make this a mini-dinner.

For our family, this worked perfectly. The boys had good energy for the rest of the afternoon and were still hungry at dinner. I made sure the dinners were appealing to children—lasagna, Mexican foods, pasta, cream-based soups, and so forth. And because they'd had veggies for their snack, they were not expected to have a whole portion of the asparagus or braised fennel.

About Dinnertime

Dinnertime is a fast-disappearing tradition, and one worth saving at all costs. Dinnertime is the prime place for the handing down of culture, wisdom, language, the art of conversation, the subtleties of social relationships, and other essential human activities. It is the time when we bring our separate individual energies back together after the day. It is the place where we are knit together again as a unit, as a family.

In earlier times, when the daily work revolved around the home and the surrounding land, families had more opportunities throughout the day for the handing on of values, for modeling cultural mores. Children learned life tasks at the side of their parents, at the spinning wheel or the plough. Even as recently as seventy-five years ago, farm children learned the intricacies of managing a family business in the course of their growing up, from home economics to animal husbandry to sound financial investing. Every aspect of managing a busy, diverse farm was discussed throughout the day, especially at dinnertime. This basic training in life skills continued into social picnics and church on Sunday. In our modern lives, as we all go off to our separate endeavors, dinnertime becomes a precious and essential time with our children.

It is tempting to make a separate early dinner of "kid food," like macaroni and cheese, hot dogs or tofu dogs, then later to prepare a quiet meal for parents to share. On occasion, this may be just what is needed. But if we make this a regular practice, we lose a tremendous opportunity to offer our children the best of ourselves. There is great pleasure in gathering together around a table filled with lovingly prepared food and the nourishment of each other's company.

If we establish a habit of coming together at the day's end and talking with each other when our children are young, it can serve as a foundation for them as they grow through the years. Some families have a tradition of telling, each in turn, a favorite aspect of their day. For our family, this was too formal. With three boys at the table, the ceremony inevitably dissolved in gales of laughter. Instead, I would begin with a small anecdote from my day, and see if I could artfully lead the conversation in a creative direction. As the children grew older, the dinner table became a place where they could voice their opinions and listen to adult perspectives about various aspects of life. We have to be careful, with older children, to sidestep the temptation to lecture. A lecture is a sure signal to a preteen to tune out. Instead we can simply share our perspective, and listen respectfully to theirs. Perhaps, like many of us, they need most to speak their own thought out loud, just to hear what it sounds like. Teenagers like a forum in which to air their current feelings on everything from religion to music, finances to utopian societies. With young children, though, we can focus on the familiar surroundings of home and family life, the goings-on in the backyard garden, the weather and its immediate effect on our lives—whether we needed our rain boots today, or if the snow will come in the night.

Dinner preparation, as with breakfast, can be simplified by thinking, shopping and preparing on a weekly plan. Try thinking of seven categories of meals, such as pasta one night, Mexican another, stir-fry another, soup and toast, and so forth. If your categories are broad enough, there should be plenty of variety from week to week, yet the system remains simple and

SAMPLE EVENING
MEAL CHART

Mon: Mexican

Tues: Chicken

Wed: Stir-fry and rice

Thurs: Soup and bread

Fri: Pasta

Sat: Quiche or pot pie

Sun: Roast and veggies

SHOPPING TIP

Stand at the refrigerator, look at your beautiful chart and make your shopping list. No forgotten ingredients!

easy to manage. You can make a beautifully decorated chart to put on your refrigerator door so that when evening arrives after the business of the day, with everyone tired and hungry, the hard work of thinking is already complete. If you shop with the weekly round of meals in mind, then all your ingredients should be right at hand, and dinner soon on the table. Remember to plan weekday meals that are quick to prepare. Save more complex, time-consuming dishes for weekends, when the pace is slower. As years go by, and your children develop new tastes, you'll make new dinner charts. If you save the old ones in your journal, they will become a family heirloom that your grandchildren will love to pour over!

As parents, we do not know what will be the result of our choices and decisions about lifestyle, schooling and spiritual direction for our children. All we can do is continue to educate ourselves in our decision-making, and do the hard work these decisions demand. It is not for many years that we will be able to see what indelible impressions we have made. We just do our best day by day, year after year, in faith that our abiding love for our children will act as our guide, that love will show us the needs of each unique child of ours.

I understood this most clearly when, after graduating from high school, my two younger sons spent a winter working and skiing in Lake Tahoe. It was their first opportunity to create a home of their own making. When I went to visit them, I was stunned and pleased to see what their choices were. After a long day playing and working in the snow, they came home to a clean house (!) and began preparing a huge dinner. As their friends, other boys their age, got off work, they began to drift in the front door. Soon there was a living room full of young men. A cloth was draped over the television; they played chess, listened to music and cooked together. There was good humor, plenty of subtle verbal quipping and the requisite amount of horseplay. When the meal was prepared, they all sat down at a large table to share this feast. This was the usual course of events for their evening, as it had been their entire lives. I understood at that moment that we parents leap off the cliff of our own heartfelt convictions, and it is not for many years that we see where we and our children have landed.

Weekly Rhythms

In the same way that we have arranged our family's meals into a weekly rhythm, we can also arrange weekly activities. Knowing our child's natural inclinations, we can think of activities she would enjoy on a regular basis. Perhaps we live close to a wooded area with nature trails, or we have a favorite park with a varied terrain and walking paths. We can create our own simple weekly rituals. Maybe we want a "Tuesday bagel day" ritual, in which we walk to the bagel shop and get bagels for lunch, with a few stale ones to feed the birds in the park. Then on Wednesday, off we go to the park, bag of bagels in hand.

We can also see what activities our community has to offer young children. We will want to choose carefully, because our children are still young and merged, in a certain way, with the environment. When you are researching what activities you would like for your child, look thoughtfully at the sensory stimulation provided. Is the place noisy, full of loud music or erratic ambient sound? Choose situations that allow a sense of inner quiet. This gives the child a way to integrate the experience. Look at the visual stimulation. Are the colors too brightly fluorescent, as in many children's activities these days? Is the visual atmosphere too packed, too busy, too much to see? Choose experiences that ask your child's eye to open into the color, to lean toward it, so to speak. When sounds are too loud and colors are too bright, the natural organic response is for the eye or ear to shut down. We are concerned not only about our child's sensory response, but also about her soul response. We want to offer her experiences that ask her to "open into" the encounter, not close down or retract from it, however subtly. If you have made a mistake in your choice of activities, your child will probably let you know about it. She may cry later in the day, or act out about some small thing. It is a rare child who will say, "I don't like this, it's too loud." But most children *will* communicate it to you in other ways.

When choosing weekly activities, remember the golden rule: Simple, Simple, Simple! A walk to the park one day, a story hour at the library another and a weekly play date with a friend is a busy week for a child up to the age of four. If your child attends preschool or kindergarten, you will want to keep the extra activities to a minimum. Save the many "enrichment classes" that are offered in your community until your child is grade-school age. The young child learns by freely imitating what she sees in her environment. Most of these classes are taught on an instructional model, which is age-appropriate for grade school children. But our young ones need environments that are free enough to allow them to use their natural gift of imitation. Activities that involve the great outdoors offer the best "sensory enrichment" possible!

MUSINGS ON RHYTHMS

In these few pages, there are dozens of ideas, suggestions, and thoughts to consider. It would be easy to feel overwhelmed, to choose nothing rather than turn your life on its head. Instead, see if there is one idea, one area in which you'd like to try subtle changes. Perhaps you'd like to try an earlier bedtime. You can begin to move it back by fifteen-minute increments, to choose a story carefully and celebrate with your child by buying a bedtime candle together. Or mealtimes may need your attention. Try shifting things around on weekends to begin with. Be gentle with yourself and set an easy pace as you move your life toward the rhythm you'd like. Abrupt changes are often too dramatic, too difficult, and therefore not successful. You can try just one thing, and when you and your child have integrated it well, then move onto the next. Most of all, enjoy!

Chapter 3

CELEBRATING FESTIVALS TOGETHER

WE LIVE IN the great round of the year, and the celebration of festivals lives deeply in our roots. Across all cultures and ages, humans have come together in observance of the progression of time, in recognition of our relationship to the earth. Although our western society has become far removed from these agricultural origins, we can give recognition to the way these rhythms still live in us through the celebration of family festivals. We can rejoice in the turning of the seasons at home with images, stories, foods and activities that evoke seasonal qualities. Many of the agricultural festivals and their closely associated religious holidays have been claimed by marketing agencies and have become overly commercial, devoid of soul. If we choose, though, we can ensoul them and make them our own unique celebrations. They can become a picture of our family life together.

In the celebration of a festival, we take a moment outside of the inexorable progression of time. We stop time, so to speak. In this way we can assess where we are right now. We can look back over the last year, remembering where we were, what we did, and who was present this time last year. We can pause to glance over what the year has brought, how we have changed and grown, as individuals and as a family. We can also cast our glance into the future, looking to see how our family will change in the coming year and what will be needed at that time.

It is important in the celebration of a festival to include certain elements that will remain the same, year after year. We also need to allow for change and growth. In order for the festival to be alive there needs to be stability, something that we can always count on, while new elements express our changing consciousness, our growth. The festival needs to speak to every member of the family, each at her own level. To create festivals for our families that will endure, and will continue to offer both stability and also the flexibility required by growth, is an art and an adventure. Let's look at some of the seasonal festivals, and at various elements that will help us to create family festivals everyone will love to celebrate.

Elements of a Family Festival

In planning a family festival, we need to consider the activities of preparation for the celebration, special festive foods, songs that are specific to the time of year, and stories that support the festival. A festival is not something that occurs on a particular day, for a few hours; it is a building toward a moment shared together in the warm embrace of family, something we can begin preparing for in advance. For a young child, the preparation, the anticipation, the slow building toward the event is as important as the event itself. We can notice a pattern of preparation, a sort of wave of energy as the day draws near. If we begin several weeks ahead, we feel the slow beginning: the telling and retelling of stories and memories, the planning. About a week before, we begin the actual work: cleaning, shopping, and so forth. In the couple of days before, there begins to be a whirl of activity: cooking, decorating, singing. The actual day is filled with all the goodness of the energy that we have given toward this day.

As adults, we may find a moment when everyone is happily eating, amidst the laughter and sweetness—right in the center of this, we may feel an inner hush. This is a moment in which we take in all the beauty, the family bonds, the joy we have worked to create. Now we can drink in the love that is being made visible right here at our family's dining table. It will not be for many years, perhaps until our children are parents themselves, that they will *consciously* know what we have made for them. But we will know.

In preparing for the celebration, we can talk together, maybe at dinnertime, remembering our favorite foods from last year and considering whether we want to introduce any variations. We can make a shopping list together, and perhaps shop with our child. You might give your five- or six-year-old the task of choosing which sweet potatoes to take from the bin, or which fruits for the fruit salad. Your three- or four-year-old will probably want to stay close, helping to push the cart or riding alongside the veggies.

Elements of a Festival

Preparatory activities

• *Discuss décor*

• *Gather natural materials*

• *Make wreath, etc.*

• *House cleaning and decorating*

Festive foods

• *Discuss*

• *Shop*

• *Prepare early*

Stories, from your childhood or the library

Songs, from childhood or library

Festival Tip

Be sure there are elements that remain the same from year to year, and also elements that can evolve as your children do!

Planning for decorations, gathering the materials and decorating the house are fun—and time-consuming, so start early! If in your family there are older grade-school or preteen children as well as preschoolers, you can involve your older children in either helping the little ones in their tasks or actually making special decorations for their younger siblings. As our children mature, they will feel more connected to the festival if they align themselves with us, the adults, in preparing an event filled with wonder for the little ones. Usually we can go for a walk in the park or a nature area to find natural decorations. In autumn, we can look for brilliant autumn leaves and dried grasses for a fall festival. In winter we'll find pine cones and bare branches, red winter berries and evergreen boughs. For spring, we can find a bouquet of flowering branches. You can buy a grapevine wreath at a craft store and decorate it seasonally for each festival, perhaps using it as a centerpiece for the table.

With each festival, you'll want to make notes in your journal, including favorite recipes, stories the children loved, or the place you found the perfect scarlet maple leaves. You can also make notes of good ideas for future years. Your journal can then become a reference book for your whole family.

You can begin singing songs and telling stories that image the season many days or even a couple of weeks in advance. Check the Bibliography for books full of seasonal songs and stories. Or take a trip to the library with your child and do your own research. You can choose some that will remain a constant, and others that will change as your child grows. This is the great fun of crafting a festival—choose year by year, gauge your child's development, and offer images, songs, foods, and activities that will speak especially to her!

Another aspect of preparation is cleaning the house for the festive day. The two-, three- or four-year-old will want to come along and join you in whatever task you are working on. This will of course take more time, so try to begin early. The five- or six-year-old will enjoy a task that you lay out for him to accomplish on his own.

Preparation of the festive foods can be started before the festival day. Because your young children will be helping, you can break it down into small increments. Your child can help cut up the potatoes, which can then be covered with water and kept in an airtight container overnight in the refrigerator. Desserts can usually be prepared beforehand, and frozen if necessary. Your young child will love to help break the eggs and whip them. Most vegetables can be prepared beforehand, refrigerated, and then be ready for cooking on the festival day. The more we can involve our child in the tasks of preparing and cooking, the more they will be invested, the more they will love the celebration. It will become their own, something that will live inside their hearts.

The Festive Table

From my kindergarten journal:

What a pleasure it is, in the twenty-first century, to set a large table with glassware, bowls and baskets of whole foods. It is morning and the table is ready, waiting in anticipation of the children. This table groans not only with food, but also with children's laughter, shared communion and culture being passed on, bowl by bowl.

The table is a living symbol of gathering, sharing, celebration and communion! Let's consider how to prepare the festival table in easy, elegant and natural ways. The simple act of laying a beautiful cloth over the table can completely transform the entire room, creating a mood of anticipation. Shaking out the tablecloth and placing it just so says, "Let the magic commence." You may want to have a special tablecloth for each family festival. This way, the cloth itself helps to define the occasion. You can go to the fabric store and buy a length of cloth to fit your table. Look for seasonal colors in quiet patterns, which will hide stains and wash easily. Hem the two ends and, voilà!—a tablecloth. In our family we had a cloth with golden autumn leaves for fall, green sprays of pine boughs for winter, and a vibrant spring floral for Easter. I didn't choose fabric from the children's section, as these designs tend to be "cutesy." Instead, I chose fabrics of my own taste. Because our festive tablecloths and decorations

---

THE FESTIVE TABLE

Seasonal tablecloth

• *Seasonal colors*

• *Patterns hide stains*

• *Not "cutesy"*

• *Washable fabric*

Seasonal centerpiece

• *Grapevine wreath*

• *"Found" decorations*

• *Seasonal candles*

Simple china, to go with patterns and décor

were of very different colors and designs, I chose a plain white embossed china that would be good on any background. You may want to consider this also. On top of the seasonal cloth, you can place your simple, elegant centerpiece, the decorated wreath. You may want to buy seasonally colored candles to go with the wreath, and include the magic of candlelight in your celebration.

The beautiful cloth and simple china, the natural "hand-gathered" centerpiece and candles, the dishes and platters full of festive foods—for your young child, these physical substances are the essence of the festival. In time your child will begin to form concepts: gathering, sharing, celebration, communion. But for now, the meaning lies in the actuality of the things themselves. So let us take care and delight in preparing them well.

An Autumn Festival

Autumn is the time of great abundance in nature, and we can create an autumn celebration to image this generosity. If you are lucky enough to live in a rural setting, it will be easy for you to find crops that are being harvested locally. In addition, chances are good that your own small town celebrates the harvest in its unique way. You can join in the town festivities and easily build a home celebration that augments and deepens the imagery for your child. If you are in a large town or small city, you can check the newspapers for farms or orchards that open their doors to the public. A family outing to a pumpkin patch, an orchard, a vineyard and such can be the beginning of a family celebration. Let these ideas be a springboard for your own imagination. An apple festival, for example, might look something like the following.

Call the orchard to find a day when the smallest crowd is expected, perhaps the day after a major holiday. Apples are picked earlier than you might imagine, so call early. Ask if the branches are low enough for a small child to reach and pick. You won't mind holding your child up to pick the beautiful red one shining at the top, but you also won't want to do this all morning. The orchard will probably provide bags for picking, but take along a large basket so you'll have plenty of apples to work with when you get home. Bring

---

An Apple Festival

Activities

- *Orchard field trip*

  Choose an uncrowded day.

  Wear long pants, long socks (poison ivy–proof).

  Bring a large basket for many apples!

  Bring water, for washing hands and apples.

  Take a long walk.

  Pack a picnic.

  Invite another family.

Foods

- *Buy hand-turned apple processor—fun!*

- *Applesauce: freeze it for winter.*

- *Dried apples*

- *Squash, onion and apple soup*

- *Whipped sweet potatoes and apples*

- *Apple pie and other apple desserts*

water to wash hands, and the apples, too. A pick-your-own organic orchard is hard to find but worth the search. Dress in long pants and long socks; poison ivy loves to grow at the root of apple trees.

On the way to the orchard you can sing the songs you have found in the songbook from the library. Or, if it is a long drive, you may want to tell a story about how the star came to live inside the apple. Did you know that if you turn every apple on its side and slice it thinly, you can see a star pattern around the core? Be imaginative and let the images be filled with wonder. Humor and cleverness can wait until your child is older. Perhaps a star child watched a little earth child playing beneath an apple tree day after day, and wanted to be closer, to hear the songs the little child sang. Maybe a young girl gazed up at the stars, longing to be filled with their shimmering light. So a star came to live inside an apple, to be baked into her birthday pie....

At the orchard, picking is only part of the fun. You can make a morning of it with a long walk through the rows of trees. If you have planned the trip with another family, there may be games of tag or hide and seek while you enjoy the early autumn sun, then a picnic snack with song and stories afterward.

Back at home, you can begin processing the apples. You can ask at any kitchen store for a wonderful device that cores, peels and slices the apples all at once, or check the Chapter Notes for ordering information. (If the store doesn't carry it, ask to see any catalogs they may have.) You can process a basket full of apples in very short order with this small device that attaches to your kitchen table and is operated by a turning handle. Your child will love to affix the apple to the prongs, turn the handle and watch the magic occur. It is easy to make applesauce in a large pot on top of the stove, with a *very* low heat, a small amount of water, and honey to taste. A little cinnamon is a special touch. If canning the old-fashioned way doesn't fit your busy schedule, you can put the applesauce in freezer jars to be brought out, defrosted and served warm on a cold winter Sunday. Or you can cook the apples slowly for a few hours, then, just before bedtime, put it all in a large casserole dish. Place this in a very low oven (250 degrees) overnight. In the morning, you will have apple butter!

You can also dry the apples by stringing them with a needle and red thread. If you have used a hand-turned apple processor, you will have a bowl

---

MORE APPLE FESTIVAL

Songs

• *Johnny Appleseed is a classic.*

• *Play "Drop the Hankie" and hum a little tune about a lost apple.*

• *Check the Appendix and your library.*

Stories

• *Your library is your friend!*

• *Your own imagination is your best friend:*

A Star Is Born in an Apple

The Adventures of the Apple Family

Windy Nights on the Apple Tree

The Day Little Apple Got Picked and Put in a Basket

You get the idea!

full of apples sliced into long spirals. Cut the apples in half from top to bottom to make crescent-shaped slices. Run the needle and thread through the top of the arc, and leave a little space between slices, for drying. Even a very young child can join in, if you say, "I will put the needle in, and you may pull the needle out." After leaving them overnight in a very low oven (as low as your oven will go) you can hang the strings of apples in the window, with red ribbon for a festive touch.

Your festival decorations might be an array of autumn leaves tucked into the grapevine wreath, with a red candle in the middle of the wreath and fresh apples surrounding it. With the dried apples and ribbons in the window, this makes an elegant and simple image for your child. The festive meal could consist of a blended butternut squash, onion and apple soup (rosemary, to taste, is the secret of this simple harvest soup), roast chicken served with spiced apple sauce, whipped sweet potatoes and apples served with honey butter, and apple pie or cobbler for dessert.

As your children grow, you will want to look for stories that grow with them, or make up your own, which are appropriate to their age. Eventually, as teenagers they may want to help plant an apple tree in a town park, or pick fresh apples to give to the local food bank. We can move from the simple enacting of the festival with the young child, to thinking about and discussing various aspects with our middle-school children, to bringing the festival into community service with our teenagers. Your journal will reflect their growth through the years, and become a family treasure.

Recently a friend took me to a local "garlic festival." There were dozens of food booths with everything from roast garlic spreads to garlic salad to garlic ice cream. Live music was offered throughout the day, some of it with a garlic theme, and a garlic king and queen were chosen. Artists and artisans offered crafts and artwork, and poetry was presented in honor of the lowly garlic. This event was a testimony to the human capacity to celebrate anything that touches our heart, and to our human desire to come together in a spirit of creativity and fun. If we can find the magic admixture of the profound and the playful, we have struck the essential balance in creating a festival that will endure.

SQUASH AND APPLE SOUP

Bake a medium-sized squash at 350°F about 1 hour, or until soft and tender.

• *When cool, scoop out flesh and blend with 1 cup chicken stock.*

• *Set aside*

Sauté in butter, until very soft:

• *1 large onion, chopped*

• *4 large apples, chopped*

• *2 tsp. dried rosemary*

Blend sautéed ingredients with 1 cup chicken stock and return to pan.

Add 1 quart chicken stock, and blended squash.

Salt to taste

This makes a very thick soup. Add chicken stock to thin. It's great as leftovers!

A Winter Festival

Most winter festivals in a temperate climate celebrate the return of the light, in one form or another. Three festivals that are celebrated widely in our culture are Hanukkah, Kwanzaa, and Christmas. This celebration of the outer light points toward kindling the inner light, the light of clarity and warmth. Here is an in-depth look at a Christmas festival, which is the tradition I am familiar with. If other mid-winter festivals of light are part of your family's culture, you can, from your own childhood memories, and some help from resource books, create a time of magic for your family!

The image of light being born in the midst of outer darkness will nourish our child's soul for a lifetime. As adults, we can conceptualize the time of solstice, the longest night in which the seeds of light are born. We can grasp that in its farthest arc, the polarization of darkness, light comes into being. As adults, we can begin to grapple with the nature of paradox. But for our young children, paradox is impossible. To talk of darkness and light, of the inverse relationship that time brings into the equation, misses the mark. For the young child, a clear and understandable image that carries this mystery perfectly is the story of a baby being born on a cold and dark winter's night. This image of the Divine born into a stable, with the animals' breath to keep the baby warm, captures all the potency of paradox and speaks it in a language understandable to a child.

Christmas is a festival that appeals to the young child by virtue of his own life experience. Very recently he has come to earth, to a very particular mother and father, in a very specific circumstance. And in his fresh innocence, each child has shone with a radiant light. In a way, the Christmas story is every child's own story. It is clear that the roots of this festival have been obscured by commercialization, but we can rescue this poignant and potent celebration by consciously choosing to research, to plan, to simplify and thereby wrest the images from the media.

If the religious aspect of the story doesn't appeal to us, we can take it out of its historical context; still the images remain intact and full of meaning. We can tell the story of an old man and a young woman who took a long winter journey. Arriving at their destination, they had no place to stay. We can include the stable, the shepherds and angels, and the birth of the "Child of Light." Our children, who still shine with an inner light, will understand this image well. And, being themselves so new, the experience of birth remains full of mystery to them.

In our family, we began the season with a low table in the corner of the living room. I draped a dark blue cloth over it. Then, week by week, we slowly celebrated the "kingdoms"—mineral, plant, animal and human. In recognizing and honoring each of these classic "kingdoms," we show our children humanity's place in the order of things. This is one of the many ways, as we weave the fabric of our family, that we show our children they belong to a greater Whole.

As the weeks went by, there was a sense of expectancy and growing anticipation as new elements entered the scene. The first week, I placed beautiful stones and crystals in the center. The second week, I displayed greens and small plants. We stabilized tiny sturdy pine boughs in soft clay, to stand upright as trees. This was the week we put up the Christmas tree. It was not until the third week that we brought out the stable, with the animals in it. Finally, several days before Christmas, we put the old man, the young woman and the shepherds into the stable. All this while, the wise men had been making their way across the living room, moving from window sill to window sill. It was not until Christmas Eve that the Child of Light came into the manger. Each evening we lit a candle, adding one more with each week, until on Christmas Eve we lit all four plus the grand "Christmas Candle." By candlelight we sang and talked about the journey, the old man and young woman, the shepherds and animals.

This slow building toward a subtle event, the coming of the Child, can act as an antidote to the societal pressures that bombard us at this time. We must remember that the atmosphere we create in our own home is the most powerful influence for the young child. It is the culture we create at home that our children will carry inside their hearts when they enter the world as young adults. To create a small corner of quiet, of gentle anticipation, of appreciation and beauty, in the face of giant commercial agencies, may make us feel a little like David facing Goliath. But if we aim well, tiny acts like these will have dramatic impact in our children's lives.

What about Santa Claus? Do you remember, as a child, the wonderful magic of Santa? This was a tradition I wanted to offer to my children,

without all the media hype. I wanted to give them a sense of Santa as a wonderful old man, kind of like an uncle, who loved children most of all. So our letters to Santa were very conversational, as if we were talking to a beloved uncle. We always wrote the letter together on Christmas Eve, and asked Santa various questions about his life with Mrs. Claus, the reindeer and elves. We also told him the highlights of each child's year, and other tidbits, so he would know us better. Occasionally one of the boys would remember to tell Santa what he wanted for Christmas, but asking for gifts was so clearly not the purpose of writing that in many years there was no mention of this at all. We wrote in colored pencils, on a large piece of paper, and the boys illustrated each letter. We left the letter under the Christmas tree, along with snacks and treats for Santa and the reindeer, too. Santa always wrote back to us, carefully answering questions and offering a word of wisdom, or encouragement, or whatever seemed necessary.

When the boys grew older and finally discovered who Santa truly was, the tradition had developed a life of its own, and so lived on. Each year we kept the "Santa letter" and Santa's reply, rolled and tied with a ribbon. We would put all the previous year's letters out, along with the new one. Of course, as the boys became middle-schoolers, their letters were full of humor, and so Santa became funnier in response. But Santa usually managed to make a philosophical statement or offer some sage advice. Even when they were teenagers, they would humor me and write a little. Meanwhile, Santa's replies became a pondering of life's questions.

The question of too many gifts at one time can be problematic. Here is the way my family handled it. Each night, for a week before Christmas, the boys got to open one gift, of my choosing. This spread the excitement out over a few days, and gave each gift its "moment in the sun." On Christmas Eve there were still several gifts left to open. And on Christmas morning they would open the very big and special Santa gift. Some children are so excited by the mounting pile of gifts that they find it hard to contain themselves, and act out in response. Opening one gift per night can be a pressure-release valve, and also add to the richness of waiting and counting the days. I have also heard of families who choose to have Christmas gifting be simpler, still. Each family member is given one large and lovely present on Christmas morning and that is all. This would truly take the commercialization out of Christmas!

A SPRING FESTIVAL

The surging joy of springtime, with its dancing, laughing energy, makes it nearly impossible to talk about. We just want to run in the spring grass and roll down hillsides. Each new blossom is a celebration in its own right. So, how to capture this delicious, raucous delight in a festival?

Eggs are a perfect symbol of this feast of Life. Each one contains a sun radiating within, the yellow disk of its orb, the white rays shining. Although our children may not entirely love the flavor of the egg, this is no reason to abandon it. In my family, we dyed, decorated and hid real hard-boiled eggs. I felt in this way the archetypal symbol of the egg remained intact. Instead of giving the boys candy-filled plastic eggs, the Easter Bunny gave them chocolate bunnies and jelly beans. I even managed to find these treats at the health food store!

A few days or a week before Easter, you can make an egg tree with your child. On a walk in the woods or the back yard, you can find a sturdy small branch, perhaps with buds just forming on it, and with a pleasing line. See if you can find one that looks like a miniature tree..

Back inside, anchor the branch in soft clay and place it in the bottom of a large clay saucer, the kind that fits under planting pots. Now fill the

---

A SPRING FESTIVAL

ACTIVITIES

• *Choose branch for Easter tree.*

• *"Plant" it in low saucer.*

• *Sprout and plant wheat grass.*

• *Blow and dye eggs.*

• *Dye hard-boiled eggs.*

• *Prepare for egg hunt.*

FOODS

• *Egg custard*

• *Bread bunnies*

• *Bread "egg baskets"*

• *Eggs: salad and deviled*

SONGS

• *See Bibliography.*

• *Check your library.*

IMAGES

• *Babies through fours: caterpillar/butterfly*

• *Fives and up: Jumping Mouse and other transformation stories* saucer with potting soil, and you have a miniature scene of a bare winter tree, standing on the naked earth. Over the next days, you can begin to build up this scene.

At the local natural foods store, you should be able to buy wheat berries, the seeds of the wheat. (You may want to set some of these aside to be baked into a sweet festival bread.) Take about one cup of berries and soak them overnight, and perhaps the next day, also. Rinse them every twelve hours. When you see a small white root popping out, it is time to plant. Rinse once more, then spread the seeds thickly over the potting soil and cover with a thin layer of soil. You can water the seeds with a plant

sprayer. If you water them too much, they will mold, so be careful. A plant sprayer also allows your child to water away happily, with less likelihood of flooding. Again, a clay pot, unlike plastic, will help to absorb excess moisture. In just a couple of days you should see green tips pushing up, and the roots beginning to grow. This is such an exciting moment for your child! Wheat grows so fast that each day there is a noticeable difference. Because it is wheat, you can "mow" the grass with scissors and nibble on it with your child. It has a sweet green taste, and is actually full of nutrition.

Now, as the festival day draws near, you can make "blown" eggs to hang on the branches of the tree. With a strong needle, make a large hole in the bottom of a raw egg, and a smaller hole in the top. With older children, a small hole at each end works fine, but for our little ones, we need slightly bigger holes. Place your mouth over the small hole, with lips making a seal, and blow the contents of the egg into a bowl well placed beneath the operation. Your small child can help, and by the time she is almost five years old she may actually be able to blow the whole egg out by herself! Keep the bowl of eggs for a special holiday treat. You can dye the eggshells (very carefully) with food color. Then loop a ribbon and push the ends carefully into the big hole. With a toothpick, you should be able to glue it to the inside of the shell. This makes a colorful hanger. Many craft stores sell small colored wooden eggs with hangers. When hung together with the dyed blown eggs, the variety of sizes is wonderful to behold, shining on the tree in morning light. With the vigorous growth of green grass below, you have transformed a bare winter scene into a corner bursting with life. If your branch had buds on it, with the warmth of being indoors its leaves may even begin to unfold, or blossoms may appear.

The day before the festival, you can bake a simple whole wheat bread (see recipe, this page) to shape into "bread bunnies" and serve with the last of the autumn's festive apple butter. Or you can try baking an egg basket: make a braided dough, shape into a small bowl, decorate with the wheat berries, place a whole uncooked egg (in its shell) in the center, and put a little braided dough handle over the top. Bake as usual, and you will have made a hard-cooked egg in a braided basket!

Stovetop egg custard is a delicious and nutritious treat that you can make after the egg hunt on the festival morning. In a double boiler, you can whisk one cup of whole milk for every two eggs. Add honey or sugar to taste, and a little nutmeg or cinnamon. Stirring constantly, in a few minutes the mixture should begin to thicken. Continue to stir as it slowly cooks, until it mounds up in a little hill in your spoon. Cool, and refrigerate, if you won't eat it immediately. You can serve it with a sweet bread full of wheat berries. There are deviled eggs and egg salads in the near future, if you have featured real eggs in your celebration. In this way, the festival continues to live and to nourish us.

In our home, we would dye hard-boiled eggs the day before Easter and leave a basket full of them on the kitchen table for the Easter bunny's convenience. My boys were happy to help the Easter bunny by leaving the dyed eggs out for her to hide. Some years, I had a bale of hay for the garden, and the boys would make hay nests for the bunny to find. One year I had many bales, and was delighted to see not hay nests, but a real hay fort awaiting her! Let your imagination dance. Like Santa, maybe the bunny will become

---

FOOLPROOF NO-RISE BREAD RECIPE

Dissolve in 1 cup boiling water:

- *4 Tbsp butter*
- *½ cup honey*

Stir until cool.

In a separate bowl, dissolve in 1.5 cups lukewarm water:

- *2 Tbsp dry baker's yeast*

Add to honey-butter and stir.

Add, 1 cup at a time:

- *6–7 cups whole wheat pastry flour.*

Knead on floured board.

Shape into rolls, bunnies, bread baskets, braids, etc.

Bake at 350°F, 40–45 min. (depending on your oven.)

Tap on top to test—a hollow sound means it's done.

Enjoy!

a beloved friend, one to whom a small note can be written in preparation for the festival.

Stories for a spring festival can image transformation. For a young child, the story of the lowly caterpillar transforming into the majestic butterfly is perfect. An older child might need a stronger illustration, such as the excellent Native American transformation tale Jumping Mouse (see the Chapter Notes). Children's literature is filled with images of transformation, and if you choose tales that speak to your own heart, your enthusiasm will carry a power of its own.

A Birthday Festival

The child's best-loved yearly festival is, of course, her own birthday. We can kindle the magic and wonder of the occasion by remembering the first moment we looked into this brand new little face and caught a glimmering of her soul. We can recollect the path we have walked together in these few years, and the way this small person has impacted in such a big way the person *we* are becoming. Keeping in mind the sense of why we have come together can help set a tone for the celebration. We can find in ourselves an up-springing joyousness, like the way the sap rises in May.

A day or two before the birthday, you can, perhaps at bedtime, tell your child little vignettes from the first days of her life. You can comment on a particular look in her eyes, or the way she liked to sleep, or what her cry sounded like. Every child loves to hear stories from her baby days, so be prepared to be asked for more and more memories. Tell her how your heart felt to look into her eyes, to begin to know who she is.

You might like to create a small birthday morning ritual. Being wakened with a kiss for each year, perhaps repeated again and again, is a good start. There might be a small birthday morning present on the bedside table for her to open. Perhaps it is a special feather or seashell, or a candle. If you can have the morning present be filled with magic—and usually it is exquisite "found objects" from the natural world that are most magical to a child—this will create an atmosphere for the day. You may want to keep a "birthday basket" in which each birthday's morning present is collected, so that in a few years it

---

A Simple, Elegant
Birthday Party

Children arrive and play

Artistic activity, to go home as a party favor

Circle game with movement and song

Beautiful birthday table

Spice cake (not too sugary)

Presents opened, thank yous

Quick good-byes

will be filled with magic feathers or seashells. If a candle is the tradition, you may want to take it downstairs and light it for the birthday breakfast, even if this is a simple bowl of oatmeal.

Your family will begin to establish how it is that you like to celebrate. Perhaps for you a small family gathering is the best way to honor the child. If you are more social, you might like, in addition to the family festivities, a party with other children and their parents. Trial and error will show you your way. However we choose, though, the family celebration will be the place where we can offer our most heartfelt wishes for our child.

If you choose to have a party, here are a few things to remember. Our society has a tendency to overdo children's birthdays, and we know the classic birthday party scenario, at which the birthday child is so overstimulated that she cries or throws a tantrum. We can prepare for a very magical, memorable party without the agitation or the tears.

A good rule of thumb for the invitation list is to invite the same number of children as the birthday child's age. In a society where fifteen or twenty guests is the rule, this will be an anomaly. Once you have experienced the wonder of a small, intimate party, though, you will be reluctant to return to the frenzy of too many and too much.

You can plan activities that are appropriate to the age of your child. The guests can arrive and have a bit of free play. Outdoors is always the best place to begin, but weather isn't always conducive to this. So, if necessary, play can begin in your open, creative playspace. (In the next chapter you'll discover how to create this space.) Parents of threes and fours will usually want to stay, and you can request this if you'd like help. Or you might want to ask a friend to come and help. The children will usually love any opportunity to play creatively, and one adult can stay in the living room, or wherever the main play area is, to help get the children's play started. In the other room, the dining room or kitchen, you and another parent can be getting a small art project ready.

For the threes and fours, the project should not be too structured. You can make a simple bread dough (see the Easter festival recipe) and have each child knead a small lump. Place all the bread rolls in a pan, sprinkle with cinnamon and sugar, bake and send home as party favors. For very young children, the party is not defined by "party games" and activities; they are

---

GINGERBREAD CHILDREN
PARTY FAVORS

Set oven at 350°F.

Cream together:

- *½ cup butter*

- *½ cup brown sugar*

Add, mix well:

- *1 cup molasses*

In a separate bowl, mix together:

- *7 cups whole wheat pastry flour*

- *2 tsp. baking soda*

- *2 tsp. powdered ginger*

- *½ tsp. salt*

- *Cinnamon to taste (we like lots!)*

Add dry ingredients to wet, a little at a time, together with ¼ to ½ cup water as needed to form a firm ball.

Roll a little out on floured board. If too sticky, add more flour. If too crumbly, add a few drops water.

Cut gingerbread family. If your child is helping roll the dough, your people will probably be chubby and thick. Decorate with dried fruits and nuts.

Bake at 350°F, 8 minutes or longer depending on thickness.

Finish dressing them with colored icing. They are charming, sturdy and not too sweet.

THE BEST BIRTHDAY CAKE

Set oven at 350 degrees.

Mix together in a bowl:

- *3½ cups whole wheat pastry flour*

- *½ cup sugar*

- *4 tsp. baking powder*

- *2 tsp salt*

- *2 tsp. cinnamon (or more!)*

With a fork or pastry cutter, cut in 1 stick softened butter. You and your child might prefer to cut the butter in with your fingers!

In a separate bowl mix:

- *1 cup milk*

- *4 eggs*

- *1 tsp. vanilla*

- *½ cup honey*

Add wet ingredients to dry with a few quick strokes. It should form a dense, creamy batter. If too thick add a little milk, if thin, add a little flour.

Pour into buttered cake pans. Bake 20–25 minutes.

Cool. Place a large paper doily on top and dust lightly with powdered sugar. Remove the doily, and you'll see a white flower on top!

---

too young for games that involve rules. Rather, the special party clothes and the festive atmosphere, the tablecloth and pretty napkins, the cinnamon roll they take home, define it.

For five- to eight-year-olds, though, party activities and games are great fun. You might want to go to the library to borrow a book of nature crafts, or check the Chapter Notes for idea books. Choose an activity that is simple, quick and easy to clean up. Maybe you would like to get a long length of white butcher paper from the deli. You can have each child lie down on a piece of paper and draw his outline, then give them wide brushes and watercolor paints to decorate themselves on the paper. This can go home with each child, rolled up and beribboned, as a party favor. For older fives and sixes, you can fashion a treasure hunt, with a basket of beautifully decorated gingerbread children (see recipe) as the treasure. Wrap each in colored plastic wrap and tie with a ribbon, to go home as party favors. The clues for the treasure hunt can be pictures you have drawn on pieces of paper. Another wonderful art project for fives, sixes and sevens, one that you will need help with from other parents or your friend, is a small sewing project. For instance, the children can sew a felt treasure bag for a polished rock to live inside.

As the art project finishes up, you can call the children together and play a simple game with them. For the very young ones, a circle game of "ring around the roses" is plenty. You can repeat it several times, telling them to "put on your little mouse feet" to tiptoe around, and then "put on your big giant feet." You can have them become kitties or puppies, too. For the older children, the traditional game of "drop the handkerchief" can be full of excitement. The children who get "caught," though, should not go "out"; rather, they should go into the center of the circle. In the Chapter Notes you will find resource books of noncompetitive children's games. Having a few of these games up your sleeve can come in handy any time you have a gathering of young children at your home.

After the play, and the games or art project, you can gather the children for the time at the table. A simple, beautifully laid table is a centerpiece of most gatherings, but especially for a birthday celebration. When thinking of the party table, try to stay away from the decorations that are designed to sell toys and videos. You can put out a richly colored fabric tablecloth, with a flower- or fruit-decorated cake as the centerpiece. Keep in mind, the more sugary the cake, the crankier the children.

A simple spice cake, with a sprinkling of powdered sugar, is just the thing. I have given this recipe to hundreds of parents over the years. Some of them are pastry chefs and some of them have never baked before. The cake comes to school in hundreds of different varieties, from something like a pudding cake to an elegant torte with raspberry filling. Depending on the skill of the baker, it doesn't always look divine, but it *always* tastes great.

Your birthday child can then blow out all the candles, and you can serve the cake. It is a wonderful touch—though a little tricky to lead in the right direction—if, as the children eat, you can guide the conversation toward each child offering a birthday wish. You can model this for them, wishing that "your heart is always happy and singing," or that "your eyes always shine with joy, as they are shining today." If the older children become goofy with wishes, you can laugh and tell them you'll want to hear all the goofy wishes outside at play. But for now, let's have the beautiful wishes at the table.

As soon as the cake is finished, it's time to open presents, give big thank yous and say good-bye! The cake and the present opening are the climax, and as with any good story, the plot needs to wind down quickly. Perhaps everyone goes back outside to play for a few minutes (and to tell the silly wishes, if they remember), and then the party is over.

There can be a tendency, even among parents of very young children, to have a "keeping up with the Joneses" attitude about children's birthday parties. You can avoid this whole trap by stepping into another paradigm. You can create a simple, lovely atmosphere in which the children are healthily engaged, the décor is a reflection of your family's sense of beauty, not an advertiser's dream, and the birthday child is honored and celebrated in an age-appropriate way. And everyone can go home without the ups and downs of too many sweets.

Remember to record birthday successes and failures, for future reference, in your journal!

WHAT ABOUT THE PRESENTS?

In the invitation, give suggestions. You can do this tactfully by saying something like: "Wondering what she'd like? How about..."

- *Art materials*
- *Active toys*
  - *ball*
  - *jump rope*
- *Imaginative toys*
  - *capes, crowns*
  - *magic wands*
- *Books*
- *Tools, child-size*
  - *rake*
  - *shovel*
  - *bucket*

THE FESTIVAL OF THE MOMENT

Rhythm is a measurement of time. All these thoughts, ideas, activities, songs and stories happen within the framework of time. As we move further into the twenty-first century, the question of time becomes more pressing. How do we manage, with all the pressures of society, to give our families time for each of these life rhythms? How do we allow enough time at breakfast, or enough time for quiet evenings before Christmas? How do we give our children enough time to grow slowly, so that they may be strong? Each of us must find our own answer, as we walk through the hours of our days. But I believe there are some common elements.

Looking outwardly at the way we arrange our days, we can try a few things. Try, for instance, unplugging the phone. Unplugging is more effective than leaving the answering machine on and listening to screen your calls. Screening still interrupts the flow of your day with the ring of the phone. It interrupts your concentration as well, as you listen to the message and decide each time to answer or not. Try not answering at all! Simply unplug, and let your voice mail take the call. You can call back later, during nap time, or outdoor time, or any designated phone time. This way *you* make the decision how your family's time is spent. Try turning off the radio, TV and computer. All these technologies, which have the potential to enrich lives, also have the potential to cut our precious time together as a family into "info-bites." You can choose carefully when they will be of help, and when a hindrance. Unplug, and watch time, yourself and your family stretch out, relax and sigh!

If we choose carefully, and follow through with determination, we can decide when we are willing to be carried along in the hurry and bustle of life, and when we will relax into the long, slow rhythms childhood demands.

Looking inward, I find that when I give myself wholeheartedly, opening into the moment with curiosity and wonder, time elongates and I am surrounded by the deliciousness of Now. Those moments that I can approach with true gratitude and wonder live somehow in the realm of timelessness. Perhaps gratitude is one of the doorways to Eternity. Our young children still have one foot in the Eternal, in Heaven. We can join them there, if we give ourselves enough time.

Chapter 4

INDOOR PLAY

*P*AY IS THE heart of childhood, the foundation of our humanity. We can retain the ability to be playful as we grow, and a playful, flexible mind can be a measure of health and grace, even into old age. Humanity is given a very long period of infancy and childhood. During this extended infancy, the brain is "wired together" for efficient learning and functioning, which will serve us the rest of our life. When we watch our little children play, we are filled with tenderness at their innocent worldview, filled with gods and fairies. But if we study more closely the brain development that takes place in these years, we will stand in awe, thunderstruck at the marvel of each child.

MOVEMENT AND PLAY

We say that children "learn by doing." This is a common way of saying that the learning process is a miraculous orchestration and integration of the *entire body*, moving a million tiny interconnected particles toward the "gestalt" that is meaning. Children *think* through movement and play. In movement and play the brain goes through all the complex processes of growth and learning. The main avenue through which the child perceives the world is the realm of the senses. Through the natural sensory input of play, the child actively makes the world his own, rather than remaining a passive observer. Neurophysiologist Carla Hannaford, author of *Smart Moves*, says, "The richer our sensory environment, and the greater our freedom to explore it, the more intricate will be the patterns for learning, thought and creativity.... Our sensory experiences, both external and internal, shape our way of imaging and therefore, our thinking."[1] *It is the life force through which the young child plays that will grow eventually into cognitive thought.*

If we watch a young child at play, we can see that through her constant sensory/physical interaction with the environment, she gains experience and understanding of the situation, of herself, and the relationship between the two. She comes to know herself, the world, and what flows between. A baby sees a bright, round object and reaches for it. At some point she manages to push the ball, and now she sees the colors dance. Eventually she learns that when she moves in such a way, she has the pleasure of the dancing colors. She learns, through the open exploration of the senses, in other words, through *play*, that she has impact not only on the world, but also on her inner experience. The movement of reaching for the ball, or any purposeful movement, sets in motion a cascade of neural communication that creates a foundation for lifelong learning.

Through this sensory-rich play, the child gains a certain mastery over her body, and her world. She also begins to understand the inner world of emotional experience. It is critical that, through play, the different areas of the brain that control thought and emotion begin to communicate. "The frontal lobe," Hannaford writes, "is able to synthesize thought with emotion through ... the limbic system to give us compassion, reverence for life, unconditional love and all-important play."[2]

When a child's younger sibling is born, she can make this experience her own through play with her doll. She can feed, bathe and nurture her doll. She may also work through aggressive feelings by "sending brother back" and stuffing the doll into a corner. Day by day she vacillates, experimenting with how feelings work and what she wants to do with them. Usually if there is a very new and potent experience in the life of the young child, you will see it reflected in her play. Given time, given your own quiet observation of the process and your capacity to "hold" your child in love, you will see the experience become integrated. Your child will develop the new and necessary qualities. As neural pathways are forged in the brain, essential qualities grow in the heart.

Children are always in motion, constantly "doing." Movement activates the brain's neural wiring, making the whole body the instrument of learning. It is our task, as parents and educators, to allow children this necessary motion in an environment that encourages purposeful movement. Especially in these times of ever-increasing overstimulation of the senses through the media, through technology, and through our hectic pace of life, we must create play environments that allow the child to discover the world at his own pace through purposeful movement and creative imagination. We must allow him the freedom to move his body and his world in a way that suits these creative impulses.

But what is *purposeful* movement for a child? When the child takes in sensory input, a motor response is catalyzed. He sees the ball and reaches for it. He holds the doll and feeds it, or he pushes it away, depending on the purpose of the moment. When children are deprived of movement, either by the physical immobility created by media exposure or by early academic programs that keep them still, sitting in a chair, the imperative to move becomes constricted. Then, when movement is finally allowed, it is as though a dam breaks, and the movement can become hyperactive or erratic. Another response to constricted movement can be a fear of movement, or a flaccid approach to movement.

We have all seen these two extremes on the playground. We see the child who rushes around, bouncing from one thing to another, unable to give himself to a particular movement—digging, climbing, swinging, etc.—for a concentrated period of time. We have also seen the other type of child, who stands immobile, unwilling to run for fear of falling, or to dig for fear of the sensation of the sand.

Let's look at the stages of play, keeping in mind our wish to create play environments that encourage the *purposeful* movement play demands.

STAGES OF PLAY

As the child matures and develops, he will move through classic stages of play. It is helpful as a parent to know a little about these stages, how each one lays a foundation for the next, and what the process is building toward.

For babies and very young children, the experience of play is a very physical experience of becoming familiar with the environment. A baby will crawl everywhere, happily getting into every corner and under everything, reaching out and tasting whatever comes his way. The toddler will do the same thing, but now will attach words and even beginning concepts to his

---

PURPOSEFUL MOVEMENT

It is imperative that we understand the necessity of purposeful movement for our children, as compared to the often erratic movement patterns that are fostered by our movement-deprived society.

STAGES OF PLAY

Sensory exploration of environment

"Ordering" of environment

Imitation of daily life events

Creative imagination is born

Intricate "chapter games" evolve

Conceptual play occurs: mental images, few props necessary

experience. The toddler points to the stove and says, "Hot!" Play now consists of turning all the baskets of toys upside down, touching, tasting, smelling, experiencing bodily the nature of the physical environment. The child may go around the room touching or banging things with the newfound toy. He is simply familiarizing his physical self with the physical nature of his world.

Soon, though, possibly with the help of an older sibling or a parent, the toys begin to become categorized. "In" and "out" gain meaning; now he puts them in the basket, now he takes them out. The stacking or nesting toys begin to be stacked and nested, not just strewn on the floor for the pure visual delight. The child may begin to put the dolls back in their beds, or to "cook" at a play stove.

When the child begins to imitate in play the daily events in her life, a new and exciting stage is opening. This repetition of the tasks she sees around her lays the foundation for a new capacity, the creative imagination. Now, after many repetitions of making oatmeal for her baby dolls, she may discover that she can make them birthday cake for breakfast, instead. Thus she begins to order her universe in the manner she wishes. Slowly this capacity grows into her ability to fulfill her wishes imaginatively, and a certain inner freedom is discovered.

Usually we see this budding of the creative imagination, depending on birth order and the tutoring of an older sibling, begin around age three or three and a half. It will grow slowly, flowering into an amazing proliferation of creative endeavors. Eventually, with the dining room chairs, the couch cushions, sheets and clothespins she will build rescue submarines and go in search of suffering sea mammals, or become the lion tamer at the circus, arranging all her stuffed animals in elaborate concentric circles around her, giving complex commands and profuse rewards. Sometimes, for a five- or six-year-old, these games become "chapter games" going on for days, evolving and transforming endlessly.

My boys played a game for many years that was called, with elegant simplicity, The Game. Often their first greeting to each other upon awakening was, "Wanna play The Game?" This game encompassed every possible permutation of their growing imaginations, and many common aspects of their days. Lunchtime, outdoor play and quiet time were all incorporated

THE CREATIVE IMAGINATION

As the young child actively imitates daily life, repeating rhythmic tasks again and again, a foundation is laid for a new capacity, the creative imagination. Thus he may discover that he needn't offer only oatmeal for the doll's breakfast, but birthday cake as well!

CHAPTER GAMES

For the five- and six-year-old, these far-flung imaginations can become "chapter games," going on for day, transforming endlessly.

into The Game. Now they cherish the memories of such unrestricted flights of creativity.

This astonishing width of imagination reminds me of the grand excesses of the natural world. Our children are Nature's crown jewel, giving a human voice to Her great imagination of what this earth might become. Can we sacrifice tidiness during playtime in order to allow our children the capacity to move their bodies and their world (our living room) toward a deeper understanding of life?

Sometime around age six or seven, we see a new development. Now our child's play becomes less dependent on the physical surroundings and there is less use of elaborate props. The living room returns to its normal, if somewhat diminished, arrangement. Now, because he is able to carry these rich images in his own imagination, he can "see" them with his mind's eye. He doesn't need to create them in the physical world because they now live inside him. A submarine might become one chair turned upside down, as he sits "inside." He sees with his mind's eye all the elaboration the game requires. All of the outer richness of the physical world has found a home inside his being, and he carries this wealth wherever he goes. Sometimes at this age games can become totally verbal. Like a good story, they can run into chapters of high adventure as he watches the images move across his inner field of vision.

It is critical that we allow our children the full progression of the development of play. This entire process builds a firm, resilient foundation for all of their academic work. The culmination of play, or the ability to create and hold inner images, is the fundamental prerequisite for all academic learning. In fact, it is this very force of the creative imagination that naturally evolves in time into the capacity for conceptual thought.

As we not only allow our children to move purposefully in their play, but also create play environments that foster this broad, diverse creative imagination, in the same measure we strengthen their future capacity for our most fundamental human activity, thinking. When we give our children a very physical and sensory-based education in play, and allow them to play through many realms of human experience, we offer them a great gift. *We offer the possibility that their future life of thought will be imbued with feeling, and with the ability to bring this heartfelt thought into action in the world. This integration of heart*

OUR CHILDREN ARE
NATURE'S CROWN JEWEL

The astonishing width of imagination is like the grand excesses of the natural world.

AROUND AGE SIX OR
SEVEN...

The child can now see, with the mind's eye, all the elaboration the game requires. All the outer richness of the physical world has found a home inside his being; he carries this richness wherever he goes. This creative imagination evolves, in time, into the capacity for conceptual thought.

forces, thinking capacity, and the ability to act with confidence is essential as we move together into our new century and create the world anew, day by day.

How do we create a play environment that will nurture and foster our child's growing capacity for creative imagination? Since at this stage our young child's brain and therefore her entire life experience is being shaped by sensory experience, let's begin by looking at the senses, and see how we can offer the finest sensory education.

EDUCATING THE SENSES

> TO EDUCATE THE SENSES...
>
> *...let the natural world be your guide.*

> TIP
>
> *If we have a choice between lighting a candle at bedtime and turning on a candle-shaped night light, let us choose the actual, life-imbued candle.*

We want to offer our children a firm foundation in understanding the physical world. We want the sense impressions they encounter to be clear, simple and true—and the natural world is a glorious model of these qualities. We can try, even in our highly technological society, to give them sensory experiences that are close to the diversity of nature. For instance, if we have a choice between lighting a candle at bedtime and turning on a candle-shaped night light, let us choose the actual, life-imbued candle. Let us allow our child to be enveloped in a subtle sense immersion: the smell of sulfur as the match is lit, the immediate flash of light, the quick heat. Then the match burns low, and the momentary question hangs in the air, "Will the wick catch fire?" The flame dances with a quiet glow as it responds to air currents in the room. Perhaps after the candle is blown out (another world of sense experience) we will need to turn on a night light till dawn's arrival. But let us not choose the electric light *instead of* the rich sense education of the senses that the candle experience provides.

A few more examples, for clarity's sake. When preparing an autumn wreath, we can choose to go on a leaf walk with our child. Out in the crisp day, a chill wind on the cheek, listening to the musical rustle as we trudge through mounds of fallen leaves, we inhale the sweet autumn musk of a leafy carpet. This is a multisensory education, compared with which the experience of tucking artificial leaves into the wreath is limited indeed. When dinner preparation time comes, how about offering our child a table knife, a wooden chopping board and a few carrot spears to slice, with all of the potential for visual, olfactory and taste delight, as well as fine motor experience? It will take a moment longer than buzzing them through the food processor, but these are moments invested in the future. Perhaps we need to use the food processor occasionally for efficiency's sake, but let's not choose it *over* a broader multisensory experience for our child.

Visual Experience

The watchwords for the education of the eye are simple, clear, and beautiful. When we are choosing visual experience for our children, think of a simple, uncluttered visual field. Less is more, visually, for a young child. We can arrange the spaces in our home with an open simplicity. We will need plenty of storage, closet and shelf space, so the visual field is clear and harmonious. We can also comb through our belongings, asking ourselves what can be given away, thrown away, what duplicates can go and what must be kept. Try going through your home one room at a time, maybe one room per week. You can slowly sift through your whole house, maybe even on an annual basis. Let's reinstate spring house cleaning!

When arranging our child's indoor playspace, again, less is more. You can go through the toy corner and give away many of the toys. When your child has too many toys, their magic is lost. Excess creates disregard. Look for a fuller discussion of this below. We can also engage visual awareness by choosing colors that are rich and warm, colors that ask the eye to *open into* the experience. We know that when colors are too fluorescent, too garish (as colors for children often are), the eye protects itself and closes down in a subtle way. We can keep this in mind when choosing our children's wall paint, bedding and clothing.

These days, there is a tendency to clutter children's clothing with advertising for the latest movie or toy, to pack a shirt's visual space with logos, with text or images. It may take some searching, but we can find, often in

---

TIP

You can go through the toy corner and choose toys to give away. Too many toys damage the magic. Excess creates disregard.

catalogs that offer natural fibers, children's clothing that is designed without the distraction of media images. Check the Chapter Notes, and the section on clothing in Chapter Nine, "Other Topics Parents Wonder About."

Sound Experience

When we choose sound experience, again, we want to use the natural world as our guide. Sound is a fundamental "shaping" experience for us as humans. As we hear, so we are shaped. Certainly we are shaped differently when we stand beside a woodland brook than when we stand by a jackhammer in the street. As with the eye, when sounds in the environment are too abrasive, the ear shuts down. We have all come out of an evening concert of amplified music a little deaf. Noise pollution can destroy the tiny hair cells of our ear's "inner keyboard," thereby reducing our hearing acuity, especially in the upper register. These higher vibrations play an important part in maintaining alertness and energy. Especially for young children, who are still acquiring all the intricacies of language, a finely tuned ear is essential. See the Chapter Notes for information on the Spectrum Center and the work of Dr. Alfred Tomatis, relevant to the critical nature of "sound experience."

Let's allow our child to be shaped by the natural sounds of family life, voices conversing, someone humming, birdsong through the window, the soft shushing of the broom across the floor, children's laughter or tears. The embryo is shaped by the sound massage of the mother's voice, and to the young child there is no more beautiful sound than the voices of those he loves. When we introduce mechanical sounds—the coffee grinder, the vacuum, the radio or television, the dishwasher—the soundscape becomes cluttered, confused. In some households, all of the family members seem to occupy themselves with their own personal machines, each machine vying for the ear! We live in this modern world, and our machines do enhance our lives. But let's choose to use them when our children are outdoors playing, or at night when they are tucked away from the noise. Before we turn the machine on, each time we can ask ourselves, "Is this the best moment?" Let's keep our child's sound experience simple, clear and beautiful.

VISUAL EXPERIENCE

Uncluttered visual field
• *Simplify toy shelf*
• *Simplify house*
Rich, warm colors, not loud or garish.
Simple, uncluttered clothes

TIP

Look for children's clothes that are not cluttered with logos or images. Try to find natural-fiber clothing in clear beautiful colors, without the distraction of media images.

SOUND EXPERIENCES

Sound "shapes" us.
Noise pollution damages upper register of hearing.
This affects language acquisition and other critical areas.
Protect child from abrasive, mechanical sounds.
Give child natural sounds: voices, running water, sweeping, etc.

Tactile Experience

The tactile world is so multi-dimensioned that we will want to pay close attention to the choices we make in this area. When we choose playthings, toys, we will want to look carefully at what the child's tactile experience will be. We will discuss toys at greater length in the coming pages, but for now we can be aware that children's playthings present great differences in tactile experience. Think of the difference between a plastic doll and one made of cotton flannel. We will also want to choose clothing carefully for our children because the skin constitutes such a large area of our tactile sensors. Natural fibers tend to be the softest, most absorbent and most "breathable." Simple cotton knit clothing, comfortably loose, with elastic waists and no buttons, belts, suspenders or other complications, can be found in certain clothing catalogs, and occasionally even in department stores. These are real winners, not only because of their durability and easy care but because of their "felt" experience of ease, softness and flexibility. Cotton knit sheets, too, are warm, breathable and cuddly. In our home, whenever we have the choice of plastic or wood, we can consider the choice tactilely. A wooden bowl is just as sturdy and easily cleaned as a plastic one, yet it has more texture, weight and scent, more body. When our child finishes his oatmeal, his tactile awareness will be better educated by licking the wooden bowl than the plastic one. The same can be said for a wooden cutting board. A wooden table, also, offers a varied tactile experience for your child as he runs his sponge over the surface, then makes bubble patterns with his hands.

Olfactory Experience

Smell is strongly linked to memory and is critical to early learning. As we know, a smell can evoke an entire "gestalt" experience, a flood of memories we haven't thought of in years. Knowing this, let's look carefully at the scent experiences we offer our child.

If we have begun a garden outdoors, as described in the following chapter, "Outdoor Play," we are already doing much to attend to our child's sense of smell. All the evocative smells of a sunny garden envelop our child when she plays outdoors. In the summer, we can turn off the air conditioner

---

TACTILE EXPERIENCE

Choose toys for tactile richness: wood or natural fiber.

Choose wood over plastic for furniture, bowls and plates, etc.

Choose soft, breathable, natural fiber clothes.

Choose natural-fiber bedclothes, cotton jersey sheets.

OLFACTORY EXPERIENCE

A garden offers a rich "scent experience."

Turn off the AC and open the windows for pungent night scents.

Choose natural household cleaners.

as evening comes and open the windows for the night air. The scents of the natural world, the dampness rising from the dark earth, the sweetly acid scent of tomato vines, the tang and musk from the herb garden all waft into the open evening house. Our children need the deep night scents, too. The scent of dark night earth is rich with sensory experience. Except in the hottest climate, we can usually leave windows open at night for six months a year. When the air conditioner is turned off, you can use old-fashioned window fans to blow not only the night scents, but also the cool night air into the house.

We can choose household cleaners made with natural ingredients, and avoid the harsh smells of typical artificial cleaners. The natural citrus cleaners are excellent for their cleaning strength and have a delicious fruit scent. Although natural cleaners still need to be locked up, as do all cleaners, for our child's sake, their toxicity is often lower than the others'. And they treat our noses, and the earth, more kindly!

Taste Experience

Scent and taste are inextricably intertwined. The appetizing aroma of good, whole foods wafting through the young child's psyche remains indelibly imprinted in his being. In some cultures, food is considered medicine, and certain foods are given in order to treat illness. Even the smell of foods prepared as medicine is considered healing. Certainly we are all familiar with the soul healing contained in an aromatic pot of soup prepared just for us when we feel bad. Recently I had a conversation with a young woman who described her childhood memories of her mother making soup for her when she was sick. She said she remembers the rhythm of the knife as her mother chopped the garlic, and the immediate sizzle in the pan accompanied by the burst of garlic aroma wafting into her bedroom. Thus began the healing process. Taste and scent are primal.

Whole, natural foods are complex and rich both in scent and taste. Prepackaged foods lose not only nutritional value but lose much of their "soul value" in that the scent and taste are designed to be predictable, to appeal to a broad audience and to preserve well. Prepackaged foods are designed to sit on the shelf for months at a time, and their flavor is often

---

TASTE EXPERIENCE

Some cultures consider food as medicine for body and soul.

Whole foods are more complex sensorily and nutritionally.

Explore the subtle world of herbs, even grow your own!

augmented with artificial ingredients because much of the flavor is lost in the packaging process. One of the wonders of freshly prepared foods is the way the tongue becomes trained to taste the *life force* when food is eaten as close as possible to the vine or stalk.

Cooking with herbs is an exciting journey, one you may wish to explore not only for your child's sense education, but also for your own creativity. A small "window garden" of cooking herbs is a multisensory experience for both of you, as is the meal preparation and the sharing of food together. If your child learns to savor the complex tastes of well-seasoned food as a young child, this will lay a foundation for a lifetime of enjoyment.

My sons went through a period during adolescence when they found it necessary to cover in catsup and mustard all the aromatic, finely seasoned foods they were offered. Eventually, though, their well-trained palates overcame teenage societal pressures, and they began to love to cook tangy, spicy natural foods, and even to invite their friends for the meal!

CREATING AN INDOOR PLAYSPACE

It is tempting to create our child's playspace upstairs, or in the room around the corner. What we may find with a child younger than five, though, is that he gathers his toys and brings them wherever we are. Our young child wants, more than anything else, to be in contact with us, his parents. We can give him this much-needed contact, while still maintaining a little personal space of our own, by arranging for his playspace to be right in the middle of the common area of our home, right where we are! Just being in our presence, or within sight, is often enough. If he says, "Play with me," your reply could be, "I will be the old grandmother washing dishes (or whatever you are doing), and you can be my little grandchild who is picking flowers in the woods (or the captain of the spaceship who has landed on the moon)." He may need a little jog of the imagination, like, "Your spaceship looks like it needs some repair. Where is the spaceship repair shop, and who is the mechanic?" He may get involved in a game and give you the running commentary, only needing an occasional "mm-hmm" from you. Wherever the most traffic is, wherever life is lived the most, that is exactly where he wants to be. If the kitchen is the central place, with the dining room off the kitchen, this is the perfect place for him. If the living room adjoins the dining room, better still.

Furnishings and Equipment

Low shelves that are easy to access are a first essential piece of equipment. Make sure they can become invisible, whether behind the couch or with doors that close or curtains that pull. This will satisfy your need for adult space after your child has gone to bed. You may be able to arrange the living room with a set of toy shelves behind the couch, if it is a sectional, or if you place it at an angle. A small wooden table for play and artwork is important. One can be bought, or made from a square end table from the secondhand store, with the legs cut to the proper length. Small wooden chairs are essential pieces of equipment, not necessarily always to be used as seats, but also as great building materials. A child-size rocking chair is a wonderful place to rest and recuperate between flights of the imagination.

Because we will have these pieces of furniture in our living room or kitchen, we will want to be sure they are beautiful and sturdy. There are many advantages to having our child's playspace in our main living area. One of them is the care we will take that our child's playthings are natural, beautiful and well kept. Not only does our child play in the midst of our life-space, we live in the midst of their toys!

Although a toy chest is a fine old tradition, I would not recommend using one. All the toys get jumbled on top of each other and are difficult to find. Investing in some good sturdy open baskets for toy storage on the shelves works better. I have found some beautiful wire baskets that last for years and years, but the tactile diversity of reed baskets is also beneficial. Be sure the baskets are simple and strong. If they are so beautiful that you will be sad if

---

ESSENTIAL FURNISHINGS

Low toy shelves that become invisible after bedtime

Small wooden table and chairs

Small rocking chair

ESSENTIAL EQUIPMENT

Sturdy baskets of various sizes

Several "handle baskets" for carrying

One or two reed laundry baskets

A beautiful "doll's bed" basket

they break, plan on buying them for yourself instead. Your child's baskets *will* break, and need replacing occasionally.

You will need at least one large reed laundry basket as a sorting basket for cleanup time. When the toys need to be put away, at day's end or before nap time, you and your child can gather all the toys into the sorting basket, bring it to the shelves and sort into the small baskets on the shelves. A large sorting basket is a piece of *functional magic* at cleanup time. It can take the tears, your own as well as your child's, out of cleanup. You will also want a few sturdy baskets with handles that do not get toys sorted into them but remain empty, ready for your child's imaginative needs. Maybe they will be needed to haul lumber to the construction site, or a small wooden boat must be tied on the handle to become a tugboat, or to become a bed for a family of mice. Another good strong basket can be lined with a soft blanket and become the doll's bed. This will be easier to tuck away out of sight at day's end than a doll bed or cradle. Be sure to have one large, strong basket in which to gather all the wooden boats, trucks, cars and other means of conveyance.

Toys and Playthings

So now we have arranged the toy shelves—out of sight, but easily accessible. We have placed some strong open baskets on the shelves, we have a doll's basket and the sorting basket ready for cleanup. The table and chairs are attractive and quaint in their little corner of the living room or kitchen. What about toys? What will fill the baskets on the shelf?

If we remember the purpose of play in the life of the developing child, we can use this as a guiding principle. The way young children think is through their play. It is the way they make the world their own, it is how they make meaning in their life. We adults make life meaningful through our thoughtful consideration of that which life gives us. A child, on the other hand, plays through, again and again, each new circumstance, each new developmental step.

In thinking of the young child's free creative play materials, a fitting motto we can keep in mind is, "Anything can be anything." But what does that mean? Children need play materials that are open-ended enough to meet new needs each day, to fill the demands of their imagination. A toy needs to be "unformed" enough to be reasonably used as many things, in many circumstances. For instance, a red fire truck, with a remote control, will always be destined to be just that. But a simple, open-bed wooden truck can be a fire truck, a farm vehicle, a bus, a lumber wagon, or even a truck that floats on water! Or, better yet, an open basket can be a bed, a suitcase, a grocery bag, a hat, or, when turned upside down, a mountain, a prison, a cave, a hiding place … anything can be anything!

Let's return to Nature as our guide. After we have pulled dried corn off the cobs and set it out in the squirrel feeder, we can put the empty cobs in a basket on the shelf. "Corncobs?" you say. "My child's new toys are corncobs?" The answer is an enthusiastic "Yes!" First of all, corncobs can be "grated" for months—two cobs rubbed against each other, over a wooden bowl—to make corn dust. The corn dust can be saved in a jar and sprinkled on icy spots ouside in winter, similar to sawdust. Your child will spend hours grating contentedly, bringing bowls of dust for you to admire and save in preparation for winter. Corncobs are miraculous toys, being useful as fishing poles for the dolls, rollers in the beauty parlor, saws for halving a small stump you might bring inside for the winter, logs to be carried on the lumber truck, corn for dinner, toothbrushes for bedtime…. And how about a basket of well-chosen sticks? They can be sanded (many more hours of happy industry) to a silken smoothness, and become fencing for a herd of small wooden horses, or necessary bolts in the construction of the ship, the bridge for the castle guard to walk over, or the plank the pirates must walk. Seashells? How about cell phones, beds for tiny fairy dolls, a walkway to the doll's house, spoons, dishes, a boat's anchor… anything can be anything!

You can take several large branches from a recent tree pruning and have them cut in varying sizes and sanded, to make a basket of tree blocks. If you have them cut level, they will function like the more traditional rectangular wooden blocks, but with the delightful shapes and peculiarities of a branch.

TIP FOR CHOOSING TOYS

Let the toys be natural and unformed.

NATURAL TOYS

Corncobs

Sturdy sticks

Seashells

Sheepskin pieces

Pine cones

River rocks

A castle built with blocks like these will be made of pure magic—Mother Nature's magic. We can let *our* imaginations go as we choose open-ended play materials from natural sources: a basket of sheepskin pieces, a basket of pine cones, river rocks from a camping trip, and... what else? Use your imagination.

Now is the time to get your journal and brainstorm: What ideas have been sparked? Where would you like to begin? What dreams do you have for reinventing your child's play? Begin with broad strokes, envision what you want. Then, chunk by chunk, plan your steps toward an enchanting playspace.

We will also want to choose ready-made toys to go in the baskets. Again, think open-ended, imagination-rich. How about a basket of knitted farm animals? See the Appendix for natural toy catalogs. After your child builds a farmyard with the tree blocks, she can place the animals in their family units, and a long game of domestic barnyard life can ensue. She may need a basket of wooden wild animals to populate the zoo she builds the next day. A few good-sized wooden trucks help with any project, transporting wild animals included. An essential toy for the four-and-a-half-plus set is a basket of braided yarn or bootlaces. These will be used to pull wooden boats and trucks as they go about their deliveries, as leashes for stuffed animals, and to tie together many incredible constructions involving the dining room chairs, toys, other furnishings and who knows what. The yarn or laces need to be thick and sturdy. They will be brought to you full of the many fabulous knots children this age are capable of, and you will want to be able to unknot them with some amount of good cheer.

What about Stuffed Animals?

Our child may love to sleep with the soft oversized bear Grandma sent for Christmas, but one very large stuffed animal is probably enough. An excellent place for it to live is in the bed, always ready for your child's sleep. These huge toys are really more for the adult's pleasure of giving; they are nearly impossible for a child to actually play with, because they are so bulky. We want to give our child toys that are easily handled and fit the scale of her other toys, to enable a scenario, a story line to develop. When

---

MAKE YOUR OWN NATURAL BLOCKS

Call your local tree surgeon.

Gather branches 2"–6" in diameter, or whatever you like.

Saw into varying lengths.

Sandpaper them with your child.

Make real fairy castles.

SOME READY-MADE TOYS

Knitted farm animals

Wooden wild animals

Open-bed wooden trucks

Open, flat-bottomed boats

Family of small dolls

Small stuffed animals

choosing stuffed animals, a good measure is to see if it fits nicely in your child's two hands.

We can also look to its visual impact. Is it a natural-looking color, is it made proportionally, what is its "gesture," what is it saying to your child? Facial features that are as neutral as possible are excellent. Your child will want to make the toy growl, smile, or cry, as the game requires. She doesn't need a smiling stuffed kitty if the game is "lost in the forest alone at night," or a growling lion if she is the vet fixing its paw. Look also to see what the texture, the tactile experience will be for your child. Some of the newer toys are imbued with an artificial scent. Better that she smell the many months of loving attention in the form of her own sweaty little hands, than some unnaturally sweet chemical. If you wish, you can buy lavender-blossom-filled sleep masks in natural food stores, in the form of animals. Or you can make with your own hands, and very little sewing experience, a lovely toy animal stuffed with lavender, or rosebuds, or whatever herbs are available from the natural food store. Check the Chapter Notes for toy-making information.

Dolls

Many books have been written on the subject of dolls, from historical, anthropological, psychological, decorative, and artistic perspectives. For our purposes, though, let's narrow the field and look at the doll that will give your child the finest possibility of imaginative use.

As the child nurtures and "mothers" the doll, he is—not simply metaphorically, but also in reality—caring for himself. It is important, therefore, that we offer a doll that closely resembles him, not so much in features but rather in proportion. The child's "felt experience" of the doll will remain with him. So let's keep the doll simple, proportional and tactilely truthful.

Of all the dolls I have encountered, the fine, handmade "Waldorf" dolls come closest to these parameters. They are made of natural materials, soft to touch, but stuffed tightly with wool. This makes them soft but firm, just like our child is. They are also designed with the correct human proportions, the baby dolls having larger heads, rounder tummies and shorter limbs, as human babies do. And the child-sized dolls tend to have the head in a

---

ABOUT STUFFED ANIMALS

Let it fit between your child's hands

Choose natural colors.

Look at proportions.

Look at its "gesture."

Check facial features.

Avoid artificial scent.

smaller proportion to the body, with the torso and limbs longer. Often the baby dolls wear a simple sleeper, while the child dolls wear actual clothes, so their small owners can practice with buttons, sleeves and waistbands. The facial features of these dolls are minimal, only a stitch for eyes and mouth, and a bit of blush for the cheeks. This encourages the child to practice the full range of human emotions through the doll. Check the Appendix for catalogs that sell these very magical, life-imbued dolls.

If, on the other hand, you would like the experience of shopping in a toy store for a doll, keep the above parameters in mind. Look for a proper proportion; for firmness, not hardness; for a soft, natural outer covering; and for simple features that don't lock the doll and therefore your child into a single emotional experience.

Now a word about dolls meant to represent teenagers or adults. Only rarely will I say, "Just don't do it." But I feel the damage that a distorted body image can do to our girl children is so prevalent and insidious that "No" is the right response. Any doll is closely tied to the child's self-image, and it may be years, perhaps when the girl is a teenager herself, before we see the results of presenting this image to her. A human being proportioned like one of these dolls would be malnourished and unable to walk, plagued by balance problems and hobbled by a series of foot surgeries!

So what shall we do if our well-intentioned neighbors give one of these dolls as a gift? I was the mother of boys, so this is not an issue we faced at home. But I have told many parents of girls what my response would be when my daughter took the doll to play with. I would say, "Oh, my good-ness, look. The poor little girl is starving. Let's make a kitchen and cook some good food. She will need a long time of eating our good food to get well again!" And another day I would say, "Let's take her to the hospital, and see if the doctors and nurses can help her get well again. Shall you be the doctor today?" Your girl may laugh and play another, entirely different game, but she will at least have heard that this image of femininity is not healthy. Each time the doll came out I would make mention, either in direct compassion for the doll or in subtle asides, that this image is not okay.

In my classroom one year I had two four-year-old girls, best friends, and each one of them sweet and firm, like a ripe peach. Both of them were given one of these dolls that year. Within a few months, both mothers came

THOUGHTS ABOUT DOLLS
The "felt experience" is critical.
Look for proper proportions.
Look for firmness, not hardness.
Look for soft natural fibers.
Look for simple facial features.
Avoid the teenage dolls.

to me, completely unbeknownst to each other. Each one told me she had overheard her exquisite four-year-old daughter say to herself, in a game or in the bathtub, "I am fat." Let's be aware of this possibility, and deal with it in a straightforward and fearless manner.

Now, off the soapbox and on to a brighter subject.

Making Toys Yourself

In the midst of all this talk of rethinking and reshaping your child's playspace, it may be overwhelming to consider making toys by hand. If so, skip to the next section. Promise yourself, though, that you will return to this delightful subject once things have settled down in your child's life of play, when you have finally stopped being astonished at her endless capacity for imaginative games, when you know this creativity to be a way of life.

If, on the other hand, you are feeling like an old hand at this approach to child's play, or if you are the adventurous sort, who is willing to jump in the river and swim, read on!

In the Appendix you will find ordering information for books of very, very simple handmade toys, using felted wool, wool stuffing, needle and thread. These toys usually take only an hour or two to make. You can pick up your sewing basket as you sit by your child's bed while she falls asleep. She will be thrilled to see you in a creative process and will want to participate, asking questions and so forth. As you make the toy, you can tell her tiny vignettes about the life the new toy will lead with her. When it is finished, it will be alive, imbued with both your and her imagination. It is critical that you begin with an easy pattern and good instructions. Choose whichever pattern looks like the easiest to manage, perhaps a mouse, a gnome or a fish. If you aim too high, deciding to make a life-sized soft baby doll with curly hair and a blue wool coat, you may give up mid-way and not return. "Little steps for little feet," as they say. Keep your own skill level in mind when you begin.

It is an amazing experience for your child to see you so engaged in his world of play that you would sew toys for him. He sees your commitment, visibly, before his eyes. I often call toys that are handmade by parents "lovies," because they are so filled with the tremendous love we carry for our child.

MAKE YOUR OWN TOYS

Your skill level counts less than your loving attention.

Choose simple patterns at first.

Sew in view of your child.

A handmade toy is love made visible.

The toy is filled with your soul and offered hand to hand, heart to heart. Believe me, a toy that you have loved into creation, no matter how imperfect it may look to your eyes, is a gift that will continue to give its magic to your child for a lifetime. So take heart, take up your needle and thread, and begin!

In the Chapter Notes you'll find a *simple* doll pattern and instructions. When you have made one doll, and feel the glow of success (this is a no-fail pattern!), try making a family of dolls. Dress two dolls as parents, and then size the one-piece body proportionally smaller to create children. Place the family in a basket lined with a square of silk cloth, and you have hours of puppet plays in the making!

Building Materials

What the young child is doing, in a very physical way, is building his own body, building the physical structure that will house him in his life's journey. We can offer our children play materials that reflect this "house building" paradigm. Luckily, with a little imagination, our living rooms, dining rooms and linen closets contain nearly everything needed for this venture. If we give our child not only the freedom to use the living space and the furniture in a creative way, but also a little imaginative help, we will be giving ourselves the greatest gift a parent can have: a happy, industrious, creatively engaged child. We will give up, for a few hours of play each day, the lovely furniture arrangement we adults appreciate, but what we are given back in exchange is ten times the price of the happy chaos. Truly, it is chaos only to our grown-up eyes. For the child these creations are the "stuff" of life, full of meaning and import, reflections of themselves.

You can help your child begin this house-building process with a leading statement, something like, "When I was a little boy, we used to build the best forts under the dining table." Or, "Your aunt and I made houses for our stuffed animals and ourselves, too, with a sheet thrown over the dining room chairs. We played there for hours." You can go through the linen closet and choose a sheet or two (flat, not fitted) as roof-making material, then place them in a basket on the toy shelf. You may need at least a full or queen size, especially if it is for a table house. Show your child how to pull the dining

WAYS TO BUILD A HOUSE

Clothespin large sheet over dining table.

Arrange dining chairs and throw large sheet over top. Clothespin.

Pull couch out from wall 8–10 inches. Arrange cushions. Clothespin sheet over all.

Line chairs up beside window, clip sheet to window molding and chair backs.

chairs out, to make more space, and then clip the sheet to the table with some old-fashioned spring-type clothespins. Buy a few small throw rugs to be brought inside as bedding, or what have you. The dining chairs can be moved and lined up to be the train for a trip to Grandma's, and a pillowcase is a perfect suitcase to pack all the supplies in. Houses will develop from both your child's and your own imagination. You might see a good window molding to clip a roof sheet onto, and then clip the other side onto the backs of two chairs—a house! Or your child might need a kitchen cupboard to be emptied, and its contents relocated, in order to make a hidden den for wolf cubs. The couch, its cushions and the space between it and the wall is a fabulous place for a whole village or apartment house to emerge. Above all of this you might like to hang some old-fashioned mosquito netting, gathered onto a hoop. Hang it from a hook on the ceiling, and a magical pavilion appears!

Another wonderful prop for house building is a basket of colored scarves. You can order a set of rainbow-colored silk scarves from one of the natural toy catalogs, or go to the local department store and look for simple, natural-fiber scarves in solid colors. These become everything from curtains at the table-house window to seat belts for a car-ride, capes and tunics, scarves and skirts, and many things in between. At cleanup time, scarf folding is a fun task for you and your child to do together.

All the imaginative games *you* either played as a child, or never got to play, may emerge as you help arrange a play environment that fosters creative imagination in your child.

Play in the Kitchen

The kitchen is a grand place to play. Often games will naturally spill into the kitchen, especially if you are working there. You can show your child which part of the kitchen is a good place to play, so he isn't literally underfoot as hot food cooks above. If your kitchen is big enough, this is a good spot for the small table and chairs. You can give him "work" to do in the context of the game, something like this: "Would the truck driver like to help the restaurant cook cut potatoes? Truck drivers like mashed potatoes, you know." Keep a basket of wooden child-size dishes and pans, so he can imitate your kitchen work.

PLAY IN THE KITCHEN

Weave your work and his play together.

Water play at the sink is excellent.

Sand in the kitchen is grand.

Water play is tremendously soothing, therapeutic and just plain fun for young children. Perhaps they remember the time, very recently, when they were water-creatures in the womb! Their bodies (and ours!) still contain a very high percentage of water, and so we will want to make water play available. Keep a small step-stool close by, or a kitchen chair ready to be pushed up to the sink. While you work at the counter, your child can have a basin of warm water and work beside you, or the basin can be put on his small table, close by. A little detergent and a few cups for him to wash can lead into thirty or forty minutes of concentrated water play. Even if the dishes are already clean, get a few cups from the cupboard and ask him for his help.

The Indoor Sandbox

Another terrific piece of play equipment, for which the kitchen is the best location, is an indoor sandbox. Don't panic! It can be made easily manageable, even for a two and a half year old, and the hours of contented play are a good trade for the little bit of mess and grit.

The magic trick for making an indoor sandbox workable is to have your child *sit on the floor outside the box* and reach inside to play. Place a small throw rug beside the box to help her visually locate the best place to be, and to protect her knees from gritty sand. A child's natural inclination is to sit inside the box, but with a few reminders, she will get used to it.

You can go to your local department store and buy a large, heavy plastic storage box. Choose a shape that is low, not more than five or six inches high, so that when it is placed on the floor your child can easily reach over the edge and into it. Perhaps you will want a long, low, narrow rectangle, 32" x 12" x 5", that several children can use at once. It can be pushed with one long side against the wall for space efficiency. You may even be able to find a color that goes with your kitchen's décor, or possibly a clear, colorless one. You can put a piece of vinyl or a throw rug underneath to protect the floor.

You're not going to want your child to use water as liberally in her indoor sandbox as she will do outside with her pool or pond nearby. Damp sand is good for modeling or sand castles, though, and you can keep a spray bottle handy so you or your child can spray the sand before play. These storage boxes come with a tight-fitting lid that will clip shut. You will want to leave

> ### INDOOR SAND PLAY IS MAGIC
>
> *Buy a low plastic storage box, with lid.*
>
> *Protect your floor.*
>
> *Get a throw rug for sitting on.*
>
> *Buy two 50 lb. bags of play sand.*
>
> *Get a few great sand toys.*
>
> *Keep water sprayer close by.*
>
> *Clean up with small brush and dustpan.*
>
> *When not in use, close box and place colorful cloth over it.*

the lid only partially shut, so the sand and sand toys get enough air flow that they don't begin to smell wet. When playtime is finished, I like to shut the lid partially and then place a cloth over the whole affair, with a kitchen basket on top.

You can buy play sand at a garden shop; usually one or two fifty-pound bags is plenty for a medium-sized sandbox. Again, when you choose the

sand toys, choose with tactile variety in mind. Garage sales or the Salvation Army usually have old-fashioned kitchenware, such as small metal bowls and sifting utensils, and you may find some treasures—egg beaters, flour sifters, ice cream scoops and so forth. You may want to place a few small figures, vehicles and animals in the box for imaginative games. Remember, less is more, so don't overfill the box with either sand or toys.

You can teach your child to keep the sand play in the sandbox, and not bring bowls full of sand over to the kitchen table. As with any guidance you give your child, *firm* and *kind* are the watchwords. Indoor sand play needs a little extra guidance to keep your life from being overrun by grit, so smile and say, "Keep the sand in the sandbox, honey." If he needs an extra nudge to remember this, close the lid for the remainder of playtime. Tell him, "We'll do better at keeping the sand in the box this afternoon." Be sure to follow through with another try later in the day. Your word is gold, so follow-through is a must. Children love sand, so he will be quick to learn the rules. Sand *will* spill out over the edge, though, and a dustpan with a small brush can be kept close at hand. Part of closing the sandbox can be sweeping up the spilled sand. This could become a beloved ritual that you perform together, as can folding the clothes or washing the dishes. When we bring joy to this work, our young child not only learns the necessary skills, but also learns to love the nurturance of life.

Rethinking Your Child's Current Toy Shelf

If you would like to move toward more open-ended, creative play materials, but your child's toy shelf is full of plastic, battery-operated toys, or other toys you are not interested in keeping, how do you go about shifting into the new mode? Depending on your child's temperament—and only you will know which way will work best—you can try a couple of approaches. With your child, you could gather the new play materials. Tell your child you need to "make room" for the new toys. Then have him choose his favorite old toys to join the new ones. When he is asleep, you can pack up the other old ones to "rest" in the basement. Gathering the new ones will be something your child will love to do with you, but packing the old ones is probably best done alone.

Another approach is to talk a little with your four- or five-year-old about what it might be like to have a new playspace and new playthings, wondering about new games that might evolve. Then, when he spends the day at Grandma's or your best friend's, you can keep the toys you know he loves dearly, but send all the others to the basement closed up tight, and create the new playspace as a surprise. Some children love surprises, and some are horrified. You know which kind of child yours is!

Make the toy shelf and the new play materials appealing, and when your child comes home, introduce him to the new scene with a game. "Look at the way we can make a roof over the table, here! Let's get the wooden boat out, and bring the farm animals to live here, close to your farm." You can then help build a farmhouse under the table. Having one of your child's friends over for a play date can help enliven the first few days of play.

If, in the first few days, your child asks for a toy that has been put away, you can remind him that the toy is resting in the basement. He may not actually be asking to play with it, just inquiring to be sure of its whereabouts. With the new play materials, he will probably let go of the thought of it easily. If, on the other hand, he asks again and again, it means there is a real bond with the toy, and you can return it to the shelf. Chances are good it will be forgotten soon, because it doesn't work well with the other playthings, and you can simply remove it with no fanfare later on.

HELPING FAMILY AND FRIENDS CHOOSE GIFTS WELL

Family and friends love to give gifts to your child for birthdays and Christmas. You can help them choose well by sending or giving them a natural toy catalog, with the playthings your child would love circled. (Check the Chapter Notes for catalogs.) You can help them understand the concept behind your new approach through conversation, describing how much more space for the creative imagination an open-ended toy offers. Remind them of the familiar image of the child who, upon receiving a remote-control airplane, pushes the buttons for a while, and then gathers the box, paper and ribbons and plays merrily with the wrappings. It may take a while, and several conversations. You may need to say it over and over, but if you persist, your extended family will begin to see the result of your insistence in the child herself. They will see how her imagination flows like a stream into each aspect of her day. They will be charmed to hear her singing her way through elaborate story lines. She will become a living statement of the choice you have made.

CARING FOR THE TOYS AND PLAY MATERIALS

Creating your child's playspace is only the beginning of a process. As we know, the success of any endeavor depends on a variety of things, and maintenance is one of the essentials. At playtime's end, we can lovingly help our child put away all his many playthings, each toy finding its way home. Let each category of toy have its own specific basket, and place the baskets on the shelf in the same order each day. Something like this—all the corncobs go in the oval basket, which sits beside the round seashell basket, which goes next to the wire basket full of stones.

To stand in the middle of the child's imaginative palette as cleanup time begins may feel to us like being in the midst of primordial chaos. I have found, though, over the years, that gratitude is a wonderful remedy for feeling overwhelmed. Not that we may feel particularly grateful for the mess, but it is gratitude for our child, and for her rich imaginative spirit, that brings a spring into our step. Our child grows, like a flower, in the warmth of this love.

HELP FAMILY AND FRIENDS
CHOOSE WELL

Give them a natural toy catalog.

Circle the toys you would like your child to receive.

Talk to them about your child's new creativity, and ask them to help foster this.

Not only at day's end do we care for the toys, but also during play. When a toy breaks or a basket comes unwoven, we can encourage our child to bring it to us, so we can attend to it. We can look carefully at the toy, ask if she knows how it broke, and if any instruction on the handling of toys is needed, we can offer it. It is helpful to have a "repair" basket into which all broken things go for further attention. We can perhaps bring the repair basket to her room, so we can work on the toys as she falls asleep, after the bedtime routine. Perhaps we'll work on repairs in the nap room, also. Caring for beloved playthings helps our child to cherish and care for everything that supports life, her toys included. If her toys are made of natural materials, they will be more easily mended, whether we are using glue, hammer and nails or needle and thread. Our children imbue their toys and playthings with the energy of their love, and it is a great gift for both of us to take the time to mend and repair them.

Certainly at this time, our lives and our environment need love and attention given at this level. To repair our child's toy is not only a fundamental lesson to "reduce, reuse and recycle," but also an embodied experience of loving kindness.

ENCOURAGING PLAY

When we create a beautiful, inviting playspace, we have gone a long way toward encouraging creative play. The structure of the playspace, the open toy shelves, the baskets filled with toys you have carefully selected—all of this creates what we will call the "container." This is the safe space where play can occur. There will be a few rules we will want to institute—"We don't throw our toys," "We save running for outside," and so forth. For the young child, it is helpful to use the golden "we." The child is not yet aware of separation, and understands better in terms of "we." You will know the rules that are needed in your home, and for your family. A simple guideline is to think of rules about damage to oneself, to others or to property. These simple, basic rules also help to establish the boundary of play.

Our loving attention to the child's playspace, and the natural boundaries of play that we have established through our rules, creates a container.

ENCOURAGING PLAY

Create a beautiful space.

Establish rules of the house

Problem-solve with new ideas for the game.

Just offer ideas, don't join the game.

Encourage the synergy of collaborative play.

Negotiating disputes? Think calm and slow.

Within the empty interior of this container exists an open space for the child's imagination to fill anew each day. Our conscious attention, held silently in our hearts, is like the "clay" of the container. Our love becomes the sparkle in the empty interior.

There are many essential skills that the child develops in play, and one critical area is the realm of social interaction. At this age, basic social skills that are essential for all of life are learned at a simple visceral level. We can help in this process by keeping an ear tuned toward our children's play. Many times young children can explore and succeed at the intricacies involved in the give and take of play. Sometimes, though, they need our help, insight and guidance. Sometimes what is needed most from us is an idea, a way in which the game can evolve, a new avenue. When we offer an idea that circumvents the difficulty, we model creative problem-solving. In time they will incorporate this respectful way of relating, making it their own. We can drop these suggestions gently like rain, over our shoulder, so to speak. After we have dropped the suggestion, then it is our children's choice what to do with it. It may be ignored completely, or taken into the game and transformed, or it may spark a whole new idea of their own.

Although it can be helpful, occasionally, to offer an idea for play, usually it is detrimental for us to bring our adult energy into our children's games. Our adult consciousness can disturb and distract our children's more mobile and fluid imagination. The best way we can join them in their play when invited is to say, "I will be the cook (or whatever you happen to be doing), and what will you be?" A better place to "play" with our child is in the creation of stories together, perhaps at bedtime.

We can encourage our children to play inclusively, to learn to incorporate others' ideas into the game, to discover the synergy that occurs in cooperative play. We can, through creating a rich play environment and keeping an ear open toward their play, help them to broaden their horizon, moving out of the natural self-oriented play of a toddler toward the exciting world of partnership. Unfortunately, most of us know some adults who have never acquired these basic skills, and we can see the difficulty it brings to their lives and the lives of those around them. Giving our children this opportunity will serve them throughout their lives.

Occasionally there will be a problem that they cannot solve by themselves. When they come to us for help, the watchwords are *calm* and *slow*. Take a breath and listen, nod quietly, say "hmmmm." This buys time for you to center yourself. In the chapter on Creating Your Family Culture, you will find a tried and true formula for helping mediate disputes. You are the foundation of your child's entire life. The way you handle yourself when his emotions run high can be a bridge for him whereby he discovers the fundamentals: problems exist, they are challenging, and they can be resolved to the benefit of everyone involved.

WHAT ABOUT GUN PLAY?

We can honor the desire for grand adventure, for the drive and daring energy that gun play involves, and still discourage the violence. I believe it is the excitement and the energy behind gun play that is so compelling for many children, not the violence.

I have dealt with this issue in different ways in my classroom than I did at home. At school, with a large group of children, I have found that gun play in any form is counterproductive to the well-being of the whole group. So I simply say, "No weapons." As we know, anything at all can become a gun if that is what the child wants. So, if fingers or sticks are being used as weapons, I say, "No pointing." What I try to offer as an alternative, though, are ideas filled with the adventure and excitement, with the hiding and intrigue that gunplay involves. I encourage them to be arctic explorers, caught in a blizzard, or paddling down the Amazon in a boat with huge pythons slithering by, or even firefighters saving dozens of people. Usually this kind of suggestion sparks ideas of their own, and they are off and running.

At home I felt it was a different situation and a different atmosphere. Although it was my natural inclination, because of my horror at war and violence, to forbid gun play at home, I felt it would, in the end, not produce the desired results. I feared the "forbidden fruit" syndrome would result and my boys would become fixated. Yet I did not want to encourage the truncated kind of imagination that gun play can involve, and I feared it would create power issues between my boys. I tried to find a compromise, a way to give

---

WHAT ABOUT GUN PLAY?

Offer game ideas full of daring adventure without the violence (see below).

If you decide to say yes,

- *Limit amount of time.*
- *Limit type of gun.*
- *Establish firm rules:*
  same team
  no pointing at each other
  everyone is having fun
- *Put toy guns away if rules are broken.*

them a "homeopathic dose," a small amount, that would resolve the question with as little damage as possible.

So I allowed them to play with little wooden rifles on Saturday mornings. The ground rules were 1) everyone had to be on the same team, 2) they were absolutely forbidden to point the guns at each other, and 3) everyone had to be having fun. If any of these ground rules were broken, the game ended, the guns were put away, and they could try again next Saturday. Because they had so much experience playing games that were thrilling and intricate without the use of guns, many Saturdays came and went without their rifles, because they simply forgot about them! If they happened to remember on a Tuesday, I would allow them to play for an hour, and then put them away.

I felt that this was a middle ground, allowing them to taste a bit of the play that is so prevalent in our society while preserving my values, and hopefully passing them along. You may find another way to come to middle ground, and it is well worth the search.

Ideas for War-Free
Adventure Games

Make bows and arrows with your child: put time into finding the right sticks. Your 5-year-old will love to "sharpen" them by rubbing them on a stone or cement.

Hunting games, Native American games, capture the wild ponies, etc., all accompanied by the bow and arrows.

Child-made, parent-supervised campfires: teach the essentials, followed by s'mores and marshmallows.

Magic potions—think berries, clover, mud, a few ingredients from the kitchen---vinegar, baking soda. Games of magic and treachery evolve.

Scrap lumber, hammers, nails (roofing nails w/ big heads); low, wide stump as work bench. Stack a few pieces and hammer together (don't make it perfect); call this a "boat." See what your child creates! Fives and under will need supervision.

Small, dull pocketknife for sixes and up: cut bush branches, windfall sticks, peel bark. Decide rules. Always supervised? Always on porch? Only when no other children playing?

Sleepovers in tent in back yard. Lots of chores beforehand: sweep clear of rocks, haul leaves for padding, make rock fire-ring, gather sticks for fire, fill water bottles, etc.

Gather wild edibles. This needs supervision, and you'll need knowledge!

Making traps: a real classic! Needs a good small shovel, sturdy sticks, grass clippings, leaves, twine, etc

Fort-building: may need parent help in tying basic stick structure together.

Your own inspired ideas!

Chapter 5

OUTDOOR PLAY

*I*HAVE FOUND IN my many years of teaching young children, and in my years as a mother of young boys, that most children are happiest at play outdoors. Young children are close to the realm of nature because they are still very natural beings. Because their consciousness is not yet separated from the environment, because they still live in the consciousness of oneness, of unity, they belong still to the natural world. In time they will belong to themselves, as the process of individuation becomes complete. But for about the first seven years, they are still at one with the world they inhabit. The process of separating from the parents and from the environment buds only around age seven. Before that, the child is moved along by life, something like the way a tree's leaves dance in the breeze. The young child responds to the environment in a very unself-conscious way, a very natural way, and the open, complex, and diverse environment of the outdoors gives him that opportunity. If, in his excitement at a butterfly, he needs to dance and pirouette dizzyingly around the garden, no one has to say, "Be careful of the table." If he needs to shout for glee or weep for sorrow, he is free.

If we are fortunate enough to have woods or a natural meadow we can visit often, or that adjoins our yard, our child will have an even more diverse experience of the natural world. Children become connected to the web of life by seeing the relationships between plants, insects, wildlife, and human beings. This "thinking from the whole" is what our children will incorporate into their own being. Our own backyard can be the foundation of environmental education and a journey of discovery for the whole family.

In thinking of outdoor playspaces, we will turn our attention not only to the play structures we want our children to experience, but also to the outdoor play environment itself: the terrain as well as the play equipment. We'll begin with the natural features of the playspace, then move on to human-made structures and equipment within the larger context of the play environment.

You might like to get your journal and make notes of ideas that inspire you. This is the time for brainstorming. After this, you can categorize ideas into "let's do it now!" and "maybe later" lists. Eventually, you'll be planning details, taking measurements and visiting your garden shop. Let's get started!

CREATING AN OUTDOOR PLAY ENVIRONMENT

Children love a large, grassy, flat area in which to run, tumble, play leapfrog and gaze at passing clouds. When caring for the lawn, we may want to research natural, native grasses, and grasses that are naturally drought- and insect-resistant. Lawn chemicals do produce a super-green growth, but they can be harmful for children and reduce the insect life—especially the beneficial insects, which we want to encourage. A fine, soft, green yard is a good start that we might augment by putting up a swing set in the middle of the grass, and a sandbox under a tree—but first let's look at some other ideas.

Children love small spaces where they can hide and tell secrets, where they can dream. Natural screens, such as large ornamental grasses planted artfully in a corner, can provide the child with this much-needed sense of secrecy, but also offer parents the ability to peer through the lacy foliage and keep watch from afar. In these secret corners, fairy huts of bark, forts made of branches and sticks, and outdoor tea parties begin to emerge.

Your child will need natural building materials for these whimsical architectural creations. You can help by gathering sticks and branches with your child after each rain or windstorm. Create a stick pile in an out-of-the-way place that your child can reach easily. If you take walks in the woods, you can gather large pieces of bark from fallen trees to bring home as building materials. A good pile of river rocks or stone is a treasure trove for young architects and masons. Old bricks gathered from nearby construction sites, or Grandma's house, are a wonderful resource, as are old tiles or soapstone pieces. Older children will put the sticks and smooth stones together to create a "knife-sharpening shop," or to make arrows. Seashells gathered from a

---

ELEMENTS OF A BALANCED
OUTDOOR PLAYSPACE

Flat, grassy area

A hill of some sort

Natural screens

- *tall grasses*
- *bushes*

"Building materials"

- *sticks*
- *bark*
- *stones*
- *bricks*
- *slate*
- *seashells*

Natural play structures made from branches/bamboo

- *tipi*
- *igloo*
- *house*

Straw bale structures

Stump creations

Classic structures

- *swings*
- *seesaw*
- *hammock*

Sand play

Water play

summer vacation can also be collected year by year and kept in a particular spot, perhaps under a favorite bush.

Bushes are another grand place for hiding, or for any game that requires secrecy. You can crawl under the bush with your clippers and hollow out a snug space, clearing away the dead branches. A few shovels full of bark mulch spread under the bush can be an aromatic invitation to your child to come "inside" the bush house to play. Flowering bushes are real gems in spring-time, as they invite elf and fairy games. In the fall, leaf games evolve under the bush—leaf beds, leaf tables, and wagons full of leaf deliveries can be trundled around the yard. A good child-size wheelbarrow or classic wagon makes an excellent birthday present that will be used for endless purposes of the imagination.

NATURAL PLAY STRUCTURES

A wonderfully whimsical "playhouse" that is open-ended and lends itself to the child's imagination is a simple branch structure. You can build it in a few hours one afternoon. If your yard doesn't offer large branches that come down in the wind, check with your town's recycling department. Sometimes cities collect fallen branches to process into mulch. Or, if you are lucky enough to live close to a bamboo grove, fresh-cut bamboo makes perfect out-door play structures (some garden shops also sell bamboo lengths). You can shape the structures like a tipi and lash the poles together at the top, making sure to sink the ends into the ground. You can also make a small, igloo-shaped structure, again sinking the ends and lashing at the top. You may want to make a rectangular structure, even topping it with "roof rafters." These structures can be enclosed with an old queen- or king-size sheet from the secondhand store. Hold the sheet in place with clothespins and take it down to launder when necessary. The beauty of these open branch structures is that day by day your children will want to go to the stick pile to continue the construction in their own fanciful way. Or they will go to gather seashells to decorate the perimeter, or collect pine needles to make a soft carpet.

Sometimes, especially with a first child, we need to give small hints, a little jog of their imagination. So you may want to say something like,

---

CREATE NATURAL PLAY STRUCTURES

Go to town recycling center for long branches

Go to garden shop for bamboo poles

Place poles for structure

Sink ends into ground

Lash tops together for "tipi," "igloo," etc.

Bark mulch for floor

Large sheet for roof

Large, sturdy stumps for table and chairs

BUILDING TIP

Keep the structure open-ended, so your child can continue to create it, day by day.

"When I was a little girl, we used to put pine needles on the floor as a carpet." Or, "I wonder what it would be like to put seashells around the outside, as decoration." Usually a few small suggestions tossed lightly in your child's direction will spark a whole flood of imagination. We can couch these ideas in the framework of "When I was little..." or "I wonder...", and they are usually happily accepted, or met with, "No, I think I'll do it like this instead."

Other delightful "play structures" have a shorter lifespan. When you are inquiring about good sticks for the back yard, ask about some large, stable tree stumps. Occasionally a very old tree will come down in a windstorm, and you can explore the possibility of hauling home a load of stumps of various sizes. These can be placed as a balance structure, with your child hopping from one stump to the next. Your child may also discover them, if they are the right size, to be a good "steamroller," or castle-building material. You can also place a large, flat stump about two and a half feet high in a central place, and put several shorter, smaller ones around it, to create a magical table and chairs.

Another type of playhouse or fort can be constructed of straw bales. I had a wonderfully educational experience with straw bale houses! I brought about ten straw bales to the school playground and stacked them in a semicircle, making to my eyes a perfect place for a play kitchen or restaurant to evolve. I placed the bales close to the sandbox, and each day would put bowls and spoons, pots and pans on the child-sized table, as an invitation to play. The children rejected my beautiful creation so completely, it was as though it was invisible! After several months, I realized it was obviously not the great idea I had imagined, so I wheelbarrowed the hay bales across the creek to the garden and dumped them unceremoniously onto the grass clipping and weed pile. The next day, the children saw the bales tossed helter-skelter in a heap and whooped for joy! They ran laughing and tumbling into the soft, sweet-smelling jumble and began to push and pull, arranging the bales into their very own creation, which was full of odd angles, crevices, and wobbly places. Day after day they returned with boards, sticks, ropes and whatnot, making trampolines, nests, balance beams, and even (as I had first imagined) a restaurant. I learned all over again to offer the right materials, with a light hand. It was my adult ideas about form that had stymied the children's creativity. When I tossed the bales aside, they became free enough for the children to make them their own. So if you create a lovely structure and your child rejects it, look carefully to see if you are too attached to it, and if there is a way you can loosen the form to set it free.

Note: If you choose to make a straw-bale house, when the bales have weathered and softened in the fall you can put them as heavy mulch in the garden, to decompose over the winter months. If you intend the garden to be their final destination, be sure they are straw, not hay, which contains seeds. If each year you bring several bales of straw home for the summer, and they eventually go into the garden, you will have not only a happy child but eventually a well-mulched garden as well.

Perhaps you'll be inspired to sketch some ideas in your journal to incorporate into your outdoor playspace!

CLASSIC PLAY STRUCTURES

Let's look at some classic play structures, too. There is nothing like a swing in the psyche of a young child. To fly like a bird, to touch the treetops, to sail the open seas, whether rocked in calm waters or tossed high in a storm... perhaps a swing is the best. Here are a few things to keep in mind when creating a swing experience for your child.

The canvas or plastic strap seats are safer than the old-fashioned board seats, and children love the way a strap seat holds them firmly. Learning to pump is easier in a strap seat, too. The child is held snug, at one with the swing.

The higher the fulcrum is, the more opportunity for the swing to grow with your child. Finding a great, strong, high branch, though, is very

> ### ABOUT SWINGS AND SWINGING
>
> *Swinging develops the brain.*
>
> *Consider making your own swing.*
>
> *A swing with a high fulcrum can grow with your child.*
>
> *Get a canvas or plastic seat.*
>
> *Bury swing set legs in the ground, for safety.*
>
> *Remember to have a hammock, too.*

difficult. Instead, I created the swing set between two tall, straight pine trees, about twelve to fifteen feet apart. About ten feet up, I had two beams bolted together and into the tree trunks. From this very sturdy beam, I hung three swings, threading the chain through large eye hooks at the top and attaching to the seats below. This way, as the children's legs grew longer, I could move the seat up by readjusting the chain. Because the fulcrum was high, the swing grew with them, continuing to offer an exciting ride. Eventually, though, when they were older, the boys wanted all the excitement of a single rope swing. Look in the toy catalogs for a small circular plastic seat. This gives the child stability as he flies in the spiraling patterns a rope swing offers.

If you are going to buy a traditional swing set, be certain that vigorous swinging will not lift the legs up off the ground. These swing sets have been known to tip over entirely, so bury the legs firmly in the ground.

Remember, current brain research shows that swinging and rocking motion, both gentle and vigorous, stimulates proper brain growth and "wire" the different areas of the brain together, so sensory integration is accomplished in a fun and natural way!

A hammock is another swinging device I highly recommend for every outdoor playspace. Completely different games evolve around the hammock than the swings. In the hammock, the child has an opportunity for a visceral "conversation" with another person. Whether snuggling with a parent or rolling, laughing and squirming with a little friend, communication happens in a delicious way.

A seesaw is an old-fashioned piece of play equipment that offers hours and even years of fun. A seesaw, too, can grow with your children. The balance point of the seesaw board can have two heights. The lower height can be about twenty inches for three-, four- and five-year-olds, and the higher one can be about thirty-two inches for age six or seven and up. If you have a square block of wood attached to the bottom of the seat, it will help prevent squashed toes. A seesaw offers great sensory-motor learning opportunities, having to do with weights, lengths, balance, velocity, and so on. This translates to hours of fun in discovering how many children, and which particular children of what age and weight, should sit exactly where on each side of the board, in order to "set the table" or balance the whole affair.

Other Play Equipment

Child-size rakes and shovels

A sturdy wagon or small garden cart

Assorted lengths of old boards

A basket of Salvation Army tools

- *wrenches of various sizes*
- *wide paintbrushes*
- *pliers*
- *lightweight hammers*
- *short roofing nails*

There are a few pieces of play equipment that are essential to maximize outdoor play. With small rakes, shovels and a wagon, your child will spend days happily digging, raking and hauling. On my kindergarten playground, the children haul logs, stumps and straw from one location to the next, building and rebuilding fire stations, zoos, log cabins and such. They furnish these structures with pine-needle carpets, pine-cone fireplaces, straw kitchens, and so forth. An assortment of lengths and sizes of old boards adds tremendous dimension to these building ventures. The wagon is in use all day. Cooperation and collaboration are key as children construct together outdoors.

Another essential element to outdoor building is a basket of the right tools. Children love to use actual tools, the kind that grown-ups use. But they need the freedom to use the tools as their imagination dictates. What to do? I have chosen to designate one of the children's tables beside the tumble of hay bales the "Workshop." This is where the basket of tools is placed. The children can use the tools on the table, or in creations close by, but cannot carry the tools too far away to be found at cleanup time. Many building materials get hauled to this place, and serious building ensues. The tools I have found to be the most useful are wrenches of varying sizes, inexpensive paintbrushes, pliers, very lightweight hammers, and a can full of short, fat roofing nails with flat heads.. One important rule about the hammer is only one child on one stump or board at a time. This means the only mashed thumbs are self-inflicted. If the nails are being used, I take care to supervise them closely. If the children are hammering together a few boards for boat-building, I check the nails to see that no sharp points are exposed. Often, though, they are satisfied to sit beside a short, squat stump and hammer nail after nail into it. Sometimes they will turn the hammer around and use the claw to pull the stump apart, discovering worlds about their own strength and the sensory banquet of fresh wood. The paintbrushes get used for "painting" with water and "plastering" with mud. Because tools are expensive and their playground use is so vigorous, I buy old tools at secondhand stores. This way no one worries if a wrench gets lost in the pine needles. Besides, it will probably be excavated at some future point, to everyone's amazed delight.

The Garden as Playspace

A remarkable addition to an outdoor playspace is a garden. Care of plant life is a fundamental lesson in outdoor play. In caring for a small garden patch, in learning to weed and water, and in delighting in the produce—whether flowers, vegetables or both—the child learns a very basic lesson in the relationship between humanity and the natural world. Whether it is a container garden on your urban patio, a half-acre of vegetables, or something in between, the close proximity of a garden deepens and diversifies your child's experience.

A marvelous way to "open" the gardening season each year is to go through the outgrown clothes with your child and choose clothes for a child-sized scarecrow. He can be stuffed with grass clippings, bark mulch, or hay, and you can make a head out of an old T-shirt, stuffed and tied at the bottom like a balloon. You can then stitch the head onto the neckline of the shirt, choose an old hat, and there he is! I have placed a small scarecrow in a child's lawn chair and put shoes on the ground under his legs. Your child will love to run and whisper to him, especially if you animate him, if you wonder what secrets he has to tell. In the summer you can place the watering can by his feet, and keep a rake beside him in the fall. As the weather gets cold, he may need a stocking cap! One way to close the garden at the end of the season is to tell your child, "He has worked hard in our garden all year. Let's let him go to bed for the winter!" You can then shake his stuffing into the compost, and put his clothes in the rag pile.

When planning your garden, you can keep in mind the idea of "grazing." Can you create a garden that will satisfy your small child's need for instant gratification, for grazing? When choosing seeds, choose some that have a short time till maturity. Baby lettuces and greens are a good choice. And if your love is a big "beefsteak" tomato, plant a cherry tomato, too, to satisfy your child's grazing memories. We humans spent a long time in our hunting and gathering cycle, so think of berries, snow peas and lettuces for gathering.

You may also want to plant with more long-term produce in mind, something that teaches patient tending, watching, and waiting. Winter squash are a delight to grow, because their leaves are as huge as a fairy-tale image. Of course, a pumpkin lends itself to an autumn jack-o-lantern, and although your child will not get to see the underground growth of the potatoes, there is nothing as delicious as fresh-dug potatoes, roasted in foil in an autumn backyard campfire. Check your seed catalogs and see what will grow best in your climate for late summer and fall harvesting.

Your children will love to participate in the daily tending, watering, fertilizing and weeding, especially if you bring a sense of joy to the work. But they will love most of all gathering the harvest, whether to bring to the table or to just pop into their mouths on the way to the fort. You may want to let your bean tipi become the children's "fort." Just be sure to make it big enough that small feet don't have to trample the vines. A few shovelsful of bark mulch will help define the floor of the tipi and help protect the vines. You might like to make a bean tipi especially for play: scarlet runner beans are ornamental, with a gorgeous flower. This could become the children's tipi, and leave the harvestable beans safe from little feet. In a small child's mind, as well as inside the bean tipi, work and play are woven together into the fabric of life.

If your yard is big enough for a full-size garden with rows and beds, you may want to plan for wide, well-defined paths. If you use golden straw as mulch for the planting beds, then you can choose a dark-colored bark mulch to define the paths. This visual cue will help your child to recognize the boundaries more easily. A child of three and a half or four should be able to play happily up and down the pathways without stepping into the beds very often.

If your yard is small, don't give up on including a garden in your child's outdoor experience. Check your library for books on container gardening. This is becoming a very popular way to garden, particularly in urban areas. Terrace and rooftop gardens are sprouting up in many cities. Don't be shy to try your hand. Ask at your garden store about soil preparation, and jump right in. The very vibrancy of a healthy, growing garden, regardless of its size, makes it a perfect companion to a young child's lively outdoor play.

INSECTS IN THE GARDEN

It is in the world of nature that young children learn to care for and nurture the other creatures with which we share our planet. The perfect complement to backyard playtime is a small wood and screen construction bug house. These are usually designed to fit a child's hand and can be found at your garden shop or toy store. Hours can be spent busily constructing elaborate sandbox palaces, complete with swimming pools, driveways, canals, and such, for the beetle who waits patiently in the bug house. At day's end, we can be sure to return the little creature to its home, where its family is waiting. To return these small lives back to their environment, offering our child the image of a waiting insect family, gives her a sense of kinship with other lives, not dominion over them.

You can choose plants that will encourage the beneficial insect life in your yard. To be in a butterfly garden in July is an amazing experience! In Virginia, butterfly bushes grow to be six or eight feet tall in just two seasons, and produce mounds of sweet, butterfly-attracting blossoms. Children love to crawl up under their bowing branches and wait for the butterflies to land, just inches away. Bee balm is another flower that is beloved by butterflies and easy to grow. In a few seasons, you will have great splashes of color, filled with the whimsy of butterflies. Bees, too, will love to graze, and you can teach your child to recognize and respect the honeybees. If you have a patch of clover, your child will love to make "clover chains" and sit in the cool green. Show him, though, how to look for bees before he sits down, and if he is barefoot, to run around the clover patch, not through it. Hummingbirds also love the bee balm and butterfly bushes, as well as some of the deep-throated flowers, like hibiscus, or shade-loving hostas. To see the tiny hummingbirds hard at work with their busy acrobatics is a gift for any child.

You can also plant flowers that are night bloomers and attract the huge, gorgeous night moths. If you leave a porch light on, the moths will come, and may still be sitting on the screen door in the morning. You and your family will delight in the tremendous variety and beauty of these night creatures. All of these moths at your light will attract toads, and you may have a little amphibious neighbor living under the porch. He can be caught and pampered, have castles built for him, and then be returned to his home under the porch.

When you plant a garden, however small, keeping in mind your children, insect life, and neighborhood wildlife, you will want to stay away from garden pesticides and lawn chemicals. There are natural, biological fertilizers and pesticides that are readily available from your garden shop.

BACKYARD WILDLIFE

Children love a diverse experience of nature. You can foster this by creating feeding areas for the various birds and backyard wildlife that you would like to encourage into your child's life. Bird feeders, squirrel feeding stations, and hummingbird feeders can provide hours of not only observation, but also interaction, in the form of imaginative games that evolve around care of the backyard wildlife. You can put out birdbaths and birdhouses, and hang a bat house, too.

An easy way to make a squirrel-proof bird feeder is to buy the kind of smooth wrought-iron or metal "garden hook" that is sold as a stand for hanging plants. Hang your feeder here. The squirrels can't climb the pole, and so your birdseed is safe. Place it where there are branches nearby so the birds can flit back and forth while they feed. You can also buy a window-type bird feeder that hangs by suction cups. Place this on the window by the breakfast nook or dining table, and your child's meal will be enhanced, with the great outdoors just inches away. To watch a family of birds is another kind of nourishment for her. If you can hang a birdhouse in view of the window, she may have the treat of observing a whole cycle of nesting, hatching, feeding and fledging! If you watch with her, this may inspire your storytelling at bedtime. Your child is interested in families of every proportion and description.

Place the squirrel feeding station in the far corner, away from the bird feeders. A squirrel feeding station may be something as simple as a low, flat

---

ENCOURAGE BACKYARD WILDLIFE

Hang squirrel-proof bird feeder from metal pole, or attach to window.

Put up a bird house just outside the window.

Place squirrel feeding station away from bird feeders.

Put up a bat house.

Hang a hummingbird feeder close by the window.

Make a toad hotel.

stump with a tin plate nailed on, and nail holes in the bottom for rainwater to drain through.

You may want to consider putting up a bat house to attract these mosquito-eaters. In one night, they consume many times their own weight in mosquitoes, making your family's evenings outdoors far more pleasant. They are, of course, very sensitive to insecticides, but will thrive in a natural environment. Bats have suffered from slanderous propaganda and are not the frightening creatures we imagine. Some manufacturers include a small book with the bat house, giving details on the care and life cycle of the bat.

A hummingbird feeder at the window is an opportunity for life lessons. These tiny, industrious workers will come to the feeder, fold their wings, and sit down on the small bar to sip the nectar. To watch them finally rest elicits a hush of wonder.

Place a broken pot upside down in the garden, and you have created a toad hotel. You can also buy whimsical ceramic toad houses in the garden shop. Whether the toad moves in or not, your child will love to check, day by day.

HILLS, SAND AND WATER

A hill of any size is a tremendous boon to an outdoor playspace. If you are lucky enough to have a natural hill, you can help your child discover its many advantages. If your yard is flat, you can import several dumptrucks of dirt to be unloaded somewhere in a back corner. The creation of a hill can be an exciting, if dirty, adventure. You and your child can get into the dirt with rakes and shovels and shape the hill the way you would like. You will need some extra time at the end of the day to fill up all the little holes your child has industriously "helped" with. If you can shape the hill with a steep side for older children and a gently sloping side for younger ones, all the better. But a hill of any description is a blessing. Ask at your garden shop about planting grass on a slope, and which season is best for luxuriant growth. When your hill is ready, many hours of fun and hilarity will ensue.

If the creation of a hill seems daunting, a dirt pile in a corner of the yard is great fun. Dirt is filled with life in a very different way from sand, and every child knows this! On my kindergarten playground, the children run back and forth between the dirt pile (which I replenish a wheel barrowful at a time) and the sandbox, announcing, "Here comes the chocolate!"

One of the best "uses" of a hill, as any young child will tell you, is to roll down it. Again and again. And again. Rolling is a healthy and necessary part of natural development. It can help the child to discover her physical "boundaries," her skin—and this can help to establish healthy psychological and social boundaries as well. On my kindergarten playground, we have a "roly-poly" hill. Each day after lunch, when every child's natural inclination is to jump and roll, we run outside and roll down the hill amidst gales of laughter. It's roly-poly time! The children also like to roll down by twos, in bear hugs. Think of initiating a "roly-poly time" in your family. When it's too cold or wet outdoors, come inside to the carpet. It will soon become a real favorite.

Hills are also good for sledding, for hiding behind, for running up the steep side and down the slope, then the other way around. They are also necessary, sometimes, when someone wants to be king. Think of planting some ornamental grasses on your hill to help define the space and create natural suggestions of forts and hideouts.

No back yard is complete without sand and water. When we think of sand, we want to think big, and lots of it. A sand pile, like we would find at a construction site, is ideal. Unfortunately, though, when sand is not contained, it drifts away. So we need to consider how best to contain the sand in a natural way that allows it to be, like a sand pile, abundantly dig-able.

At our house, which is in the forest, we had the natural material of fallen trees available. We rolled a fallen pine down to the yard and cut it into sections, which when placed together created an octagonal "box." You can look around at the natural materials available in your area and let your imagination fly. Perhaps you can find stones and mortar, or old timbers from a neighboring barn. Be cautious of considering old railroad timbers or old telephone poles. Yes, we want to use recycled materials when we can, but you will want to research the preservatives that may have been used in the wood, as they can be highly toxic. Buying good, solid timbers from the lumber yard is also wonderful, but you may want to play with the shape of the container so your child has a fanciful shape to spark the imagination, rather than the rectangle the boards may suggest.

You can take your child on a visit to the sandlot to see the different quality of the sand. Look carefully at the color of the sand; it will be coming into the house, and will be walked into the carpets. A white "play sand" may be best where cleanup is involved. Remember, don't put a bottom in your sandbox—how will your child "dig to China" if you do? Your child will exult in having dug deeper than the sand, down to the mud, or rather, the "chocolate." A bottom can also retain rainwater and make the sand begin to smell stagnant. When you look at sand toys, remember that the typical plastic toys will usually deconstruct within one or two seasons. You can go to the Salvation Army, though, and get old pots, pans and serving utensils that will survive your child's entire life in the sandbox. A sandbox cover is usually a necessity, given the possibility of neighboring cats. If you have made a nice, big sandbox, a wooden cover can be unwieldy. I have been content with a forest-green, construction-grade tarp, which folds back easily. I have also heard of making a Plexiglas cover with hinges that will fold when not in use.

Water is essential for sand play. If your sandbox is big enough, your child will discover the magic of making waterways, canals, swimming pools, lakes and even the ocean! A good source of backyard water for creative play is a small wading pool. Place the pool in a spot far away from the sandbox to encourage plenty of running and physical activity. We want to give our children the opportunity to move in a purposeful way, using their whole body in meaningful physical tasks. Running back and forth, bucket in hand, is full of meaning and purpose for your child, as is creating great river systems in the sandbox!

Recently, some child psychologists have begun using "sand tray therapy" with their clients, observing their play and imagination. Often, not only will the therapist better understand the child's difficulty, but the child, through

---

REMEMBER THE WATER

Try a small wading pool, placed far from the sand.

Water-carrying is excellent skill building: strength, balance, steadiness.

Water in the sandbox is fun.

- *soups and pies*
- *canals for ants*
- *swimming pools*
- *river systems, and more!*

TIP

Sand play is good therapy. Malleable, soothing and easy to manipulate, sand is an excellent medium in which to "solve" problems from the creative hemisphere of the brain.

play, will find insight and solutions for her challenging life circumstances. This fact inspired me to place many small plastic farm animals and wild animals in our outdoor sandbox. These figures are constantly being played with, lost and rediscovered, much to the children's thrilled amazement. If we give our children access to sand, water and free creative play, we offer them an open stage upon which to experiment in safety with life's big questions— who am I, where do I fit, what are my needs, what do I have to give? All imaginative play offers this opportunity, but the malleable sand and water carry a specific magic all their own.

Sand play is the perfect time for us to suggest a nurturing attitude toward the small insect life in the back yard. Your child may come with tales of a huge daddy longlegs in a corner of the sandbox. This is the moment to get out the bug house, gingerly deposit him there, and suggest a fine sand castle for the insect, complete with waterworks. Your three- or four-year-old may forget this project in a couple of minutes (and may need a reminder to release the daddy longlegs), but your five- to nine-year-old will carry it through, with many refinements.

A necessary adjunct to sand and water play is a basket full of old towels that lives by the back door. Meet your child at the door with a smile and a towel, and rub down—first stripping off the outer layer of clothing if necessary. Usually a bath is not required immediately, if you rub well. If your sand is white, probably only the sparkles will show up on the carpet.

Water in the outdoor playspace enhances every aspect of your child's experience. Sandbox water is only one possibility. You may want to research a backyard pond, complete with pump, pools, water plants, and so forth. A human-made pond is a lovely addition, and one that always takes a little attention to maintain. Your garden shop should be able to tell you what kind of time investment it will require so you can make an informed decision. The natural life that occurs around a small pond is diverse and amazing. Outside my kitchen door runs a tiny stream, and the "wildlife" that it attracts is a year-round pleasure. Birds, of course, come to drink and bathe. But the diversity of toads, water-skaters, salamanders, minnows, crayfish, and even a raccoon that comes to wash his food, is remarkable. If we create environments that are designed with the needs of various creatures in mind, in time they will find their way into our lives.

KEEP "SAND TOWELS" HANDY

Keep old towels in a basket by the door.

Rub your child down before he comes inside—maybe strip off the outer layer.

White sand shows less inside.

ABOUT A BACKYARD POND

Enhances insect life

Enhances wildlife

Enhances soundscape

Enhances your child's outdoor life

It is critical, especially now, as our environment is so threatened, that we teach our young children, through doing, to love, nurture and respect the other forms of life with which we share our world. Our young child will learn to love the water-skaters on the surface of the pond, not by hearing about them, but by interacting with them, through play.

SOUNDSCAPE

A very subtle way to improve our child's outdoor play experience is to attend to the "soundscape." Many of the ideas mentioned before will diversify the soundscape. Encouraging beneficial insect life enriches the sound experience, as your child plays with bees buzzing close by and dragonflies flitting over the pond. Backyard wildlife, with birdsong at dawn and the chattering of squirrels, makes the sound experience very life-filled for your child. Wind whispering through the tall ornamental grasses at the foot of the hill tells summer secrets, and the laughter of a stream trickling into the pond is a song of its own. That hummingbirds actually "hum" is an amazing fact for a child. You can also hang beautifully tuned wind chimes in the branches of a tree, choosing which tuning is perfect for your family. You might also like to hang a few smaller wind chimes from low bushes, or from an ornamental garden stake, so that your child can reach out to touch them as he runs past. Nature is never silent, and we can help encourage all the richness of her symphony as we also create an enticing playspace for our child.

OUTDOOR ACTIVITIES

As society becomes more removed from the natural environment, it is essential that we give children a deep immersion in the natural world, in the simple experience of our own back yard. In good weather you can consider doing many activities outdoors. Perhaps you would like to have your snack outdoors. It is lovely to put out a bright flowered tablecloth and uncomplicated food, with berry tea shining in the sun. You could consider having the evening meal outdoors whenever possible. Your bat house will make it even more pleasant, as these night-shift workers will have consumed hundreds

BRING YOUR LIFE
OUTDOORS

Eat outdoors.

Do art outdoors.

Have story time in the hammock.

Have a backyard campout.

of mosquitoes. There are also citronella candles, for atmosphere as well as insect control. There are many non-offensive natural insect repellants, too.

You could consider bringing artwork outdoors, as well. You will need a picnic table and a good weatherproof tablecloth. It is a stunning experience to quietly paint with watercolor and a wide brush on a large sheet of paper, as the birds sing and the light and shadow play through the leaves. Story time in the hammock is the perfect precursor to nap time, rocking both your child and yourself into a relaxed, happy state. Every back yard needs the quiet comfort of a hammock, whether for dreaming, snoozing, or riding a boat on the high seas.

Let's look at our days, and see which activities we usually do indoors that might be experienced as well in nature. Don't let the weather deter your resolution. In my kindergarten, we have a picnic lunch nearly every day of the year! The picnic table is at the foot of a poplar tree, therefore densely shaded in hot weather but bright and sunny when the leaves fall. It is a great joy to bundle up in our layers and run out to a sunny winter picnic!

Don't forget the nighttime. A backyard camp-out with the whole family can be a grand adventure. The very familiar back yard becomes mysterious with night sounds and scents. You will need to gauge your child's temperament and development to know when it is the right time to sleep outdoors.

Colder Weather Outdoors

Autumn playspaces can be full of wonder, even as the tomato vines wither and the leaves fall. Your child will love pulling out the old squash vines from the summer garden, ready for the compost. He will remember the fun days spent playing up and down the garden paths, and the taste of fresh berries. If your yard has shade trees, after you and your child have raked huge piles of leaves (and re-raked them after they've been jumped into), you can finally wheelbarrow them into the compost heap. It a great lesson in the cyclic nature of things for your child to see part of her playground, the straw bales and leaves, going into the garden. She will begin to understand that decomposition acts to nourish the future, her own garden playspace!

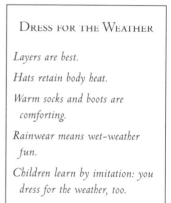

Colder Weather Outdoors

Put the garden to bed.

Rake leaves.

Put away the pool.

Fill wildlife feeders.

Begin to wear layers.

Dress for the Weather

Layers are best.

Hats retain body heat.

Warm socks and boots are comforting.

Rainwear means wet-weather fun.

Children learn by imitation: you dress for the weather, too.

When a chill comes into the air, this will be the time to empty the sandbox pool of water. Putting away the pool is also a lesson in the cycles of life. You can hang it in the garage, to wait for warm days to come again. In the fall chill, you will want to pay special attention to your wildlife feeders. As you fill one feeder after another, you can tell your child stories about the animals who go to sleep for the winter, and about the brave, cheerful winter birds who stay awake to keep us company.

If we choose our child's and our own wardrobe well, we should be able to go out in nearly all weather. Layering is the answer to just about any question about cold weather wear. Better to have several layers, including long johns, turtleneck, sweater, and a couple of weights of jackets, than one large, bulky winter coat. A coat can easily be too warm when our child is actively running and tumbling, and then too cold when she is busily digging. With layering, the outer jacket can be shed during a "tag" game, and then retrieved for a secret meeting in the fort. Think of layers to wick away the moisture of body heat, and even layers of socks for warmth. Keeping feet warm and dry, and heads covered, is a great secret to happy children at outdoor play. Although it is currently not in fashion to wear a hat in winter or to button the coat, if we can train ourselves to wear a hat and button up, our child will be happier when we insist on her warmth. Remember, she learns by imitation, and if she sees us shivering outdoors, she will assume that is the right attitude, and will want to adopt it herself. We lose so much body heat through the top of our heads, and there are now so many wonderful, whimsical, fun and even elegant winter hats that we can easily join them in the fun, and warmth, of hat wearing. Good, warm, waterproof boots are also an essential to fun outdoors. Some children's boots come with felt liners, and these are optimal. The liners can be taken out and set beside a stove or heat register to dry. If we also invest in a good rain slicker, for ourselves as well as our child, we can have the rare pleasure of being completely dry, warm and protected while enjoying the great blessing of rain. Sometimes it is too muddy to play in the yard, but we can taste the freshness and cold of the outdoor air with a rain walk. Children usually love the rain. It is our parental wish that they not get wet and catch cold that keeps them indoors. If we dress them and ourselves properly, they can have the freshness of the rain-washed air and stay healthy, too. Dressed properly, we can join them in this communion with the weather.

To create a balanced, diverse, vigorous outdoor playspace for our children is not only a great gift we give to them, it can also be an adventure for us. Imagining ways we can bring more and more of our living outdoors brings our whole family into greater connection with the natural world. As parents, we may also discover a natural joyous part of our essential being. We may rediscover the art of play!

Chapter 6

THE WONDER OF STORIES

ONE OF OUR most human capacities is the ability, as well as the need, to create stories. It is through the medium of story that we make meaning of our life. We each have our own personal story, which dynamically changes as our understanding and integration expand. Bruno Bettelheim tells us that the young child achieves "understanding, and with it the ability to cope, not through rational comprehension... but by becoming familiar with (life) through spinning out daydreams—ruminating, rearranging, and fantasizing about suitable story elements in response to... [life] pressures."[1]

Through the use of story, we can give our children powerful tools necessary to make sense of their lives. Stories offer our children examples of *solutions* for the difficulties they will encounter as they grow and develop. They also image for our children various *qualities of character* that will aid them in these difficulties. These images can lay a foundation of strength that will serve them for a lifetime. For a "true" story, like all good literature, appeals to readers at many different levels of their being, and also speaks to different stages of development. The stories and potent images we give our children offer new dimensions to their imagination, ones they could find difficult to discover on their own.

Not only does the realm of story help growing children make sense of their inner experience, it can help them understand the way the outer world works, as well. In all early societies, from the most ancient rendering of story as paintings on cave walls through the long and hallowed tradition of oral storytelling, to the evolution of story into print, always story has served the larger society. Through the images offered, the child is shown the subtleties of human interaction, as well as the qualities both admired and rejected by the social group. In this way stories have shaped social behavior, and culture has been passed on from generation to generation. The fact-oriented nature

Through the use of story, we offer our children qualities of character that will aid them in discovering solutions to life's difficulties.

Story images show the child the subtleties of human interaction, as well as qualities both admired and rejected by the larger society.

of history is always embellished with that which captures the human heart, the stories of the people whose lives are involved in the history-making.

LANGUAGE ACQUISITION THROUGH STORY

We cannot underestimate the function of storytelling in the acquisition of language. The child's first impression of the mother tongue occurs in the womb. After birth, the baby is held in his parents' loving embrace, and in the warm flow of language that surrounds him. This is why it is so important to offer the infant and young child the sounds of the natural human voice, and to limit his exposure to mechanical or electronic voices. It is not just the content of the words that is critical to healthy development; it is also the feeling quality, the *human* quality carried in the voice. The mother holds her baby and talks soothingly during diapering and nursing. "Oh," she says to the baby, "are you wet? Let's make you warm and dry." "You must be hungry!" or "Here comes daddy. He loves his boy!" Already at this early stage, the baby is learning about himself, his world and those around him through story. In the simple natural verbal recounting of Baby's life, physical sensation, feelings, and eventually images are being created and recreated. Through hearing the "story" of his days unfold, by associating words with people and things, slowly the child begins to live into language.

For the baby, this simple tracking of experience through language can be enriched by "finger and toe" games. The classic rhyme "This little piggy went to market" tells a story in rhyme and gesture. This kind of story is told in Mother or Father's lap, with rhyme and gesture referring to Baby's physical body. It lays a foundation for language development, and also the development of memory, upon which meaningful cognition depends. Because finger and toe games are rhythmic, rhyming and bodily based, Baby's verbal memory is augmented by a kind of motor memory in which body sensation calls up the next image or word. The classic nursery rhymes, when repeated again and again with your child in your lap, give the baby, toddler and preschool child a wealth of experience in rhythmic language and a solid foundation in image formation. This capacity to form mental images is the prerequisite for all academic learning.

For babies, language can be enriched by using "finger and toe" games. Use rhymes from Mother Goose and create your own games, with a tickle of ears and nose, belly and toes, at end-rhymes.

You will want a copy of Mother Goose to be one of the first books you buy for your baby. At first, think about using it primarily as a reference book. You can leave it open on the kitchen counter, and as you go about your work, slowly build up your repertoire of the beautiful, funny and nonsensical rhymes it contains. While holding Baby on your lap, make eye contact, and in the spirit of fun, repeat the rhymes in a slow, clear, rhythmic fashion. Using "This little piggy went to market" as a model, you can punctuate the end-rhymes with a tickle of fingers, toes, nose, ears, belly button, and so on. Be certain that you use the same gestures in the same way each time you say a particular rhyme with her. Again, this helps to develop motor and later cognitive memory function.

It is best, for our two-, three- and four-year-old, to find stories that are told in verse, with simple images that reflect her small world. All children love the rhyme and rhythm of poetry, so check your library and bookstore. Elegant use of language is a treasure in these times when much of modern children's literature has become "cute-ified," with the language reduced to its lowest common denominator. We want to offer our children, beginning at an early age, language that is richly textured, varied, and melodic. If we think of language as a river in which our children are carried along, let us look to the quality, purity and life force of this water. Check the Bibliography for book ideas.

For two-, three-, and four-year-olds, stories told in verse are excellent. Look for elegant use of language

Three- and four-year-olds are discovering the wonders of their own small world. Look for stories that tell of simple happenings in the course of a simple life.

STORIES FOR THREE- AND FOUR-YEAR-OLDS

Stories that re-create for our children activities from their own days—the warm brown smell of oatmeal in the morning, the acrobatics of the squirrel in the tree outside the kitchen window, cool silken sand between bare toes—these stories help them bring language to their everyday life, and thereby make sense of it. In your library, you can search for picture books that tell the story of simple happenings that occur in the course of a simple life. For your very young children, see if you can find the ones with little story line, just poignant illustrations of an event. Simplicity is the watchword here, as it is in most choices you make for your young child. Look for stories that picture, for instance, a young child's experience of a kitten purring in her lap, or the wonder of waking up snuggled in the blankets as a bird sings outside the window.

You may also discover the wonder of "wordless books," which tell a story in pictures only. These are not only delightful for your child, who can relax and gaze wonderingly at the progression of pictures, but also for you! They provide you an opportunity to practice your skill at creating stories. Your child can join you in story-making, also, if you point to a picture and say, "I wonder what is happening here." A homemade story is a gift from heart to heart.

Three- and four-year-olds are busy becoming aware of the natural world. They are like little Buddhas, very present in the sense impressions that each moment offers. Nature offers them a subtly and slowly changing variety of sensory input within a broad context of constancy. Because they are still very natural beings, they are attracted to the green world outdoors. Books and stories that sensitively render the simple splendors of the interconnected web of life are perfect at this age. You might find in your library an illustrated story of the yearly cycle of a tree, as it buds, flowers, leafs out, drops its leaves, and finally makes nuts or berries, which the deer come to eat. Or perhaps you could find one that creates a picture of a little child wishing for snow as she blows out the evening candle. Then the silent descent of tiny diamonds, till at dawn her house is nestled in snowdrifts. Simple, simple simple.

A perfect way for a three- or four-year-old to understand the interdependent relationships in nature is through the story imagery of a large and loving extended family. We can read and perhaps create our own stories of Mother Earth as she cares for her many "children," the leaves, insects and small animals. We can describe how she puts them to bed in the fall, keeps them warm in winter with a snow-white blanket, and wakens them to wear their flower dresses in the spring. Other family members are Father Sun, Sister Rain and Brother Wind, who each play a significant role in the ordering of life on Earth. You can make up stories that tell of the "Weather Fairy Family," the rain fairies who come to care for the spring garden, the mist fairies who sprinkle pearls along the spine of each blade of grass, the snow fairies bringing warm white blankets for winter. Your children are just discovering the nature of "family" firsthand, and will love to hear their own experience portrayed in this imaginative way.

Discover the magic of "wordless books" and practice making up your own story.

Books that sensitively render the simple splendors of the interconnected web of life are perfect for threes and fours.

Tell your three- or four-year-old stories of the large and loving extended family of Nature. Peopled by Mother Earth, Father Sun, Brother Wind and Sister Rain, as well as the cousins, the Rain Fairies. These stories enlarge your child's growing sense of family.

Animal stories are also excellent for three- and four-year-olds. You will want to focus on stories about animals that are familiar to your children, through their backyard experiences, and save the savanna animals of Africa or marsupials of Australia for a later stage of development. Stories of family pets, farm animals, backyard wildlife, insects and water creatures are good at this age. You will want to look for imaginative renderings of these, a kind of anthropomorphism, rather than a scientific examination. We want our children to develop, at this age, a *feeling quality* for the animals and for nature. This they can do by beginning to form inner pictures that are born out of their own experience.

Remember to put your little one in your lap and read slowly, allowing time for him to "digest" the language as well as the images. Your child will ask for the same story over and over, and it is important that you read the text in the same way each time to strengthen his language acquisition, memory and sequencing. This "layering up" of visual, auditory, and tactile experience is a gift we can give that will last a lifetime.

After a little practice making up finger and toe games with Baby, and creating stories to go with the wordless books, we will enjoy the next natural step. If we make ourselves familiar with the simple, home-oriented themes appropriate to our three- and four-year-olds, we can begin to really take pleasure in the adventure of making up stories of our own imaginings. Remember to keep the themes close to home and familiar. Keep the plot very minimal. Allow the clarity of the images you create to carry the day.

Here are two examples of impromptu, "homemade" stories with themes appropriate for three- and four-year-olds. Even the fives and sixes love a simple story like this sometimes, too. Don't forget your journal. You can create simple stories like these, out of your own imagination. Your child will love *your* stories the best!

~ *The Rain Garden* ~

ONCE UPON A time, on a dim and dreary day late in November, little George sat on the great windowsill of his bedroom. He looked out at the garden, which had been so bright in summer, filled with the ripe, red tomatoes he and Father had planted. He remembered the tall spears of the

Animal stories are also excellent for threes and fours. Look for books and stories of familiar backyard, woodland, or farm animals. Save exotic animals for a little later.

Have your three- or four-year-old sit in your lap, and read slowly, in the same way each time. This "layering up" of visual, auditory, and tactile experience is a gift to last a lifetime.

Try your hand at "homemade" stories. Keep the themes close to home and the plot minimal. Allow the images you create to carry the day.

gladiolus, with their scarlet blossoms whispering secrets to the warm breezes. But today the garden lay in a gray and tumbled heap.

Suddenly, he saw a little brown head bob up and down below the great, bending stalk of his favorite sunflower. It was so big, he had built a fort of sticks beneath it in July. He squinted his eyes, to see a little better. There again, the bobbing! Now he saw the flap of a tiny wing, and suddenly he

could see the chickadee, busily pecking for sunflower seeds. He watched as the small brown bird pecked beneath the huge gray sky.

Then he had an idea! He jumped down from the windowsill and scampered down the stairs, all breathless. In the kitchen, he opened the pantry door. "What do you need, honey?" asked his mother. "I need to grow longer legs!" he said. But instead he pushed a kitchen chair across the floor and stood peering into the dark corners of the pantry. Where was that jar? The one he had worked so hard to fill at harvest time, while Father was digging potatoes and Mother made peach jam. He pushed cans and jars and packages this way and that, as Mother said, "Carefully, go slowly!"

There it was! At the very back of the high shelf. He stretched and reached for it with both hands. Climbing down from the chair, he showed it to his mother. "There are the seeds from your very favorite sunflower in the garden!" said Mother. "Where are you going with them?" But little George was in such a hurry he couldn't answer.

At the back door he pulled his jacket, hat, and mittens from their hook. Now he was big enough to put everything on by himself, even though the zipper was hard to manage. Just as he was ready to open the door, Mother came to him, saying, "Georgie, it has begun to rain." So now the yellow slicker went on top of everything, and even the big yellow hat, which made everything sound funny when he was underneath it.

In the garden, he breathed the sweet musk of autumn leaves underfoot. As he walked across the old tomato patch, he was surprised to smell the tang of last summer's tomatoes still clinging to the fallen vines. The sound of the raindrops on his great yellow hat was louder than the raindrops on the roof!

The chickadee had been watching him. Now that he came close, she opened her tiny wings and flitted to a nearby branch. She watched with her bright, sharp eye, as little George stood beneath the sunflower stalk. He bent low, and searched the brown soil. Only a few scattered seeds remained. He smiled as he opened the jar and sprinkled a handful of shiny black seeds over the damp earth.

Now the wind blew a sharp gust. His raincoat flew up, and the flaps of the yellow hat sprayed a cold mist on his cheek. He shivered, and ran to the swing set close beside the garden. Looking up, he saw Mother's smiling face at the kitchen window. So little George swung and skipped, dug and ran, as the rain fell gently around him. He was warm inside all his layers, and glad to be playing while the rain fairies danced around him.

Finally, as he settled into busy tunneling in the sandbox, with a swoop of wee wings, the chickadee returned to her pecking. She pecked, seed by seed, and little George tunneled, scoop by scoop. They were both very happy.

Later that evening, in the bathtub, little George sang a merry song about a chickadee and shining seeds, about summer sunflowers and autumn rains. He fell asleep smiling in his snug bed.

~ The Rain Fairies' Winter Coats ~

ONE BRIGHT MORNING, Great Mother Rain Cloud gazed down on the earth below. There she saw a girl, digging with busy industry in her garden sandbox. Her baby brother sat close beside her, waving his chubby arms. Nearby, a tall man with brown arms bowed low over the garden beds. He stood and straightened his back, shaking his head. "Well, honey," he said to his wife, who worked in the pea patch nearby, "we really need some rain." Lifting his head, he shaded his eyes. In the distance he saw the Great Mother in her pearl-gray, lace-trimmed dress. "Maybe the rain is coming in our direction." The little girl glanced up from her bridge-building, and whispered, "Oh, please, rain fairies, come visit us today. I need water to fill my river, here below the bridge." Her little brother curled and uncurled his tiny toes in the silky smooth sand.

From above, the Great Mother listened carefully. She loved the humans of the earth, as well as all the many winged and four-legged creatures. And she especially loved the scaled fishes, the toads, and the insects. She heard the girl's tiny whisper; she heard the man's concerned voice. Then she went to the deep horn with which she woke her children, the rain fairies, when there was work to do. The voice of the horn boomed out as she blew mightily. "Thunder!" cried the man. The little girl jumped up and down. The baby squealed, while the woman smiled and pushed a curl from her forehead.

Now, from deep inside the cozy skirts of the Great Mother, sleepy rumpled heads started to pop up from lavender and blue blankets. Amidst all the tossing and turning, a pillow fight began. The rain fairies laughed merrily, throwing the fluffy cloud-pillows, hiding under the covers. The Great Mother's eyes twinkled at the antics of her children. "Come, children, we've work upon the earth to do!"

One by one, her children filled their tiny buckets from the reservoir of the Great Mother's lacy skirt, and hurried to the garden below. The peas perked their curly heads. The pods puffed up with pride. The corn shook its silken hair. The man and woman hurried inside, scooping up the baby with them. The little girl sat, quietly breathing as her sandbox river slowly filled.

So day by day the rain fairies visited the earth, watering the corn and peas, filling the creeks and rivers, making the minnows, farmers, and children smile. Thus the summer unfolded, until finally it turned its leafy green head toward autumn.

Late in autumn the Great Mother Rain Cloud's uncle, the North Wind, began to blow his shivery breath. The garden lay quietly sleeping. The children were busy at play indoors. Now the rain fairies began to beg their mother, "Oh, please, can't we go visit our cousins in the North Country? They have so many fun games to play!" The Great Mother nodded. "Yes," she said. "I believe that is just the thing for us to do!" She packed her children cozily in her lacy cloud skirt, and swept away.

Far in the north, at play with their cousins the ice fairies, the rain children began to shiver! They scurried back to the Great Mother. "We are so cold!" they cried. "Here, then," she replied, "Here are your winter coats." The rain fairies' eyes sparkled! Mother had made for each one of them a shiny white coat that glistened with rainbow glints, and twinkled in the light. Each child put on his coat and snuggled warm in its feathery softness. Now there were games of sledding and ice-skating, with snow porridge for breakfast and snow ice cream for dessert. It was a grand visit.

At last the Great Mother gathered her children and said farewell, and so they came swooping back home. The rain children were proud of their brilliant new coats. Never had they seen such beauty. "Can we show the human beings the gift you gave us in the North Country? Please, mama, please?"

The little girl said her evening prayer, kissed her mother and father goodnight, and blew out the candle. She heard the baby breathing in little puffs from his crib. In the night she shivered. Then she felt a cozy comforter pulled high and tucked beneath her chin.

When she opened her eyes, the room was filled with a soft glow. She threw back the covers and padded across the floor. Then she looked out her window, and cried for everyone to hear, "Look! Look! It snowed!" Her eyes shone as brilliantly as the rain fairies' new coats. Everyone was happy indeed.

GUIDING STORIES FOR THREE- AND FOUR-YEAR-OLDS

We may find situations with our three- and four-year-old in which a subtle kind of guidance is needed. As we become more familiar with the creative process of "making up" stories, we can give indirect but very effective guidance to our little ones. We can, using the imagery appropriate to this age, give strength, consolation, courage and enthusiasm.

We can create, in the story realm, a situation that mirrors closely the difficulty our child is experiencing. Often at this age we can make the story parallel the actual occurrences, placing it in the animal kingdom. For instance, if a child is experiencing the difficulty of a new sibling, we can perhaps tell a story about a Little Squirrel, who is happily ensconced in his life with Mother and Father Squirrel. Much to his dismay, a new Baby Squirrel arrives and disrupts everything. The much-beloved romps in the treetops with

> ELEMENT OF A "GUIDING STORY"
>
> *Let the story parallel your child's difficulty.*
>
> *Place the story in the animal kingdom.*
>
> *Lay out the problem and give descriptive details.*
>
> *Show the resolution in vivid story images.*
>
> *Let it all end "happily ever after."*

Mother are far less frequent and shorter in duration. Father Squirrel, who is great fun to crack the really big nuts with, is now the one to tell the bedtime story. Remember that the young child lives life through the details, so fill your stories with colorful detail. You can describe Little Squirrel's response, hiding in the hollow log beside the stream, feeling very alone. The beauty of stories is that they can happen more quickly than life does. Resolution can be pictured *now*, and give real hope for the future. After laying out the problem, you can jump to the next season, when Baby Squirrel is a bit bigger. Now she needs to learn all the important squirrel secrets, which Little Squirrel happily passes on: hide and seek among the roots of the oak tree, where to find the perfect sticks for playing acorn-ball, and especially the art of walking on branches upside down. Through a story like this, your young child learns that in time, with patience and perseverance, a situation that looks at first to be dreadful, can in the end enrich life tremendously.

FAIRY TALES FOR FIVES AND SIXES

For children of five and older, though, a need for something new emerges. With their newly found skill levels, with the corollary independence this brings, and with maturing cognitive development, children now need images they can turn toward for courage, intelligence, and generosity. This is the time for the introduction of fairy tales. Fairy tales will serve the needs of the developing child until seven or eight years of age. Like all true world literature, though, fairy tales speak to all ages and stages. We parents, too, can take meaning and guidance from the tales we choose for our children.

The child of five or six is beginning to experience the presence of "good and evil" in her own life. She may experience this in being teased by other children while at the park, or even in the simple interactions of visiting cousins! Generally the young child is not yet capable of recognizing these oppositions within her own being, but she certainly recognizes them in her outer world. Well-chosen fairy tales can show her, through simple, clear imagery, and characters that are painted in broad strokes, positive ways to deal with the condition of her humanity. These tales can help to shape her moral development, as well.

Five- to eight-year-olds need images they can turn to for courage, intelligence, and generosity. Now we introduce fairy tales.

The child of five or six is beginning to experience the presence of "good and evil" in her life. Well-chosen fairy tales can show her positive ways to deal with the condition of her humanity.

Fairy tales characteristically state a problem in clear, unmistakable terms. The plot is laid out simply, and the characters are drawn in bold, unambiguous strokes—the evil queen is, truly, evil incarnate, the youngest son has a pure and golden heart. It is imperative for the child of this age that the characters embody *qualities* rather than complex human individuals. The child does not yet possess the discernment necessary to evaluate figures drawn more closely to life, figures filled with the ambiguities that are true of us all. At this point, the child needs to see the various "qualities" of the human soul laid out in understandable terms, personified in the different figures in the tale. We see opposite qualities laid side by side: one sister is virtuous and industrious, the other lazy and cunning. One brother is selfishly cruel, the other compassionate. One parent is all good, the other all bad. Laying these opposites side by side gives the child the opportunity to see what these characteristics bring to fruition in the lives of the figures as the story unfolds. The cruel brother is turned to stone, while the compassionate one wins the love of the princess forever. And is it not true that cruelty hardens the heart, while kindness opens the doors of love? The lazy sister is covered in "pitch," while the industrious one is clothed in gold. We know only too well that our inner laziness creates lethargy, while inner striving, regardless of outer result, shines out in wealth of heart.

Seeing these opposites laid side by side, the child can begin to imagine what kind of person she would like to become. She does this by identifying with the various characters, feeling what they feel, "trying on" different ways of being. Often in fairy tales the negative figure has temporary ascendancy, and the child may feel attracted to the power, cunning or might of this figure. As the story unfolds, the child is shown the result of such an egoistic orientation, and can experience this imaginatively.

The young child does not yet possess the conceptual ability to "choose" between right and wrong; rather, she identifies with the character that arouses her sympathy or antipathy. The more simply and clearly the character is drawn, the easier it is for the child to identify. And we must keep in mind that it is not the figure's essential "goodness" that appeals to the child; instead she identifies with the condition of life that this goodness creates. Through these tales, she learns that goodness brings good results into her life, and that egoism eventually brings great limitation into life.

The child needs to see the various qualities of the human soul laid out in understandable terms, personified in the different figures of the tale.

Seeing these qualities laid side by side, in the characters of the tale, the child can begin to imagine what kind of person she would like to be.

Remember, it is not the figure's essential "goodness" that appeals to the child; instead she identifies with the condition of life this goodness creates.

Some fairy tales do not so clearly lay out the opposites; rather, they pose a question and show solutions. The child can see in the diverse figures of the story that there are many different kinds of people, and various ways to approach problems. The little girl outwits the bear and finds her way home. The poor woodcutter generously shares his crust of bread and is given sustenance forever. The youngest brother looks kindly on the bees, which then help him choose the sweetest princess. The prince goes out into the world, and by his own pure heart and perseverance at the tasks given him, he wins the princess and the kingdom as well. The girl must sit vigil three nights and withstand the visitation of monsters to discover that the kingdom is rightfully hers. We adults can all relate to the above fairy-tale themes: A keen intelligence "outwits" the most confounding circumstances. Generosity begets generosity tenfold. Kindness toward others brings much-needed help into our own lives. Purity and perseverance make our hearts rich. Calmly facing our inner "monsters" returns us to our true selves. What better way for us to pass on to our children these hard-won truths than to give them the actual "felt experience," as they identify with the fairy-tale characters?

Let's look at the internal structure of the fairy tale, and see what elements differentiate it from other traditional stories such as myths and fables. A fairy story is always set in the middle of everyday life. A fisherman is at his nets, a woodcutter is in the forest, a child is playing with a golden ball. This implies that what is about to happen could happen to any common person who is going about his daily business, including you or me. The hero and heroine are not named; they remain in the archetypal realm and are simply called, for instance, the Youngest Son, or the Good Queen, which leaves them openly available to be identified with. Myths, in contrast, are set in the grand realms of the gods, and the characters are clearly identified; sometimes their lineage is set out. The fairy story unfolds in a humble, conversational manner. Even the most fantastic elements and occurrences are told in simple, clear terms, with very little fanfare. This casual tone helps make it believable that even an ordinary person, small and insignificant (as the child may feel), could accomplish these wondrous feats. The myth asserts, on the other hand, that only demigods and heroes could reach such heights. Fables, rather than impressing the listener with the grand scope of things, take on a more didactic tone, assuring the listener of the moral of the story. A fairy story leaves

---

Essential Elements of a Fairy Tale

It is set in the middle of everyday life.

It unfolds in a humble, conversational manner.

It has a fundamentally optimistic tone.

The hero or heroine is not named and is easy to identify with.

Discovering the inner meaning is left up to the child.

Always, the hero/heroine lives "happily ever after."

the inner work of assimilating meaning up to the child. A major element that differentiates a fairy story is its fundamentally optimistic tone. The central figures go about their tasks, facing insurmountable odds. They are visited with help at every turn, usually due to their good character, their courage or generosity. They face the impossible with faith and perseverance, and are rewarded a hundredfold. Always, they live "happily ever after." Myths and fables, though, acting as morality stories, often end in tragedy or loss. For young children, a tone of simple, optimistic faith is critical. It is because of this faith, says Bruno Bettelheim, that children are willing to engage in the challenges and adventures of growing up.

GUIDING STORIES FOR FIVE- AND SIX-YEAR-OLDS

Often in fairy tales the hero must, through unavoidable circumstances, go out alone into the world. Through inner confidence and resourcefulness, while also making relationship with the world, and with a touch of magic as well, the protagonist finds an abundance of love and goodness in a new home. The original home, as well as the parents left behind, are returned with great jubilation. Integration of the old and the new is celebrated.

A sense of separation from the parent and the environment naturally begins to dawn on a child of six or seven years. Childhood is a long, slow process of individuation. The child grows ever more confident and, by adolescence, needs the support and guidance of parents less. As our society becomes more and more fragmented, though, it is easy for our children to feel, rather than a secure growth toward separation, instead a sense of isolation. A "guiding story" in the form of a fairy tale can act as an antidote, bringing comfort, courage, and healing.

Sometimes we will see our child struggling with a dilemma that she cannot solve. Or we may see her establishing a pattern of relating to others, or situations, that is limiting or unbalanced. When we become familiar with this internal structure of the fairy tale, and understand the role of the different elements in the growing child's life, we can then begin to weave our own magic. Taking our cues from the realm of fairy tales, we can create for her stories that pose the hero in similar internal struggles. Our story can show her, stated very simply, the problem, a central figure with whom she will identify, and a journey that allows for the aid of beneficent helpers, as well as her own inner resources, to manifest. We can empathize with her struggles and, with our more mature perspective, offer her *qualities of character* that will help toward resolution. We will want to be sure that the resolve is obvious, the protagonist is rewarded and everyone lives happily ever after. Remember to tell this story in the same relaxed, informal tone that we use for other fairy tales. Although you may feel a particular emphasis, just retain a simple conversational approach.

Here is an example of a homemade story you might choose to tell your six- to eight-year-old who is showing anxiety about leaving a familiar situation and moving into a wider circle. Perhaps she is moving from kindergarten and making the leap to grade school, or moving from one town to another. This would be a story to tell a child who has a natural inclination toward *kindness*. Following this is another story for a child in the same situation, who has a natural attraction toward *courage*.

~ The Princess in the Woods ~

ONCE UPON A time a princess lived in the castle of her mother and father, the King and Queen. Her parents' lands spread out from the castle walls as far as she could see. Beyond these well-tended fields, there stood a dark wood.

The little princess loved the formal flower gardens, full of roses and lilies, that surrounded the castle. But she loved the kitchen garden best. There she played for hours among the sweet and pungent herbs, nibbling on peas and baby lettuces. Year by year, the castle's gardener taught her all the secrets of the garden: the starting of seeds indoors, the feeding of soil with rich black compost, the pulling of weeds. The castle's cook taught her herbal secrets to flavor the game meat brought by the huntsmen, as well as the great pots of stew that simmered for hours at the open hearth. The little princess was happy amidst the garden and kitchen by day. She was also happy to sit beside her father at dinner, listening to visitors tell tales of foreign lands. At bedtime, her mother brushed her auburn hair and told her fairy stories.

One day, as she played in the warm sun, a honeybee landed on her nose. Although she was frightened of its sting, she sat very still. She remembered that the small, round bees gave her honey, which sweetened her bread each day. The bee sat daintily, and soon buzzed away. As it left, she called out, "Thank you for your sweetness!" Turning around, she saw the cook's son, a tall boy twice her age, aiming a slingshot at a ring-neck dove cooing on a low branch close by. "Oh, don't!" she cried. At the sound of her voice, the dove flew away to find its mate. That evening, while the princess was at table, an old woman came begging for a crust of bread. The little princess climbed down from her high seat and gave the beggar woman her own bowl of stew, saying, "This will warm you and give you strength." For her heart was as warm and shining as her bright copper-colored hair.

The following day, as she played in the garden, there beside the fence stood a baby fawn. It cried to her pitifully. Determined to help the poor creature find its way home, she opened the gate, laid her hand upon the fawn's back and set her footsteps toward the dark wood. "I will go only to the wood's edge, and then hurry home before darkness comes," she murmured to herself. But when they approached the edge of the wood, coax and encourage though she might, the fawn would not run along to find its mother. "I have an hour's light before it is dark. So I will go only a little way further to help the fawn."

An hour goes quickly, though. Just as darkness fell, the fawn bleated with joy and leaped forward. There in the shadows stood its mother, who nuzzled and licked her baby. The two woodland creatures, reunited, began walking away, but glanced backward, as though asking the princess to follow. Looking behind her, she saw in the deepening dark that she had lost the path home. And so she slept the night in the open air, snuggled close to the doe and fawn.

At morning's light, she found her companions gone and her stomach rumbling. What would she do for food, and how would she find her way home? Then she heard a buzzing close beside her ear. It was her friend the honeybee, who whispered in a buzzing voice, "Because you love our sweetness so, we will help you now." A swarm of golden bees led her through secret and winding forest paths, till they came to a great hollow honey tree. There in the warm sun, the princess ate the sweet honey, happily licking her fingers.

When she was no longer hungry, she looked around. She now knew she was lost more deeply in the tangled woods.

To her surprise, a softly cooing voice said from a nearby branch, "Follow me." The dove she had saved from the boy's slingshot glided from branch to branch, guiding her finally to a small hut in a clearing in the woods. At the door of the hut, the old beggar woman stood waiting. Now she was not gaunt and hungry-looking. Rather, she was round, with merrily dancing eyes. "I came to the castle to test your strength of heart. Your kindness has served you well. Now there is much I can teach you."

So the little princess lived with the old woman in the hut in the woods. Year by year, she learned from the old woman all the herbal lore of the forest, how to make healing potions and poultices, how to heal broken bones. Her knowledge of the healing arts was surpassed only by her radiant beauty. For she had grown to be as lovely as the ethereal woods, the copper of her hair reflected in the vivid autumn leaves.

One day, as she gathered soft plantain from a sunny spot beside a stream, she heard a hunting horn echo among the trees. In a moment, flashing through the woods, a huntsman on a swift steed leaped the streambed. The rider lost his hold as they vaulted, and tumbled to the ground. He lay close by, softly moaning. The princess was frightened of the man. She had seen no man for many years, only the old woman and her woodland friends the animals. But she hurried to his side. Bending over him, she saw he was badly bruised, but not mortally wounded. With the fresh herbs, she tended his injuries. She saw the stranger was strong and fine-looking as well.

When he regained consciousness, he found her bending low above him. Her beauty shone out in the afternoon sun. His heart fell from his hand, and he said to her, "I am the son of a great king. Because you have healed me, come with me to my castle. There I will make you my bride."

The wedding was celebrated with great ceremony, and invitations were sent forth to all the kingdoms far and wide. The last guests to enter the hall were an old king and queen, who wept when they saw the shining princess. Finally they had found their child, lost in the deep woods so many years before. All were united in great joy. And so, they lived happily ever after.

~

Here is a story for a child in the same situation who is attracted to the quality of courage.

~ *The Prince and the Ogre* ~

ONCE UPON A time there was a young prince. He lived happily in the castle with his mother and father, the King and Queen. He loved to see the great processions of knights, all in radiant colors, with their flags and pennants waving as they rode by. Sometimes the armor-master allowed him to shine their vest-plates till they glinted in the sun. The master archer taught him to aim the bow straight and firm, and to pull back the taut string to let the arrow fly direct and true. When the work of the day was finished, he loved to sit at table and listen to tales of foreign lands. And as his mother tucked him into bed, she told him fairy stories, filled with magic.

Alas, great sorrow came to the land, and the prince was sent far from the castle. In the care of his father's trusted servant, he journeyed far. But in the deep woods, robbers overcame the servant. Now the prince found himself alone in the world, without a friend.

He sat upon a stump, wondering which way to go. In a twinkling, there stood beside him an old beggar man, bent and gaunt. "I have not eaten all day," said he. The little prince, who was kind as well as brave, reached into his pocket, and took out his last piece of bread, saying, "I will gladly share my bread with you." So they sat together in silence and took their midday meal. When the old man stood up, though, he was no longer small and wizened, but tall and majestic. "Because you have helped an old man," he said, "now I will help you. Take these three gifts; you will need them on your journey. Here is a loaf of bread, a simple stone, and a vial of rosewater. You will throw away the bread, you will trade this stone for another, and you will spill the water on a rock. Far away beyond the horizon, there is a kingdom ruled by an ogre. A fair princess has become enchanted and is kept there as his prisoner. With these gifts, you will have all you need." He gave the prince the loaf of bread and a small velvet bag. In the blink of an eye, the prince stood alone.

So the prince made his way, day and night, longer than we can imagine. Finally he came to an ancient stone wall. Following the wall, he soon found a gate, guarded by a fierce dragon. Flames burst from the dragon's mouth. He threw the bread into the dragon's open maw, and when it began to eat, the iron gate opened. The boy crept past the dragon, which, busy with the bread, did not notice him. The dragon lay down in the sun to sleep. Now the boy came into a crumbling, ruined castle. In front of him stood an ancient throne, where no one sat. Only a parrot rested in a cage close by. He crept up the stairs to the empty throne, where he found nothing but a simple gray stone. Remembering what the old man had said, the boy took his stone from the bag and traded it, placing the ogre's stone in his velvet bag.

The parrot cried loudly, "Thief! Thief!" The boy could hear the castle tremble at the ogre's echoing footsteps, and ran for his life. When he was well beyond the sleeping dragon, he called, "A thief has stolen the ogre's stone!" With a roar, the dragon sprang awake and, nearly before it had opened its eyes, tore the pursuing ogre in two.

Now the boy sat down on the dusty road to catch his breath. He was hungry, and hoping to find a bit of bread, he opened his bag. Not a crumb was to be found, but there he saw the vial of rosewater. He took it out, looking at it with curiosity. He remembered that he was to spill the water upon a rock. No rocks lay close beside the road, though. So he stood and slung the bag over his shoulder, preparing to go on his way. It was then that he felt the weight of the ogre's stone at the bottom of his bag. Quickly he pulled the stone from the bag and poured the rosewater over it.

In a twinkling there stood before him a beautiful girl. Her eyes shone, her cheeks flushed pink, and her lips were red as roses. "I am the daughter of a King and Queen. The evil ogre turned me to stone, and I was made to sit upon the empty throne until the enchantment was broken. Your courage has set me free."

When the prince and princess returned to her castle, they were wed with great ceremony. Invitations were sent to all the kingdoms far and wide. Amidst the merriment, the doors opened, and there entered a noble King and Queen, who wept to see the brave and handsome prince. Finally they had found their beloved son, who had been lost to them in their sorrow. All were united now in great joy. And so they lived happily ever after.

OTHER "HOMEMADE" STORIES

The very best gift we can give our child is the gift of ourselves. One of the most satisfying ways we offer ourselves to our children is in telling them stories about ourselves. Our children want to know everything about us. So we can tell them a delightful type of story: When I Was a Little Girl (Boy). Your child will hang on every word you share about your growing-up years. These stories can emerge in the course of an average day. For instance, at mealtimes you can tell about the favorite dish your mother prepared for you. Or the food you most despised! Or the favorite thing you learned to cook for yourself, or the time your brother slipped with a plateful of spaghetti. You get the picture! Offer your child bright little snapshots of your life.

Keep the stories light and filled with sensory details. Tell your child about the way your mother's hair smelled when you brushed it for her, or how the garage was always chilly while you helped sweep it up. Talk about the way the wallpaper beside your bed had pink and purple stripes, and when you crossed your eyes it made a new color. Tell your child how you set out the chairs in your room so that in the middle of the night you could crawl from chair to chair and not have to touch the cold floor on the way to the bathroom. You can tell her silly little goofy things you liked to do. It will make you that much more human. Or tell about the things that made you cry. Your child can empathize.

You can tell these little anecdotes in the midst of the daily rounds of life, or make a mental note when you think of them, and save the telling for a bedtime story. Here are other ideas from your childhood to tell your children about: mealtime routines, favorites foods and least favorites, bedtimes, what pajamas you liked best, favorite stories from your dad, best games you played with brothers and sisters, best "neighborhood games," worst games, climbing trees, tree houses you had or wished you did, sliding down the stairs, what you got in trouble for, what the consequence was, what you thought it ought to have been, what your brother (sister) was best at doing, what you tried so hard to do but never quite could, what you shone like a star at doing, your worst household chore, how your sister made you laugh... the list is endless. As you go through your days with your child, if you pay attention to her world, if you notice what is important to her, if you empathize with her evolving consciousness, you *will* be reminded of similar situations you encountered as a child. Share this with her. It is easy to feel very small, and that the big people know all the secrets. Let her know, in vivid sensory pictures, that you have been in her shoes.

Your children will have favorites they ask for again and again. For your three- and four-year-old, tell the story in the same way, with the same details, each time. As you know, this lays a foundation for language development, memory, and sequencing, and provides a sense of security. When your child is five and older, though, you can retell the story, and then add, "But the part I haven't told you yet is…" A little embellishment can be considered poetic license, and children of this age are beginning to appreciate tall tales. So if you stretch a little in telling exactly how big that year's pumpkin was, you can give your child a little wink. Children this age are just beginning to really understand the "twist" entailed in a joke, so a little humor can spice things up a bit. If at the end of your tall tale he says, "No, *really*, Mom, how far did you throw the ball?" you can fess up with laughs and hugs.

If your older child loves adventure, you can also tell adventure stories from your own life. He would love to hear about the camping trip you took when it rained for five days, or the time you met the bear on the trail, or when you climbed higher than the eagles' nest and watched as they played on the air currents below. More mundane stories, also, can have a special appeal. Tell how very red the cardinal looked against the glittering snow on your fifth birthday, and wonder together where the color red came from. Or how the birds flew in synchronicity, like a school of fish, as people hurried on the sidewalks below. Do we really live in an ocean of air?

Another type of homemade story is what I call a chapter story. This is a story that evolves over time, one that is born out of a moment's inspiration and continues to live day by day. Usually a chapter story is more appropriate for our five- to nine-year-old, but if we can intuit the right theme, we may be able to create this type of story for our three- or four-year-old, also.

A chapter story for our threes or fours might begin with the life and activities of the squirrel family who live outside our kitchen door. Or perhaps the secret life of the family cat, or the mouse family that lives in abundance at the back of the garden shed. We can begin, as with all stories for threes and fours, with simple images from daily life.

If we choose a theme from our own backyard, we will have abundant story material presented to us on a daily basis. A story could begin the morning after a windy night, as together you look out at all the fallen branches. Perhaps a large branch now blocks the squirrel family's front door, and you offer some simple descriptions of their efforts to dislodge it. But the day is saved when a little boy (your child) comes along in search of the perfect stick. The story can ramble on about the uses of the stick, and then back to the squirrels' jubilation in the treetops. More chapters can follow regarding the squirrel's discovery of the new bird feeder, the human intervention to save the bird food, the acrobatics involved in dismantling the squirrel-proofer, and the arrival of the elegant squirrel feeder. Then on to the way the squirrels bury a cache of acorns in the garden, and how oak seedlings sprout in the pea patch the following spring. As you can see, this can become a never-ending story. Also, you won't have to search your creative mind for tidbits of story material. All you have to do is be observant when you look out the window.

When children ask me for a story, sometimes I will reply, "Let me listen for the story-angel; she whispers the story in my ear." I say this because it is true. All creative artists listen for the promptings of the Muse. When we are committed to telling our children chapter stories, we learn to listen to all the stories the world offers us. We listen to what is whispered in our ear, and then retell it for our children. For our threes and fours, as mentioned above, nature stories and stories from their own lives are affirming, reassuring, and true.

For our five- to nine-year-olds, though, we can expand the horizon a bit. As I mentioned earlier, when my boys were this age I began a chapter story called The Grandpa Story. One cold winter morning as we were on the way to school, driving through the rural Virginia countryside, we saw an ancient log cabin. Much to my boys' surprise, a thin blue ribbon of wood smoke arose from the chimney. "Who lives there?" they asked in amazement. I knew that an old patriarch of a large Southern family insisted on continuing in the old family cabin. "A very old Grandpa lives there," I replied. My boys were full of questions, including, "Isn't he awfully lonely?" Thus arose the first chapter of The Grandpa Story. Three boys, lost in the woods, stumbled upon the cabin, and so began a story of several years' duration. The boys in the story led lives similar to those of my boys, who also lived in the woods. And so adventures of jumping off rocks at the swimming hole, building tipis in secret hollows of the hills, careening down sledding hills, scraped knees, and much more ensued. As they grew older, the adventures led them far afield from their homely hills, but always they had each other, and their old Grandpa.

Again, if you look into the common happenings in your life, a story theme, simple but packed with adventure, will present itself. Listen carefully, though, to the whisperings of the story angel. And keep your journal close by. These stories are gems!

You may also find your way with your older child into a co-created story. This is a story that you and your child create together. It could evolve from questions your child asks, to which you reply, "Hmmm, I wonder...." In the pregnant pause, your child might come up with a whole new idea, by way of answering her own question. And there you go, off on a new adventure together.

READING BOOKS TOGETHER

When choosing books for our children, we can follow all the developmental guidelines mentioned above. Remember, also, to choose books that are illustrated with open, fresh colors. The purity and clarity of the color will ask your child's eye, and also his soul, to *open into* it. Garish or dissonant colors tend to close down our visual receptors. You can look for books with a flowing watercolor effect. This "impressionistic" type of illustration, again, asks your child's imagination to open up, to "fill in the blanks," so to speak. You will find many books of this type in the Bibliography. A more linear or realistic illustration leaves not much to the imagination. Also, look for illustrations that have one central image, with a few supporting figures per page. This allows your child to gaze deeply into the "gesture" of the image. You will want to avoid the types of illustrations that are packed with minute detail. This kind of orienting to two-dimensional detail can wait till your child is older, perhaps when he begins to learn about map reading. For now, look for illustrations that allow him to relax into the image, to spin daydreams as he gazes.

Remember that all of us, especially children, are shaped by images, both internal and external. This explains the principle of self-fulfilling prophecy; what we think of ourselves (our self-*image*) is what we become. Our children do not yet possess the internal filters that we have developed as adults. So let's choose books that present the world as good, beautiful and true. Keep in mind the noble gesture of fairy-tale images, and measure the books you choose against these shining qualities.

Chapter books can come into play by age five or six, but we need great discernment in choosing chapter books for children of this age. Most chapter books are geared to the development of older children, age eight through ten. Check the bibliography for a list of books for late fives, sixes and up.

Chapter 7

ARTISTIC EXPERIENCES FOR
YOUR YOUNG CHILD

ARTISTIC EXPRESSION IS an essential element of a balanced "diet" of experience for our young children. In artistic work, we accomplish two essential tasks of childhood: the training of the hand and the training of the heart. Together these lay a firm foundation for the training of the mind.

I wrote this in a summer journal as I watched the children modeling natural clay, with total absorption, at the stream bank:

I see their hands move lively and quick. Unconsciously they live the gift of an opposable thumb. Today I am thinking of our ancestors, all the way back to the cave, and the central place of the hand. In every culture, until perhaps the last forty years, hand-education has been an integral part of growing up. Hands were taught to carve stone arrowheads, to weave baskets, to mold clay pots, to hunt, to cure, to cook, to spin and weave, to sow and harvest. What are hands taught in the twenty-first century? At what expense do their hands lie limp in their laps? As their hands languish unused, so follow their minds. How can we measure the impact of a well-coordinated, steady, finely-tuned hand? What riches does this hand bring into their life? What do these well-trained hands have to offer the world?

In his book *The Hand: How It Shapes the Brain, Language, and Culture*, neurologist Frank Wilson shows us the pivotal place of the human hand, equipped with our amazing thumb, in the evolution of the species. He argues passionately for the education of the hand, assuring us that people who use their hands, woodworkers, artists and plumbers alike, have a way of knowing the world that is inaccessible to those who have less hand training. We know that the density of nerve endings in our fingertips is enormous, and when these are engaged in childhood, the brain is enriched beyond measure. Through artistic expression, the hand, and therefore the mind, is introduced to its own astonishing creative potential.

The heart, too, is cultivated through the arts. As we look, below, at the various artistic media, let us remain aware that the child explores not only color, form, texture, density, elasticity, and so forth. Through the physicality of this exploration, the child discovers her own self. Each of these avenues of expression elicits a feeling response from the child. In this way the child, who in early childhood does not differentiate herself from the world, begins to experience parameters that in time will become an "I." Through art, the seed of self is watered and nurtured.

The young child also makes relationship with the world through art. Children come to us from other realms, "trailing clouds of glory," as Wordsworth says. Through all their multifaceted experience, they begin to know this world of density and form. And it is surely through the focused intention we parents bring, in the shape of artistic experience, that they find rich ways to reply to what the world speaks to them: they learn to make relationship.

To explore the self and to love the world: this "heart-knowing" is learned by hand.

WATERCOLOR PAINTING

Let's consider, now, specific areas of artistic process, beginning with a "wet-on-wet" watercolor painting technique. In this process we use small pots of liquid color, with wet watercolor paper and a wide brush. Because of the mobility of water on the damp page, the child is allowed to experience the purity of moving colors, unhampered by the restrictions of form. The young child, himself, is still living in the realm of pure movement. The need for the restrictions of form in the physical realm, such as movement lessons and dance classes, will come later, in grade school. Likewise, the need for artistic instruction occurs later. We want to offer him a painting experience that mirrors his own developmental stage. Wet-on-wet technique is perfect for this.

With a large piece of good-quality watercolor paper (12 x 18 for children five and up, 9 x 12 for younger ones) pots of pure pigment mixed with water, and a wide brush, the child can begin to make relationship with the realm of color; he will get to know the colors themselves, like new friends. It is the freedom of the wet colors as they move, each in their own unique way, across the damp paper, that allows the various "natures," or feeling qualities, of the colors to be known. Painting prompts discovery not only of the various qualities of the colors, but of the nature of your child. To witness the miracle of a child's unfolding sense of himself in relation to color is a great gift. The way the child moves with sensitivity and curiosity toward the colors and their various relationships can be a window into his soul. Is yours a child who vigorously applies two colors to the page, and crows with delight when a mysterious third appears? Or does he lay the colors down carefully and slowly, breathing in their feeling qualities, then look at you with silent wonder as purple emerges from his red and blue?

The way your child paints is a window into her soul. Does she crow with delight or wonder silently?

If you have not painted in this way before, you will want to experience this heart-opening discovery by painting alongside your child. You will find ordering information in the Chapter Notes for paints, paper and brushes, or you can make a trip to your local art supply store. Ask for help selecting a good, heavy paper that is affordable but can take a beating, and ask for the three primaries, red, yellow and blue, in shades that will combine to make clear, beautiful secondaries.

Your child will imitate your care, curiosity, and love of the colors.

In my classroom, as in all Waldorf Early Childhood classrooms, we use only the primary colors. We uncover the miracle of the secondaries ourselves. We make a slow progression throughout the seasons, exploring each color in depth, and finally, late in the drear winter months, we begin using all three primaries together. By this time the children have an intimate knowledge of each primary and its close neighbors.

Let's look at the progression through the colors and a way to give instructions through story. Remember, your child learns through imitation, so use *your* materials well as you work side by side. Then we will see how to best arrange the painting table.

The Color Journey

In the fall, I begin our "painting journey" with the color yellow. Each week on painting day we set out the pots of yellow color, the wet paper, the rinse jars and wide brushes, the small sponges and the painting aprons. The children all gather around me as I tell them a "painting story," one that conjures up the feeling and experience of yellow. Perhaps I would tell of a little leaf on a poplar tree, who awoke one autumn morning to discover he had been transformed to yellow. As I tell the story, I paint on my own paper, then, with this inspiration and subtle instruction as well, the children go to paint on their own. After the exploration of yellow, I move on to red. This is the perfect opportunity to inspire your child with the kind of homemade stories we explored in the last chapter. Here is a good story for the color red:

Tell a Story about the Color

One autumn morning, a little girl woke suddenly from her sleep. She had heard someone call her name. She rolled over in her bed, and listened... but not a sound did she hear. So she closed her eyes again, and was just drifting off—when she heard her name again! Now she looked out the window. No one else in the house was awake, but old Father Sun was just waking and rubbing his eyes. She could see the pink and red streaks in the early morning sky, and sat up to see the luscious color spreading across her window. Did she hear a soft whisper again? Was someone calling her? Who might it be? She opened the window and listened... yes! She was quite certain she heard a small voice calling her.

Quickly, she hopped light-footed from bed and tiptoed downstairs barefoot. She would just sit on the big front porch and listen some more. Sitting silently on the porch step, she looked out into her front yard. Dawn's rosy light washed everything in red. The sidewalk was a warm pink, the white mums she had planted yesterday were now proud of their fine red dresses, and even her own house glowed like a morning cherry.

Suddenly she heard a small whisper. She stepped down into the cold dew, which hung like tiny rubies on each blade of grass. Her feet were instantly wet and the hem of her nightgown, too, but she hurried toward the voice.

ONE IDEA FOR COLOR
PROGRESSION

Late Summer: Introduce yellow. Tell a story of the little child and the giant sunflower.

Early Fall: Introduce red. Tell about the reddest apple, or reddest leaf, and the child who found it.

Mid-Autumn: Use both yellow and red. Tell about the pumpkin who hid at the sunflower's feet, and the child who made a Halloween lantern.

Early Winter: Introduce blue. Tell about the nights growing long, and the many blankets on the bed.

Holiday time: Use red and blue together. Tell about the cold outside (blue) and the warm hearts (red) of the family inside.

Deep Winter: Continue with red and blue. Tell about the seeds sleeping deep underground, and creatures, too.

Late winter: Use blue and yellow. Tell of a little child who dreamed of summer grass and woke to see the first green bud appear.

Spring: Now use all three primaries! Tell of the color fairies returning and painting the meadows back to life.

Summer: Continue with primaries. Continue with stories of Mother Earth, her creatures and a small child's adventures.

She stood beneath the giant old apple tree, the one that shaded her family's house all summer and gave her and her brothers fine rosy apples in the fall. Her family made apple pie, applesauce, apple butter, baked apples, apple pudding... every imaginable apple dish! Looking up, she was surprised to see that the entire ancient tree—its trunk, leaves, and of course its apples—were as red as her red wagon. And something here was whispering her name!

Barefoot in the dawn light, she began to climb the familiar old branches, which lovingly held her safe. The higher she climbed her old tree-friend, the better she heard her name. Peering through the branches, she saw her own bedroom window. As she looked in from the outside—instead of looking out, as she usually did—she heard her name again, and climbed to the very top branch. There she saw, glowing in the sun, the biggest, juiciest, *reddest* apple! Certainly it was the tree-spirit whom had called her, to show her the way. Here was the finest, reddest apple of the fall! She whispered a happy "Thank You!" then plucked the apple and scrambled back down.

When her family awoke, they found that each person's breakfast bowl was laid out on the table. In each bowl an apple slice shone. Cut sideways, the star, enfolded in rose petals—did you know inside every apple a star is shining, all wrapped in rose petals?— glowed pink in the morning light.

Paint with Your Child

As I tell a simple story like this, I paint, slowly and with curiosity, watching as the red moves around the page. My purpose is not to create a formed image, but rather to really experience the feeling of red! By the time we are painting with five- and six-year-olds, though, we can begin to look for form that *wants* to emerge from the color, such as round strokes slowly bringing forth the image of a ripe, juicy apple. I rinse my brush in the jar of water and pat it on the small sponge each time before I reach for fresh color. I move the brush across the page in steady, graceful strokes. The children will learn this kind of attention to technique best by simply taking it in through imitation, rather than through direct instruction.

Having begun by painting several yellow pictures, now we will paint several pure red ones. By pumpkin time, we are ready to put two primaries together, and—hey, presto! A small miracle occurs on our page. Believe me, for a child who has lived deeply into yellow and then red, the appearance of orange is mysterious and wonderful! You might tell a garden story. Or, better yet, a compost heap story—did you ever get the best volunteer squashes growing from your compost pile? I have! Tell about the yellow of the late autumn sunflowers, and the red of the early morning light. Tell about the child's surprise to find a bright orange pumpkin growing at the foot of the sunflower in the compost, as the rosy light shines. The child might bring both "compost sisters," the sunflower and pumpkin, indoors to decorate the family's dinner table.

Are you beginning to see the methodical way we can move through the seasons with color and stories? The mood of the story supports the mood of the color and vice versa. In early winter we can move on to a blue color experience, telling of the long blue shadows thrown by the bare branches of trees, or the blue and white experience of a sunny snowy day. Add red to your blue, and you move toward the deep, purple darkness of winter, with its long nights and our longing for the light. Late in winter, give your child the blue of winter with the beginning yellow warmth of spring, and green emerges. Your child will nearly jump for joy to discover green all on his own, just at the time he is longing most for a green bower. Having made an intimate relationship through story and painting, with each of the colors—yellow, orange, red, purple, blue and green—your child is now ready for the delight of using all three primaries.

When the colors are introduced slowly and with care on the adult's part, we can see that the children use the paint differently. They approach color with wonder and respect, like they are playing with best friends. It takes planning and effort, but this is a tremendous gift you can give your child and yourself. Chances are good that you have never experienced color in this way, either. You will find that this can be a calming, centering and healing time for both of you.

Arrange the Painting Table with Care

You and your child can work together to arrange the painting table. She can soak the paper in water for a few minutes, then, with your help, place it on the "painting boards." These can be as simple as acrylic cutting boards from the kitchen store, or you can buy boards specifically designed for the purpose (see the Chapter Notes for ordering information). Be sure to buy a large size, to accommodate the large paper. After placing the paper on the board, *lightly* sponge off the excess water. If your child is under age five, you will want to be the one to stir the pigment and water together. But by five, she should have the dexterity to stir alone. Use baby food jars with lids, and you will only need a tiny amount of pigment, less than a quarter of a teaspoon, with a quarter jar of water. Mix and use small amounts at a time. If the colors remain clear after painting together, you can put on the lids and re-use them. If the colors are muddy, pour them out and re-mix next time. Together you can place the painting boards and paper side by side on the table, and put the pot or pots of color between them. Place the rinse jar (a pint-sized canning jar, or old spaghetti sauce jar that's not too tall) above the paint pots, and the sponges for patting your brush dry below the pots. Be sure to protect your table and yourselves. Special aprons used only for painting contribute to the ritual aspect. When finished painting one picture, consider well whether you want to paint another. Keep in mind the saying "Less is more." If you go deeply into one painting, it may be enough. But if you and your child are still hungry for color, paint just *one* more. Then set the painting boards aside to dry.

Something you may want to consider is creating a very quiet atmosphere in which to paint. I always tell the children, "Let's whisper, so we can hear what the colors are saying!" It is a very different experience to paint with quiet concentration rather than amidst chatter and clatter. Not only will your child be surprised by "what the colors want to say," but you too will be delighted to hear their message.

One year I had a parent who collected all of her child's paintings and then displayed them all together in sequence, one panel of consecutive colors, on his bedroom wall. The effect was gorgeous, to see the slow progression through the seasons and the colors, like seeing a color wheel in motion. Or you might like to record, in your journal, the painting stories that you tell, color by color, through the seasons.

BEESWAX CRAYONING

How do we understand the great proliferation of our children's drawings? Filled with color and movement, what are they telling us? If we understand them properly, we can see them as icons along the course of our child's developing consciousness.

The first "drawings" our child will offer us, as a toddler, are the simple tracings of movement. The child of this age is compelled to discover his environment, and thereby himself, through movement. The first drawings we see trace this exploratory path. The toddler's consciousness *is* the movement itself, and this is what we see on the page. Put the paper in front of him and a crayon in his hand. His hand is already always in motion, and now this new object, the crayon, makes his movement visible to him. Remarkable! Soon he learns that the brightly colored thing consistently obeys as his hand moves back and forth. There will be much repetition of this tracing of movement, which makes its own developmental journey. At first we will see light strokes of color, a few tentative marks on the page. Then, with repetition and the development of eye-hand coordination, the strokes become stronger.

You can encourage this experience by joining your child in crayoning. Simply lay color down on the page, with delight and attention. Move the crayon in your hand back and forth, back and forth. As with painting, at this early stage, do not be tempted to create form. Wait until your child shows you her own beginnings of form.

Allow yourself to enjoy the color as it emerges on the page, simply for its own sake. Choose different colors and lay them down together, side by side. *Play with them.* Your interest and enjoyment will draw your child more fully into her own experience. If she puts a few strokes of color on the page and says, "I'm finished," you can reply, "Here's a beautiful purple for you, and here's one for me. Let's color purple." A very young child will want to hop up in a minute or two, but you can coax her to stay a bit longer, saying, "I'm going to make all my white paper shine with color." Eventually, she'll stay longer, and with a stronger capacity for will, her paper will shine with color, too.

Sooner or later, this tracing of movement will begin to form a circle. Your child may practice for a long time, repeating the mystery, discovering

---

ONE DEVELOPMENTAL JOURNEY THROUGH CRAYONING

(Remember, children develop at different speeds, so ages are very approximate.)

TODDLER—*Traces movement, a few simple strokes of color. With much practice, this becomes...*

THREES AND FOURS—*Vigorous colorful movement on the page. Now the page is full of color.*

FOURS AND FIVES—*The strokes of color become a circle, and a face appears. With practice this becomes...*

FIVES AND SIXES—*Many colorful figures dancing, floating across page.*

SIXES AND SEVENS—*Now the figures come down to earth and trees no longer float but have roots. A central figure is attended by other bilateral figures.*

again and again how a line can manage to find its way home, right back where it started. One magic day, you'll discover two little dots in the circle, and your child will say, "It's me!" Or, "It's you!" This portrait-making begins with the human face, a circle with two dots for eyes, and maybe a dash for the mouth. You will notice that usually the arms and legs sprout right out of the head. These limbs can be very disproportional, long and tentacle-like. The child is showing us pictorially how critical it is that he explore his world with these fabulous powerful tools, his arms and legs.

The formation of a trunk with limbs attached often waits until the child is close to five, and we may wait a while longer for the limbs to come into proportion. Now the central figure begins to be attended by many supporting shapes. Trees, birds, clouds, rainbows—or, along another track, backhoes, boats, trains— all these figures dance merrily across the page. Frequently they "float" in space together, gloriously disproportional and more indicative of the child's interests than of the actual object. They can remind us of the splendid joy in life we see in ancient cave paintings, filled with vigor and innocent wisdom.

Sometime around the age of six (remember, these ages are approximate) these figures become grounded. Terra firma appears at the bottom of the page, and the arch of blue sky soars above. The central figure walks with feet firmly planted on the earth, and by now the arms and legs are more proportional. Attending figures tend to be bilateral, that is, evenly placed on either side of the central one. Harmony and balance reign.

We can see every child's drawing as a self-portrait, showing us where she stands upon a natural developmental path. One of the markers we can look for in determining when our child is ready for academic work and grade school is the appearance of this grounded little person, who no longer flies through the air with the rainbows, but walks upon the earth with rest of us.

Another artistic path your child's drawings might take is a non-representational, geometric progression. Rather than figures, your child might be drawn to the purity of shape and color. As with the progression along the representational path, your child may be drawn at an earlier stage to simply color shapes that randomly fill the page with riotous color.

In time, this shape-making begins to have a relationship to the page, and you may see your child draw a large central cross on the page, thereby quartering it. The cross is a universal symbol used by most ancient peoples. It is a symbol of the self, the "I," as it emerges from the mists. This quartering can grow into graphs, the page filled with horizontal and vertical lines. Encourage her not only to create the graph, but to decorate the interior spaces with color.

You will see this graph-making become more precise, and by about age five, the lines move toward a diagonal. The corners of the page may be colored diagonally and move, like a "god's eye weaving," toward a central focus.

Look for the day your child draws, not a cross, which is an earlier developmental stage, but an "X" from corner to corner. Vibrant color decorates this new stage. This capacity to envision and create a cross-lateral form is an indication of a specific stage of brain development. The child simply cannot do this task until the brain grows into this stage.

The Brain Gym system works with helping children with sensory integration problems accomplish exactly this, cross-laterality, as well as many other "brain calisthenics." I play a game with my school children that works with cross-laterality. Sitting on the floor with knees bent, we touch opposite elbows to knees. I ask them to have the first morning sunbeams (elbows) kiss the mountaintops (knees). The little ones merrily touch right to right and left to left. The fours and early fives notice that I am doing something different, but have no clue what it is. The late fives and sixes proficiently touch right elbow to left knee.

So look for this cross-lateral shape to appear. It tells you your child is moving toward academic readiness.

ANOTHER
DEVELOPMENTAL JOURNEY
THROUGH CRAYONING

Toddler and Threes / Fours proceed as above.

Fours and Fives—The page becomes quartered and the colorful shapes become more orderly.

Fives and Sixes—Lines move toward the diagonal and "god's-eyes" appear

Sixes and Sevens—A large "X" appears, quartering the page in a new way, vigorous color decorates the new stage.

Now a word about crayons. Do you want a sense delight? Look in the Chapter Notes for information on where to buy beeswax crayons. Why beeswax? First of all, the colors are so pure and gorgeous, you will have to see the difference for yourself. Also, in terms of educating the child's senses, beeswax crayons are a feast. They actually still smell like honey! And the felt sensation in the hand is delicious. You'll be surprised by the subtle but powerful difference in types of crayons. It is good to have a nice mix of both stick crayons and block crayons. Stick crayons help a child develop proper pencil-holding skills, and block crayons are the best for shading large areas or mixing colors on the page.

I recommend two grades of crayon paper. You can use a ream of simple copy paper for everyday use, when your child wants to sit down and fill page after page with color. And it is also a real pleasure to keep a ream of good-quality drawing paper (see Chapter Notes for ordering information) for special occasions: a get-well card for Grandma, or a love picture for a special little friend. Your child can help you choose which paper he wants today. He may simply like the texture of the good-quality paper, and ask for it often. Collect these drawings and gather them into "books" that he can give as gifts at holidays.

To make a gift book, gather the drawings and, with a hole-punch, make three holes down the left side of the page. Now run richly colored ribbons through the holes. Leave the ribbon a bit loose, so it doesn't cut the paper as the pages are turned. These homemade gifts are real "keepers," and will be pulled out often for viewing!

MODELING MATERIALS

Every child loves to shape malleable materials, and I cannot overstate the importance of offering a variety of modeling experiences. Modeling is an excellent training of the hand, strengthening, sensitizing, and creating dexterity. Below we'll look at modeling in sand, dough, beeswax, and clay.

GREAT GIFT IDEA!

Save your child's best drawings, and make them into a "book." Bind with brightly colored ribbon and voila! A book!

WET SAND

...is endlessly malleable and forgiving. If it's not quite right, mash it down and start over. Sandboxes, creeks, lakes, the beach—explore them all.

Sand

Sand is the original modeling material, and you will find descriptions of the use of sand in the chapters on both Indoor and Outdoor Play. Every child needs an outdoor sandbox, and I also recommend an indoor one. The outdoor sandbox lends itself beautifully to modeling because water can be used liberally. Younger children will want to get their hands into all sorts of "sand kitchen" creations, mixing birthday cakes and soup pots, up to their elbows in sand and water. Older children can work for hours and days, creating great waterworks systems, shaping and endlessly repairing canals, rivers, lakes, and dams. Of course, days spent at the beach give everyone in the family a chance to luxuriate in sand and water. Try sand castling with the whole family! You'll be enchanted, even as an adult, by the compelling malleability of wet sand.

Bread Dough

The next most natural modeling material is homemade bread dough. Look in the chapter on Festivals for a foolproof bread recipe. The good news about this recipe is that, because of the use of whole wheat pastry flour, it can be kneaded, rolled, shaped, squashed, flattened, and generally played with for a very long time. When it is the right consistency, it will need very little flour for kneading, hence very little sweeping up after. If your child plays with this dough for twenty minutes or longer, and then rolls it up into a dinner roll–sized ball, you can pop all the rolls immediately into the oven at 350 degrees. You will end up with not only edible, but *delicious* rolls. If one of your weekly activities with your child is baking bread, then when a festival time comes she will be familiar with the use of dough and may create special shapes: bunnies for spring, or stars for winter. Our festivals always include bread, in one form or another, all variations on this same terrific recipe.

Play Dough

Of course, the classic take-off on bread dough is play dough. There are many recipes for cooked and uncooked play dough. This one was given to

---

BREAD DOUGH!

Use whole wheat pastry flour, and you get the sturdiness of whole wheat, and the elasticity of pastry flour. See the Festivals chapter for a no-fail recipe.

me by my nieces, and is the best so far. Cooking it in the microwave keeps it from burning, which is the main problem with the stove-top recipes. It cooks easily and keeps beautifully. I only make two colors at a time, a primary, and one of its secondaries, such as yellow and orange, or red and purple. This way, when the colors get mixed they will create a beautiful third color.

Children love to practice rolling out with a rolling pin, and cutting shapes with cookie cutters. I have a collection of small animal-shaped cookie cutters, and after they have rolled and cut a few, I then encourage the children to play with them at the table. They can roll a little more play dough to make fences, or a barn, or nests. This encourages them to use their hand-dexterity in service to their imaginative skills. Great training for life!

Clay

Earthen clay is an experience all its own. The healing properties of clay have been known for millennia, and when our children play with earthen clay this sense of depth and healing is palpable. The perfect place to play with clay is by the creek-side, where it is naturally found! Water is available to keep it moist, and the availability is limited only by the child's ability to dig. Cleanup is quick and easy, too.

Assuming most of us do not have this source available, you can look in the phone book for local potters. They usually have a bag of clay out back somewhere that does not meet their standards that they'd be happy to offer at a reduced price. You can also buy clay at an art supply store, but it is more expensive this way. You will need an airtight container large enough for your amount of clay. Each time the children finish playing with clay, you will want to return it to the container and sprinkle a little water over it, to remoisten it. Check it a few days later to see if you added the right amount. If it is too wet, leave the lid ajar a few hours. If it is too dry, add a bit more water.

Unlike some of the other modeling materials, clay cannot be played with for long periods, because it tends to dry out quickly. For this reason, I would recommend it as a regular artistic medium for older children, five and up. Younger children lack hand strength and can be easily frustrated. Rather than offering it *regularly* to younger children, you can plan a special

---

MAKE YOUR OWN
PLAY DOUGH

2 cups white flour

1 cup salt

½ cup cornstarch

1 Tbsp. alum powder

1 ½ cups water

1 Tbsp. cooking oil

Combine dry ingredients in 2-quart glass bowl.

Gradually stir in water and oil, until smooth.

Microwave on high 4–5 minutes, stopping to stir each minute, until very thick (mixture will be lumpy).

When the dough is cool enough to handle, knead in food coloring as you knead out lumps.

Store in airtight container in refrigerator.

Remember to make only two colors at a time, a primary and its close secondary, like blue and green.

Gather a collection of small animal cookie cutters and small rolling pins. Enjoy for months!

For the best price, look for a local potter. But go to the art store for the non-firing type.

project, to be finished in a short amount of time. Maybe you would like to make clay beads for Thanksgiving, honoring the native peoples. These beads can be made from the non-firing type of clay, strung on waxed linen thread and left to dry. You *will* need to go to the art supply store for this clay. Then, using your watercolor paints, you can decorate them in washes of luminous color.

Older children will love to make pinch pots, cups and saucers, modeled animals—the sky is the limit. As the clay dries out, you can dampen it and return it to the container, then get another little piece and have fun. Remember, their hands are small, so especially with earth clay, give them small pieces, one at a time. Some potteries have an open firing day, so you can save the very special pieces to be glazed and fired.

Beeswax

An especially beautiful and appealing material is modeling beeswax (check the Chapter Notes for ordering information). This beeswax comes in a rainbow of luminous colors and can be worked with again and again. The essential ingredient needed is warmth, as the beeswax will soften with warmth but harden with the cold. Again, this is a challenging material for very young children, so with them I save beeswax only for special projects. You will need to warm the wax in your own hands first, and probably re-warm it as well, for the younger ones.

Older children are able to hold the beeswax between their hands to warm it up. I tell them, "Put it in your little oven. Now shut the door, and keep it closed." Often, as they are warming their beeswax, I will tell them a story. I like to make up stories about the bees and what their life in the hive is like. Remember, we're not teaching science, we're feeding the imagination. So, when you tell a beeswax story, look at your child's day, and reflect back to her similarities between her day and a little girl bee's day. If she woke up on the wrong side of bed this morning, make up a reason the little girl bee did the same thing. Perhaps she awoke in her golden bed in the golden hive and was afraid the farmer had mowed her own special, secret bee-balm flower, hidden among the bracken at the back of the garden. As you tell the story, her warm hands will soften the beeswax, and it will be ready to be shaped, perhaps into

---

EARTH CLAY

... dries easily, so use it on a regular basis with older children, and save it for a special project with younger ones.

BEESWAX

...comes in light-filled colors, still smells like the honey comb, and needs warmth to make it malleable.

Like clay, use it as special projects for younger children and on a more regular basis with older ones.

As your children hold the beeswax to warm it, tell a story— imaginative, not necessarily scientific—about the life of a little bee.

her own beeswax flower. Small pieces work best, about the size of the end of your thumb. Not until grade school will the child be able to handle large amounts. When she is finished, you can shape it into a small pancake and put it away for next time. She can play with any given piece several times before it begins to lose its "oomph." When you see it losing malleability, let her finish the piece, then save it, perhaps on a low shelf, as a decoration.

CRAFTWORK FOR FESTIVALS

As you can imagine, there are libraries full of gorgeous craft books for children. My favorite, though is by Carol Petrash, titled *Earthways*. (See the Chapter Notes for some of the other books I use, and ordering information.) In this beautifully illustrated book, Carol walks us through the seasons, offering simple, easy crafts, using materials taken from nature. The remarkable gift of this book is that it designs crafts appropriate to the skills of preschool- and kindergarten-age children! I cannot recommend it highly enough. You will have seasons of crafts to last an entire childhood.

For now, though, let's look at one simple craft for each season. If you have planned a festival for each season, make a craft using the same theme. This will enhance the festive atmosphere and broaden your child's experience. Remember, we want a festival to be a multisensory feast, filled with sights, smells, stories, and activity. If you make festival notes in your journal, you can look back over the years and remember what craft projects you have offered in the past, and this will help you choose for the future.

Year by year, as you move from one festival craft activity to another, staying within a seasonal theme, your child will build up a layered experience that can become like a subtle watercolor painting in her heart. This experience, slowly building and expanding as her skills do, will act as a reservoir of inspiration and powerful energy in her adulthood.

Bark Boats for Summer

Summer and water play are inseparable. Here is a simple little boat to while away the hours at the stream, the pond, or the backyard wading pool.

The layered experience of festival artwork will become a fountainhead of energy and life force in your child's adult life.

SAIL AWAY IN BARK BOATS

Gather or buy your pine bark.

Help your child bore a hole in the center.

Thread a leaf onto a good sail-sized stick

Place the stick in the hole.

Screw a teacup hook to front of boat.

Attach a string for pulling.

Look for sailors to sail the seas.

1) Go for a walk in the woods, looking for old pine trees. At their feet find both large and small chunks of pine bark. If a pine forest is not close by, go to the garden store and check the bags of pine bark mulch carefully. Buy a coarser grind, and see that the pieces are one half to three quarters of an inch thick. Sort through, and choose varying sizes.

2) Help your child bore a hole in the center of the bark. Check the Chapter Notes for a small hand-held awl for children. If using an ice pick, bore the hole yourself.

3) Help your child thread a sturdy leaf onto a stick properly sized for the hole, and place the stick in the hole.

4) Screw a tiny teacup hook into the front of the boat and attach a string for pulling.

5) Look for special small stones, or make tiny beeswax figures to be the passengers.

6) Make a fleet of boats, and invite friends to a boating party!

An Apple Banner for the Fall

1) Go on a walk with your child and pick up several small branches, about the diameter of your thumb. Cut them ten inches long.

2) Go to the fabric store and buy a quarter yard of cotton muslin. Wash and dry it, then cut it into eight-inch squares. Plan to use one for each of your children and one for yourself. Put the others away for future fun. Pull loose threads until you have "fringed" it.

3) Mix red and yellow watercolor paint, a bit thicker than you do for painting. Cover the bottom of two aluminum or glass pie pans with the thickened paint.

4) Cut a fine red apple in half sideways, so the star inside is clearly visible. Remove the seeds. You may need to cut several apples to find the perfect star. Now notch the rounded "back" of the apple so you have something to grip, a handle, so to speak.

5) Place the muslin, the paint, and the apple on your table, being sure to protect the table and yourselves. Craft aprons are perfect here.

6) Holding the apple halves by their "handles," press them into the paint, and quickly onto the muslin. This prints the apple's star onto the fabric. You can print several stars, dancing inside their apples, across the banner.

7) Attach the banner to the branch by staples, or by sewing. Then tie a bright red ribbon to each end of the branch, and lay flat to dry.

AUTUMN APPLE BANNER

Go for a walk to gather sticks.

Buy muslin and cut to size.

Mix red and yellow paint, thick.

Cut an apple sideways.

Look for the star.

Remove the seeds.

Print the star, in colors, on the fabric.

Attach the banner to the branch.

Hang the banner by the festival table... celebrate!

8) Hang beside the festival table on the special day!

If you have chosen a leaf festival for autumn, you can follow the same process, and print a perfect leaf, or a medley of leaves, on your banner.

Pine Cone People for Winter

You can make the shepherds for your winter festival from pine cones, hazelnuts (filberts), acorn caps and bits of wool felt.

1) Go for a walk with your child to pick up pine cones. Or, if no pine trees are available, buy a bag of cones at the craft store.
2) Match up the perfect pine cone and hazelnut. Look for the cones with flat bottoms, for stability.
3) With tacky glue or carpenter's glue, glue the nut on top of the pine cone to make a fine round head. You may have to remove the top spire of the cone to make a spot for the nut.
4) When this is dry and sturdy, place an acorn cap on your shepherd's head and dress him or her with bits of wool felt glued together. Remember, it is winter, so your shepherds will need mufflers, warm skirts, and tunics.
5) You can make two small dots for eyes, but don't overdo the facial features—let your child imagine, instead.

Make several of these homely folk, or a whole village, depending on your children's ages and interest. They can join the stable when the Old Man and the Young Woman enter, in the fourth week (see the chapter on Festivals for details).

Wool Butterflies for Spring

Even a small bag of raw sheep's wool makes for days of fun and many spring projects. Here is only one project:

1) Look in the phone book under Fiber Arts or Livestock, or call your County Extension agent, and see if you can locate a sheep farm. Your local knitting store or fabric store may have this information, too. A field trip to the farm is always fun. Just seeing, smelling and petting the

---

WINTER PINE CONE PEOPLE

Gather your pine cones.

Buy a bag of hazelnuts.

Match a pine cone and nut.

Glue the nut on top of the pine cone. Allow to dry.

Dress with acorn caps, bits of felt and wool for hair.

Make shepherds for your winter scene, or an entire village!

sheep or lambs is a rich sensory education. Be cautious about going on shearing day; the sheep can be nervous, and sometimes the clippers nick them and they bleat pitifully. Come home with a bag of raw wool.

2) If a farm is not available, check the Chapter Notes to order wool.

3) Days can be spent washing and cleaning the wool. The picnic table is the perfect place for this work. Soak wool in a series of *lukewarm* baths infused with Woolite. Do not scrub it or agitate it in any way; this will felt it. Simply lay it in the lukewarm Woolite water. You can push it around with your fingers a bit, to dislodge dirt, but don't let the fibers scrub up against each other. Keep the water temperature the same as it goes from bath to bath. When the water runs clear, give it a final *lukewarm* rinse. Lay it flat on a towel to dry, or hang it over a clothes rack.

4) After many washings, the wool may still have small sticks and grass tangled in it. When the wool is dry, you can comb it to help the fibers lie side by side, and to remove the last of the debris from the field. This process is called carding, and you can buy wire-bristled pet brushes for this purpose. Have your child hold one brush, bristles up, on his lap, and hold firmly. Place a small bundle of wool over the bristles, and brush it in one direction with the other brush. I say to the children, "This one is the holding hand" (the hand that holds the brush stationary on their lap) and "This one is the working hand" (the hand that brushes the fibers). Show your child how to brush in only one direction, not back and forth, as this will tangle the wool. Children love the carding process, and you can keep a large basket of the cleaned but uncombed wool on hand for moments between pretend games. Keep the small pet brushes in the same basket, so they are always ready for use. I keep a separate smaller basket right beside this for the carded wool. If the wool gets played with, it can then go back into the uncarded basket, to be re-combed and made ready again.

5) When the wool is clean and carded, it is time to dye. There are fabulous plant dyes, but for a small project like this, Rit dye is fine. I buy a rainbow of colors, primaries and secondaries. In bowls as small as soup bowls, I place about one cup of boiling water and one teaspoon of dry dye powder, and stir well. When these are warm, not hot, I place them in a row, a spoon in each bowl, on a low, protected surface, maybe the bench of the picnic table.

6) Protect the children's clothing with aprons or old oversized T-shirts, and have them take a swatch of wool, a puff that fits on an open palm, and place it in a bowl of dye. With the spoon they can push the wool

underwater and stir slowly and gently. It is best for each child to work on one color at a time.. This way the children can really observe the process, how their own activity can change white wool to a luscious color. After two or three minutes of stirring the swatch in the dye, it is ready to be taken out and rinsed. This is your job. Take it out with the spoon, place it in another bowl, and run the garden hose very gently over it. Lay it flat to dry on an old towel, as the towel will become dyed, too. Now dye another color, repeating all the steps, then another, to your heart's content. Lay flat to dry.

7) When the swatches are dry, shape each one into a lovely, dense square. You may need to fold the wool bundle in half to accomplish this. Wrap a green pipe cleaner around the middle and twist at the top, leaving a bit at the ends to make the antennae. Stitch the body in place, in case of vigorous play. Shape the wool to create two diaphanous wings. Loop an embroidery thread through the middle of the "back," so your child's butterfly can go fluttering away! Soon you will have a butterfly garden to replace the egg garden from your festival. You can hang the butterflies on the branches of the egg tree when they are not being played with.

THE WONDER OF WOOL

Puffs of cloud-like sheep's wool can find their way into many games, becoming snow on the ground, a bowl of popcorn, hair from the beauty parlor, clouds in a puppet play and so forth. If you have made the wool butterflies for spring, above, you will know how glorious sheep's wool is. Wool felting is another superb way to spend a morning with your child.

Wool Felting

1) In a one-inch-deep baking sheet lay down a thin layer of the white, washed and carded wool, all going in the same direction. Now lay down another thin layer of wool, going in the opposite direction, so the first layer is horizontal and the second, vertical.

2) You can lay the leftover dyed wool from your spring butterflies on top of these two white layers, arranging the colors in a pleasing way. Now you have an impressionist's palette of wool in the basin. Pat the wool all over, checking for thinness, and add more white to thin spots.

HAND-FELTED WOOL

Put wool, white and colored, in 1-inch-deep baking sheet.

Pour hot soapy water over it.

Enjoy the tactile pleasure: warm water, wool, soap bubbles....

Now rub-a-dub-dub.

Keep rubbing!

Rinse and lay flat to dry.

WHAT TO DO WITH
SO MUCH FELT?

Be creative:

- *Make a bedtime cuddly.*
- *Make a wall hanging.*
- *Make bags to play with.*
- *Make coasters.*
- *Make presents.*
- *Make necklaces.*

3) Make a pitcher of hot, sudsy water, using a natural soap like Dr. Bronner's, or a dish soap. Pour this slowly over the pad of wool, pushing the wool down into the warm wetness. Felting is a process of helping the tiny "barbs" on the wool fibers catch onto each other and form a solid mass. To do this, you and your child can simply mess around in the warm, sudsy water. Pressing down, watch the suds billow up between your fingers, feel your hands in the slippery wetness together—all of this is full of sensory enrichment for your child. You'll have to help your child not wad the wool up in balls, but just push it up and down in the suds. If he accidentally *does* wad it up, you can just push it back into shape, keeping the colored wool on top. A friend of mine, a fellow teacher, likes to use potato mashers when the water is hot, at first, and feels that for the younger child this is easier. When it cools a bit, though, don't forego using your hands. The tactile experience is unforgettable. The longer you continue the felting process, the stronger the felt will be.

4) When you feel it beginning to hold together, you can begin to rub it gently, then later to rub more vigorously. When it feels like one unit, turn it over and rub the other side.

5) When it feels like it is one solid piece, and you are sure the colored wool on the front is secure (you may need to rub this longer, for staying power), pour the suds out, keeping the mass of wool on the cookie sheet. Then fill with rinse water, swish and rinse again.

6) When the felt is well rinsed, lay it flat on a towel to dry.

Now you have a pad of soft colorful wool felt just the size of the cookie sheet. What to do next?

1) You can fold it in half, colored side out, and run a blanket stitch around the edge of the whole pad. This can become a "cuddly" for your child at bedtime. Or,

2) Blanket stitch the edges and hang from a dowel as a wall hanging by her bed. Or,

3) Cut it into several long rectangles, fold each one in half, and then sew the sides together to create a bag. Add a long finger-knit handle, and you've enhanced the toy shelf. Make bags of different sizes, one for a polished stone, and one for a small doll. Or,

4) Cut it into rounds or squares, blanket stitch, and use as coasters for the coffee table. Or,

5) Cut it into heart shapes, blanket stitch, and send to grandparents just for fun. Or,

6) Cut it into a small heart, a moon, and a star. Blanket stitch and string them on colorful ribbons. Hang the ones with long ribbons by the dress-up corner, as necklaces, and make short ribbon-hangers to put them on the Christmas tree.

As you can see, there are as many uses for handmade wool felt as you can imagine. The trick is to felt it long enough to be strong, and blanket stitch the edges of whatever you create, to help it stay in shape.

Water, paint, clay, dough, apples, nuts, pine cones, wool—through artistic relationship with all these treasures, and through the gift of the human hand, the child comes to know herself, to love the world, and to reach out toward Life with an inquisitive mind. We parents are blessed to be in the position to help guide this journey. Best of all, we ourselves get to make artistic relationship with the world as well.

Chapter 8

OTHER TOPICS
PARENTS WONDER ABOUT

OVER THE YEARS, parents have asked many questions. The previous chapters have addressed questions that need in-depth consideration. Before we tie everything together with a chapter on creating your family culture, I'd like to address some questions that can be answered more briefly, but still figure largely in a parent's life. I have arranged them in terms of the frequency with which they might be expected to arise in daily life. Whether you are looking for solutions to the "clothing battle," how to help with nightmares, a direction to go toward when your child asks about death, or aspects to consider when choosing a child-care center. I hope this chapter will help smooth your way.

CLOTHING DOESN'T HAVE TO BE AN ISSUE

The world of fashion would like to usurp the children's clothing arena, and require as much concern from parents about the "right" thing for our preschoolers to wear as we give to our own adult dress. Let's think about our child's "fashion statement" as a declaration of ease, comfort, independence, freedom of movement and beauty, too. Here are a few things to keep in mind.

Remember when you are choosing clothing to look carefully at the fabric content. Synthetic fabrics tend to not breathe well, and a child who is hard at work playing can feel damp inside. Natural fibers, as you would expect, breathe naturally. A child can play hard, get sweaty and cool down to a clean dryness inside natural fibers. Some cotton fibers now are even organically grown, and therefore kinder to the skin and also the environment. If you are interested in having your child wear wool in winter for the incredible warmth, but are shy of the "itch factor," see the Chapter Notes for sources of children's wool long johns and outerwear that are machine-washable and guaranteed itch-free. I know these claims are true, because I wear them myself.

Check the seams of each item you buy, especially socks. Run the seam across the inside of your wrist. If it feels scratchy or rough, your child will be feeling this at wrists, arms, neck, waist, cuffs, and down the inside of his legs. Children's sense of touch is often far more sensitive than ours. If it feels like it would bother you, it will bother your child even more. Some children's clothing is made with itchless seams, so the seam is sewn down on the inside of the clothes. (See the Chapter Notes.) This is ideal! You may, as a matter of course, cut the tags out of the neck seam. In my kindergarten, I am asked to cut many, many tags out of children's clothes.

Select for ease of movement. Knowing everything we know about the child's essential need for movement, let's shop with vigorous movement in mind. Watch out for tight jeans and belts, or stiff fabrics. Also be cautious of the current trend that children's clothes be worn oversized. This can be as restrictive to movement as tightness. If you want to buy with "grow room," be sure you roll the sleeves and cuffs up, and see that they stay up well while your child plays.

Little girls, who love the frivolous beauty of dresses, also need the freedom of active movement. Think of closely woven tights or leggings under those pretty dresses in winter. It is quite cold on my playground, so I ask that girls wear fleece pants under dresses. For warmer weather, you could try shorts under a summer dress. Not until they are five will they be worried about their panties showing, but you can get them used to this layering before they arrive at the age of embarrassment. Remember, being upside down is great for brain development, so dress your girl for the monkey bars and spirited swinging. See the appendix for catalogs that sell girls' clothing with layers for play in mind.

Layering for all weather is always the right way to go. Especially in spring and fall, the weather can change dramatically in a short time, and you will want your children to be comfortable for many hours of outdoor play. In spring and autumn, think of a short sleeve, a long sleeve, a closely knit sweater, and a jacket. Sometimes in this season, shorts underneath long pants are great. Several layers that can come and go as the sun goes in and out behind the clouds are a better option than one winter coat that is too hot for playing tag, but too cool for playing inside the shady bush house.

It is so important to choose the right shoes for active play outdoors. Shoes that have a closed back and are well fitted, with both grow room and toe room, can become an extension of the child's foot. To experience ease, comfort and support in their bodies is more empowering to a child than we can imagine. Shoes that are too big, too small, too loose, too tight, too floppy, too high-heeled, too pretty, or too slippery encumber the child's ability to play.

Recently, little girls' shoes have been made with an open back, clog-style. These are impossible to run, climb, jump, or hang upside down in. Even girls' sneakers are made to slide into. Others are made with the beginning of a high heel! This throws the girl's developing spine and posture off center. Looking at the damage high heels do to their mothers' feet, legs, hips, spines and shoulders, let's give them the gift of being able to develop as Nature intended. Let's not send her to the modern-day foot binder just yet. She can make her own decision regarding damage to do, or not, to her own spine, when she is an adult.

If your child attends preschool or kindergarten, dress her for ease and maneuverability in the bathroom. For the three- and four-year-olds, usually elastic waists, without belts or sashes (to go up and down easily at the potty) and knit cuffs at sleeves (easy up and down at the sink) work the best. The complications of suspenders, belts, one-piece undergarments (leotards) and buttons at cuffs can make for accidents, even under the best of circumstances. Save these more complicated clothes for the "home days" when there is no line of peers waiting outside the door. Let her struggle to develop more complex fine motor skills at her leisure. By the time she is five or six, if she can consistently manage them in a timely manner, then she is ready to wear them to school.

When shopping for clothes, remember that we want to offer our child an open, uncluttered visual field, and that this extends to clothing, too. Many lines of children's clothing are really advertising in disguise. Look for clothes without media images, slogans, logos, brand names, or the current toy that is on sale in the next aisle.

Yes, it is difficult to find natural-fiber clothing in clear, uncluttered colors that is also affordable. When you have discovered a good source, shop the sales and buy in quantity, sized for next year, too.

If I had another career allotted to me in this lifetime, I would invent a line of children's clothing that came in washable all cotton, wool, and silk blended knits, in a rainbow palette of gorgeous solid colors, so everything matched with everything. I would make a tank, a short sleeve, long sleeve and sweatshirt, one cut for boys and another cut with feminine lines for girls. Everything would be made with elastic waists, knit cuffs and no-itch seams, and would need no frills, because of the beauty and grace of the line of the cut. I would do the same with pants, shorts and vests, plus a skirt and dress. All sized from infants to parents! Wouldn't we all be happy, comfortable, worry-free, and exquisite to behold?

Meanwhile, we'll do the best we can!

What Can We Do about Nightmares?

Some children have nightmares and some don't, and I really don't know what the cause is. Although this was not a problem for my children, I have answered this parental question for years. So, while I can't speak from family experience, I can tell you what the parents of my students find helpful.

When I was a little girl, each night as my mother tucked me into bed, after hugs and kisses, she told me to scoot *way* over in my bed to make room for my guardian angel to get in bed with me! I remember having a sense of a huge being, made of starlight and the diaphanous veils of the Milky Way. I always scooted as far as I could, but I knew my angel would never fit in the bed—he was almost too big even to fit into my bedroom!

Many children are told that their angel is with them. But I think the physical response of making room for the angel, right there in my very own little bed, was remarkably powerful. It took the angel out of the conceptual realm and located him a heartbeat away. Usually this reassurance, along with the bedtime ritual and prayer (see Chapter 2) invoking the angel's presence, is just the right remedy for a night of peaceful sleep.

If your child does wake up with a bad dream, here are some other ideas. Telling your child there is nothing to be afraid of is usually unproductive. Clearly he is afraid, and the nightmare image gives form to this fear. So accept exactly where your child is, and tell him that you are with him, and he is safe. Have him tell you the dream. Have him describe to you what the "bad thing" looks like, what it feels like, and so forth. Hold him close, to bring his heart rhythm in synchrony with yours.

Listen, as though you were problem-solving one of his daily challenges. Where does it come from? Where does it live? And so forth. Does it live in the closet? Close the door and put duct tape across it, saying, "Sorry, you can't live here." Does it live under the bed? Consider storing a few things there, so "It doesn't have enough room now. I guess it will just have to move somewhere else." Is it just the darkness itself? Leave the light on. Although my son did not have nightmares, he needed to have the overhead light left on, all night. This went on for a couple of years, until the night he asked me, somewhat casually, to turn it off as I went out the door.

Do the small things you can, to show him that you are listening and you believe him. These small things may become part of the nightly ritual, as leaving the light burning was for my son. Your acceptance of his fear, and even your acceptance that the "bad thing" exists, validates his experience of himself. It is helpful to approach the "bad thing" with equanimity, thinking of a solution as though you were figuring out how to solve a plumbing leak. If you approach it with valor and bravery, this can actually add fuel to the fire. The child may think, "Uh-oh, Mommy and Daddy are afraid, too." So, in a respectful, understated way, make the symbolic gestures necessary to reassure your child. Usually bad dreams will pass after a short while, when approached in this simple, respectful way.

How Do We Talk about Death?

Every parent must deal with this question. Because the answer lies somewhere within our own belief system, a good way for us to begin is to examine our feelings and beliefs about death. Elisabeth Kübler-Ross has written extensively about the question of death, and her work can act as a helpful guide for us. This inquiry is a life's work; the answer will change as we grow and evolve. Humanity has been probing this imponderable since we lived in caves. We parents continue in this tradition of inquiry as we wonder how to approach death with our young children.

I'll share with you what my approach has been, with my own children and in the classroom. Over the years, we have had various classroom pets die, so it has been my responsibility and my privilege to help guide the children's understanding.

I feel that children have just come to birth very recently, and their task is to understand what this life is about, to discover its purpose. "How do I help them to find this sense of purpose?" is my daily question. This, then, is what imbues my approach. What is the purpose of death, in terms a small child can understand?

When we celebrate the children's birthdays, I tell them their very own story, the story of their journey to earth. I tell them that a heavenly child lived in a heavenly garden. She was very happy there, living with her angel and the other heavenly children. I describe the games they liked to play with the clouds and the stars. Another very special game, I tell them, was to look over the edge of heaven and see what they could see of the games the earthly children liked to play. Then I give some descriptions of the games the school children that particular year like to play. Finally, the heavenly child says, "I wish I could go down there to play!" So the journey with her guardian angel begins. I then tell details of her babyhood and early childhood, until she reaches this day, her birthday.

When children come to me with news of a grandparent's death, I feel I can extend the story a little. Because the child has been imbued with a sense of having come to earth with a purpose, to play and explore, I can let the story have its natural conclusion. I will often say something like, "I wonder if Grandma is back in the heavenly garden now." You should see the children's eyes light up! A typical reply is along these lines: "Maybe she's playing with my kitty who died last year. Do you think they are together?" Other children are always ready to contribute, and a long discussion can ensue, wondering if various grandparents are meeting each other, or pets playing together.

I feel this entire story, including birth and death, gives the child a sense of the cyclic nature of life. It is akin to the way growing a garden imbues a sense of renewal. Both of these kindle, in images, an understanding of the way Life and Death walk had in hand.

Let me tell you the story of a very recent death in my classroom. Early in the year, I unexpectedly rescued a very special little dog. She was the prototype of sweetness, so we named her Priya, which means sweet. Every morning she ran to the door, tail wagging, and gave each child a special greeting lick. She had her tiny bed in a corner of the room, and loved to participate in the children's games. She had her own chair at the snack table and sat daintily, waiting until given permission to hop down and "vacuum" under the table. At circle time, she joined the fun, trotting around in the circle with us, and even put her head down at the quiet times. She was another member of our class.

A few short months later, she left us, just as unexpectedly. She was gone from this world within a few minutes. Not only did I have my own grief to deal with, but I had twenty children to help through their own feelings.

I called the parents and asked them to tell their children before school the next day, and possibly have them draw a picture for Priya. Many of the children brought pictures, which I carefully saved. As each child asked me "Where is Priya?" I replied, "It was time for her to go back to the heavenly garden." Each question that arose, I answered within this framework.

Child: "Why did she have to go so soon?"
Sharifa: "I wonder what work she was needed for, up above."

C: "Will she be allowed to sit at the table in heaven, like she did with us?"
S: "She learned her manners so well down here, I am quite sure she has her own chair up above!"

C: "Will she get to bark at the squirrels in heaven?"
S: "She will get to run and chase and bark, just the way she loved to do with us."

This went on for many days; the children discussed all the various possibilities of her life in heaven, and had a marvelous time elaborating their imaginings. But they missed her presence. One of the children's parents sent in a precious book called *Dog Heaven*. This book assured us that dogs who go to dog heaven get to come back to earth, and spend some days silently and invisibly with the children they have left behind. This comforted the children tremendously. Occasionally a child would scoot over to the edge of her chair, and say "I'm leaving room for Priya to sit with me."

I felt that having a way to talk about this very powerful event was excellent, but we all needed to have action. We needed to *do something* with our bodies to express our sorrow. I had buried her on a little hill above the garden playground. On the first day, I asked the children to go to the stream, which runs close by, and choose a very special stone to put on her grave. We then made a little burial mound of sparkling stones, and I put a beautiful garden stake at top. I had taken all their charming drawings, put them in a sealed plastic bag, and attached this present of love, with ribbons, to the stake. Day by day, the children, of their own accord, would bring special stones, or more pictures for her. Priya's burial mound became a favorite place for the children to play, arranging the stones in this way or that, and building "fairy huts" with the natural objects they found in the garden and playground.

Indoors, they wanted to play "Priya games." They came to me asking to play with her bed, her blankets, her leash and collar, and even her little sweaters and coat. They took turns "sleeping" in her bed and being led around on her leash. There was such a sense of love and beauty that surrounded these games. And the children played very sweetly together, as though they were sensing her small, canine sweetness.

Several weeks later the school year ended, and I felt we were just coming to the end of our process. Her life with us was such a gift, and even her death gave us a chance to experience loss within a framework of safety and beauty. The parents, too, were grateful not only for her life and all the tenderness she brought, but also for her death. It gave us, adults and children alike, an opportunity to find our way into one of humanity's essential questions.

Choosing a Child-Care Setting

One of the most important passages we make as parents is the moment we choose to open up the circle of "family" and allow our child to be cared for by others. Because we know that our young child experiences himself as being "at one" with the environment, we will want to research this decision very thoroughly.

The Human Being Is the Pivot

The first aspect we need to consider is *who the human being is* that will care for our child. As parents, we endeavor to be a person worthy of our child's imitation, in all of the large and small acts of love we offer. You can use this as a measure, also, when you look toward the care provider. *Balance* is the key word. You are looking for a person who is working toward balancing many aspects of herself, and can offer this balance to your child. Trust your heart in this decision. If you feel warmth and trust, if you feel she is accessible and responsive, if you see in her a sense of responsibility as well as kindness, these are excellent qualities.

What Culture Is Created By the Caregiver?

In the same way we look at our own family's "culture," we will want to see what kind of "culture" the teacher establishes in the environment. We can use the same measures we use for our own creation of culture. We will want to see what kind of a "container" is in place, offering firm, safe outer structures (classroom rhythms, healthy indoor as well as outdoor playtimes, etc.) balanced with adequate inner freedom for exploration. As we do at home, we will want to see that there is a sense of purposeful work made available for the children. Are they involved in the daily preparation and care of the environment? Do they help with snack preparation, care of toys and so forth? Hand-in-hand with work is play. Be sure there are many hours available for open-ended creative play, both indoors and out.

See if the teacher has good group management skills, as well as keen attention to the needs of each individual child. Within a sense of orderliness for the whole group, does the teacher allow time to care for the needs of the individuals? A healthy daily rhythm is essential for this. But she needs to use flexibility as well, so that the typical unforeseen events in a small child's life can be attended to in a timely, generous manner.

What Discipline Strategies Are Used?

Look carefully at the provider's use of discipline, seeing that it is instructive, not rigid, halfhearted or irresolute. Remember the watchwords you keep in mind for your own discipline measures: *firm* and *kind*. Is she firm and kind? How does she re-direct? In a disciplinary situation, does she look to the long view, offering life skills, not judgments? How does she handle children's quarrels? What happens when someone hits? What consequences pertain? It is essential that we not only observe keenly, but also *ask* these questions, and consider carefully the reply.

The Children Must Be Allowed to Move

As we have discussed, movement is critical to your child's healthy development in every arena, from brain development to skeletal-muscular growth, to emotional balance. Are the children allowed and encouraged toward healthy, purposeful movement? Is their movement trained by a robust, gesture-rich circle time? Is the children's creative play free and active, not impeded by battery-operated or computerized hand-held toys and games? Look carefully at the play materials. Do they encourage the use of the imagination, which always requires an active response? *Is the media used to baby-sit, keeping the children motionless in front of the screen?* Look at the movement of the children in the child-care setting. Is their movement grounded, deliberate, and healthy?

How much time are the children allowed to run and play outside? Is the outdoor play free and creative, or are peewee sports being coached? What is the outdoor playspace like? Look carefully at the teacher's attitude toward the children's movement.

The Physical Environment Is Essential

We can look at the physical environment with well-trained eyes. We have created, at home, a physical environment that fosters our child's growth in many ways. Look for an environment that expresses similar values. Remember that early childhood is the time to educate the senses. Look carefully at the play environment. Are the senses being stimulated in pure, simple ways?

What about the visual field? Look at the use of color. Are the colors warm and inviting, not garish or dissonant? See how cluttered or clear the space is. Look at the storage of the toys. Is it pleasing to the eye? Look for a sense of visual harmony; this way the eye can relax and gaze openly into each circumstance encountered.

What is the experience of sound? Sit quietly in the play environment and listen. This is what your child will be experiencing each day. Is there a busy hum in the air? I like to think that the sound a group of children make while busy at play is like the sound of a beehive. Happiness has a particular sound, and you can hear this if you listen. Is there, instead, the clutter of machine noise in the playspace? Is a radio or television on in the background? Is "children's music" being played? Or do you hear the natural voices of the teacher and the children singing and humming? Listen for a simple, clear, and beautiful soundscape.

Get a "feel" for the tactile environment. You can run your fingers over the toys and play materials. Touch the dolls, the building materials, the table and chairs, the blankets. Natural materials and fibers are pleasing and multidimensional to the touch. The feel of wood has far more variety, grain, weight, and texture than plastic. Silk, wool and cotton are warm and alive to touch, not damp or "clammy," the way synthetic fibers can be. See if there is access to water and sand. For the younger child, it is excellent for both of these tactile experiences to be available both indoors and out.

Olfactory delights. The scent of good food cooking can be one of life's great pleasures. But the smell of old food, or unclean corners and cupboards, can hang on longer than we wish. Breathe deeply while in the playspace. As parents of young children, we know how hard it is to keep our children, their clothing, their toys and their environment clean. When there is a group of young children together, it takes real attention to detail to keep the space clean, fresh, and sparkling. Often the sense of smell is most accurate. Notice, also, if there is the homey smell of good food, or berry tea.

The taste of life. What foods are served here? Look for shared values in the foods chosen, and in their preparation. What is the attitude about food? Is it a grounded, fundamental, delight-filled daily experience? Is it approached with an eye toward beauty and also gratitude? Food is such a fundamental human need, and its preparation such a central human activity, that you will want the child-care setting to reflect your family's values in this area.

When you visit the child-care setting, observe the *furnishings and equipment.* Look for natural materials, keeping the education of your child's senses in mind. What materials are the toy shelves, the table and chairs, the dollhouse or castle made of? Are furnishings in good repair? Your child will perceive whether they are cared for or not. Children have a built-in "love meter" and will know, even if the materials are old, whether they are loved and cared for. Look at the floor. Is it hardwood? Is there a carpet? Remember that your small child spends most of his day very close to the floor, or directly on it. Is it a floor you would like to live close to? See if the windows are sparkling, look for a quality of sunlight in the space. If there is a kitchen area, see if the food preparation materials are cleaned and put away after each meal or snack. Look for an artistic sense of beauty and harmony in the kitchen.

Now you can look more closely at the *toys and playthings.* See that the toys are open-ended and encourage creative imagination and free, purposeful movement. Examine the materials used for the toys, looking always for the variety and texture natural materials offer. Again, check to see if the toys are in good repair. If the toys are obviously cared for, the children likewise will care for them. If, on the other hand, repairs are neglected and the toys are not kept clean, the children will become careless, also. See how the children interact with the toys; see if a care for the physical environment is being modeled. You will see this in their play.

Don't Forget the Outdoor Space

Look at the outdoor playspace. An understanding of children's outdoor needs is becoming more common now. A few years ago, the typical children's playground was a flat, mulch-covered area containing a swing set, a climbing structure, and a sandbox, with a flat, grassy area adjoining it. We are beginning to understand, finally, that the perfect outdoor playground is a natural setting. There, the swells of hills and the mystery of bushes and tall grasses call to the children. Look for plenty of natural building and play materials, good sticks for digging and building, some heavy, flat stumps, good stones and so forth. For your fives and sixes, ask about tree climbing—are there any trees with sturdy low branches? When considering safety issues, remember the old saying, "A broken bone is better than a broken spirit."

Artistic Experience

Look for a balanced approach to artwork. Look for seasonal craftwork, color experience and hand training. Listen to the stories that are told and the play-acting that can ensue. Notice the presence of singing and natural music wafting through the environment. See if the *atmosphere* of the classroom is artistic, as well.

The Sense of Rhythm

Check the daily rhythm to see if, like at home, it is an open, "breathing" rhythm. This will include times of *expansion* in outdoor play and creative, imaginative indoor play. Also look for times of *focused attention*, at story, art, and circle time. See that there is a sense of "enough time for everything." As at home, we do not want our children to feel rushed. See if the program offers a sense of the rhythm of the year: are festivals celebrated? Are parents invited to join in these festive times? This encourages the reality of home and school working together in partnership.

Waldorf Schools

Good programs will offer some, or many, of these essential aspects. Shop around and see which program offers the best of these. If you are fortunate enough to have a Waldorf School close to you, you will be pleased to discover that each aspect we have discussed is addressed in the Early

Childhood classroom. Each subject is studied in depth during teacher training, and many Early Childhood teachers continue to study throughout their teaching careers.

You may want to get your journal and make notes on the specific areas you are looking at, and the details you are looking for. Then make notes of what you see, and what you *feel*. Use your head, follow your heart, engage in the "search" with your senses, and you will discover the child-care setting that is right for your child and for your family.

Chapter 9

CREATING YOUR FAMILY CULTURE

*I*N THE EARLIER chapters of this book, we've discussed how you can begin to establish the rhythms of your family's life through the rhythmic activities you share together, the way you organize your days with regular mealtimes and bedtimes, and the festivals you choose to celebrate. You can also create play spaces that foster physical, emotional, and cognitive exploration. You can choose carefully the artistic activities you offer your children, and tell them stories you love. In all of this you are making decisions that establish your family's culture. Culture is nothing more or less than the way we live our lives. Although this "culture making" is going on all the time, the *quality* of the culture pivots entirely on the awareness we bring to it. We are fashioning our family's culture with each decision, so let us bring as much consciousness to this process as we can.

If we do not work toward this conscious shaping of our family's culture, that culture will be shaped unconsciously by the larger societal norms. These, in turn, are shaped to a large degree by the mass media, by advertisers, by the "spin doctors" of our society. To raise children who, as young adults, can freely create their life as they envision it—this is our task. We do this by fashioning a space in which, with a delicate balance of guidance and freedom, our children can discover who they really are.

With each decision we make, we are showing our children what we value. As adults, we have the capacity to look at each other's choices and know whether we agree with these values or not. Our children have not yet gained this power of discrimination. Because our very young children experience themselves as being at one with their environment, they deeply internalize the value system we offer them. In consciously choosing to value life in all its forms; in choosing to foster health, well-being, self-respect, and respect for others, we show our children that we value *them*. Perhaps more than anything,

> *The quality of our family culture pivots entirely upon the awareness we bring to it. Let us bring as much consciousness to this process as we can.*

our young children are *alive*, like the first day of creation. In showing our children that we value Life, we affirm through every action that we love them, in all their liveliness.

AWARENESS OF THE FAMILY ORGANISM

It is through all the choices we make, large and small, and through actions more than words, that family culture is established. Our children come to learn that they are an essential part of a living organism called "our family." Through this clear sense of family, our children eventually learn the cardinal place they have in the larger family of the world. They know that they belong. At this time, when humanity suffers from the life-negating forces of alienation and disenfranchisement, a sense of belonging is more crucial than it has ever been. If, in our family culture, we show our children that we value *all life*, through gardening, through caring for backyard wildlife, through hiking, bicycling and other nature-oriented activities, they in time develop this larger sense of belonging. When we tell our tiny child a story about the rain fairies who come to care for our garden, or about the great father oak tree who puts his leaf children to bed each autumn, we plant in their hearts seeds that will grow into a strong sense of belonging to Life itself.

We can also show them, through this sense of family, the intricacies of social behavior. Many times we can call on the larger entity of "family" to explain how things work. We might say, for instance, "In our family, we don't hit each other, we talk about things instead." Or, "In our family, we like to sing grace before we eat." As the children grow and visit other families, they will begin to notice that people do things differently. Usually their reporting will be something like this: "Katie gets to stay up until 10:00," to which we can reply, "In our family, we go to bed with the birds!" Calling on the larger entity of family not only helps explain things and gives a sense of belonging, it can help us sidestep a power struggle.

During adolescence, our children will become more aware of the differences in families. They may choose to "adopt" a friend's family, or conversely we may find our child's best friend eating dinner at our house often, or sleeping overnight every weekend. We can intuit our way toward creating an

When we tell our child stories of our friends the rain fairies or the great father oak who cares for his leaf children, we plant seeds that will grow, in time, into a sense of our belonging to Life itself.

Calling on the larger sense of family can help us to sidestep a power struggle. If one of our children does not want to join a family outing, we can reply, "But this is a family adventure! We need you!"

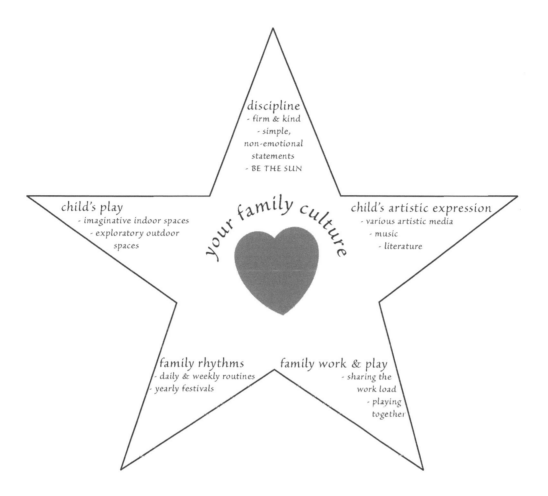

atmosphere that draws our children's friends toward our family. When my boys were teenagers, I knew food played a central role in their lives. Because I wanted them to love being at home, I kept the refrigerator stuffed with foods they liked. Their friends were often at our house on weekends, cooking huge feasts late at night. I insisted that they leave the kitchen clean, but otherwise gave them carte blanche. I knew the money spent in groceries was an investment in their sense of self-worth and belonging. And better spent now than on visits to a therapist later, dealing with alienation issues! You will find ways to make your home and your family a magnet for your child and her friends, too.

What begins to develop, over time, is a sense of pride. The children know they are an essential element in something that is uniquely "our family," full of life and evolution. If we plan a family outing, and one of our children does not want to join us, we can lean on this. "But it is a *family* adventure. *We need you!*" We can point out in conversation qualities that our family carries, something like, "Our family loves to cook together," or "Ours is an outdoorsy kind of family." In time, and with exposure to other families, our children will tell us what they think of our togetherness, with comments like, "Our family laughs a lot, don't we?" This is a powerful basis for a healthy sense of self-esteem. With this strong foundation, our child steps confidently toward self-discovery.

CREATING THE CONTAINER

Our family is the container, the safe space in which young souls are cultivated. They grow in this atmosphere, with the mixture of necessary elements. When they know themselves well enough, they step outside the family, into the strong wind of their own life.

I believe there is one central task that each parent is given with the birth of his or her child. This is to carry for the child, until he can carry for himself, the fundamental human question, "Who am I?" When we look into our beloved child's face, we can look down the long corridor of his life, inquiring who the man will be. It is crucial that we allow this question to remain open, that we not close the door with our preconceptions. Too often in families, children become pigeonholed. "Emily is our worker bee, but Johnny wants to play all day." Our assessment of the child may be correct, but we must remember how malleable, how "unfinished" the young child is. It is not until much later, at the close of adolescence, that the young adult will have the capacities necessary to begin to mold himself into the person he wants to become. He needs a clean palette to work with, not one clogged up with parental biases. As parents, we certainly will see particular characteristics, tendencies, in our child. We will offer much love and effort in guiding these inclinations in the right direction. But this work must be done in secret, veiled from the child. Our goal is to have the young adult step into

When we create the "container" of family, we work with the opposing principles of firm structure and open flexibility, or freedom. When both of these forces are in balance, the container fulfills its purpose—to help the young soul discover itself.

Firm structures—life rhythms—give the child a sense of safety. Out of safety grows inner freedom. Freedom is fostered through self-expression.

this "self-making" with freedom. We foster freedom by holding open the question, "Who are you?"

The container of the family is the vessel in which we carry this question. If we look at a ceramic pot, a container, we see opposites come together to fulfill a purpose. We see the firm solid exterior of clay, and the open, empty interior space. When we create the container of family, we work with both of these principles, firm structure, and open flexibility. It is only when both of these opposing forces are in balance that the container fulfills its purpose—to help the young soul discover itself.

When we create firm structures, regular and rhythmic life habits, we give our child a sense of safety. Out of safety grows an inner sense of freedom. We can foster the openness of freedom when we give our children multifaceted opportunities for self-discovery and self-expression. They may experience this through open-ended creative play, through the arts, through stories and music, or through the exploration of Nature.

We can think about creating the container in the same way we envision creating an orderly, predictable play environment. The toys are mindfully selected and lovingly cared for. Each toy or play material has its "home" and at playtime's end finds its way into the proper basket. Everything is brought to order and to rest. But during playtime, there is spaciousness, "anything can be anything." There is tremendous freedom to explore, to create, to experiment. It is in this weaving back and forth between the mindfully structured orderliness and glorious open space that the strong container full of emptiness is created. This is Family Culture.

We can hold this image as we move through the many questions that will arise in our parenting. As situations present themselves, we can ask ourselves, what are the firm boundaries this situation calls for, and how can my child experience freedom within these boundaries? By holding this question, we recognize and care for many needs of our young child's being. The child needs physical safety, warmth, and nurturance; emotionally, she needs love, guidance, and modeling. Spiritually, she needs inspiration and freedom to become the person she will be. The right balance of structure and freedom will meet these diverse needs.

But how does all of this apply to your young child? At dinnertime, if your child turns up his nose at the cooked carrots, you can put a little on his

> *Every parent's question: "What are the firm boundaries this situation calls for, and how will my child find freedom within these boundaries?"*

> *It is through our inner attitude that we show our love. It's not just what we do, it's who we are in the doing of the things, that speaks to our child.*

plate and say, "Just a taste!" This creates the structure and boundary. After the taste, it is his freedom to join the rest of the family in enjoying the carrots, or not. At nap time, if your child says "I'm not tired," you can follow through with the nap-time ritual, requiring that he be horizontal, but he can lie in bed and play quietly with his stuffed animals if he can't sleep. If you take the carrots off his plate, or let him get up from nap after a few minutes of wakefulness, you have weakened the container. Conversely, if you force the carrot issue, insisting he eat them all, or you insist that he lie stock still, the freedom of the spirit has been hampered. At this time in our society, contrary to earlier times, our tendency is to err on the side of weakening the container. In more authoritarian times, we erred on the side of a loss of freedom. We *can* find a middle path, offering both structure and freedom. *Both are essential in discovering the evolving answer to "Who am I?"*

> *Let us approach the incessant round of ordinary life-nurturing activities with an extra-ordinary attitude. This is love made visible.*

WORKING TOGETHER

A major way we show our children that we value them is in undertaking the never-ending round of "caring" activities life requires. It is not only in housekeeping and the preparation of food, in the arranging of the flow of life, but it is primarily through our *inner attitude* that we show our love. It is not just what we do; it is *who we are*, in the doing of the things, that speaks volumes to our children.

> *In earlier times, it was understood that in "keeping the hearth" all the essential elements of life come into play, and through their alchemical mingling, something new is born. Transformation!*

For example, think of all the small and large tasks involved in cleaning the house. Think of dusting, picking up each thing, rearranging. Think of sweeping, scrubbing, shining, and vacuuming. Think of fluffing the pillows, cleaning window sills, sweeping cobwebs, digging into corners, reasserting order. Some people may think of this as drudgery, something to be completed and forgotten as quickly as possible. But there is another side, an *inner* side, to housekeeping. Have you noticed when you finally sit down, how each thing shines with its own particular light? Have you seen how the air sparkles with life, the rooms silently sing? I believe this shining quality is the hymn of the life force, which you, through your loving work, have brought alive. This is love made visible.

When we approach the incessant round of ordinary life-nurturing activities with an extra-ordinary attitude, when we understand what we are doing on a subtle level, we can free ourselves from the prevalent societal attitude that household tasks are of less value than tasks of the mind. Certainly for our young children, these tasks are essential. They are essential not only for furthering daily life, but also for the child's beginning understanding of the meaning of our humanity. This is work that our children can actually witness with their own eyes, unlike so much of the technological work we do. As they join us in this work, they can practice contributing toward the whole family. This prepares them to contribute, as adults, to the larger society. Our joyful attention to these tasks creates an atmosphere in which our children can grow. Our gladness in these tasks is the tilling of the soil, the weeding of the garden, the life-giving water in which their souls take root and flourish.

In earlier times, and in other cultures, tasks associated with caring for the household have been considered essential, even of sacred value. In the East, each household had a nook where the kitchen gods were honored. In some early societies it was considered a sacred duty to keep the fire alive. It was understood that in "keeping the hearth," all the essential elements of life come into play, and through their alchemical mingling, something new is born, a transformation occurs.

In medieval times, these "essential elements" were categorized as Earth, Water, Fire and Air, with their corollary properties of stability, purity, transformation and spaciousness. It may be helpful to us to see these elements at work in our daily tasks, bringing a primal sort of transformation even into the twenty-first century.

For instance, we work with the stabilizing element of Earth as we bring a balance to indoor and outdoor activities, as we bring indoors bouquets from the garden or colorful fallen leaves, as we care for the indoor plants, as well as the yard and garden. We experience the purifying element of Water in all the many washing activities throughout the day, and in our child's free, exploratory water play, or in the exuberant joy of the bathtub. The transformative powers of Fire come to us as the raw vegetables slowly become soup, with the scent of fragrant herbs filling the air. If we have the luxury of a fireplace or a wood stove, we are immediately aware of fire's essential power as we lean

---

THE ALCHEMY OF HEART AND HEARTH

Earth—Stability
- *Balance of activities*
- *Care of growing things*

Water—Purity
- *Washing activities*
- *Water play*
- *Bathing*

Fire—Transformation
- *Cooking food*
- *Warmth in winter*
- *Bedtime candle*

Air—Spaciousness
- *Inner calm*
- *Outer openness*

The kitchen is the room most filled with the rich tapestry of life force, with all the elements weaving together to make our family's culture palpable.

toward its warmth on a cold night. The spaciousness of the Air element is more subtle. We find its transformative power in the way we count to ten, breathing in and then out again, before we respond to the honey spilled on the floor. The subtle openness we create in quiet moments with our child, or the sparkle in the atmosphere after a brisk cleaning, are qualities of the air element, also.

Perhaps the place in the home in which all of these elements come into play the most often is the kitchen. All of the transformative activities of cooking, eating, cleaning, conversation and laughter take place in this central area. Is this the reason why the kitchen is often the best-loved room in the house? It is the room most filled with the rich tapestry of life force, with all these elements weaving together to make our family's culture palpable.

In earlier times, people knew that there was tremendous power in working with the elements, these building blocks that give form to the world— and that the alchemical interaction of the physical elements and their more subtle corollaries even shaped the human soul. They understood that in the keeping of the hearth also lived the keeping of the heart, and therefore the keeping of the whole society.

It is a relatively new attitude, in our human history, to devalue the tasks that nurture and further human life. In a market society, these tasks do not necessarily bear quick profits. It takes many years to see the return we get from a well-brought-up human being. As we turn farther away from the valuing of these simple, life-affirming tasks, mundane though they may be, as we strip them of meaning, we find proportionally headlines asking "Our Nation's Kids: Is Something Wrong?" The answer of course is "Yes, we adults are wrong-minded in our lack of understanding of true values."

But how, in this frenetic life, do we manage to value these simple daily tasks? It is the challenge of our times to bring consciousness to all these activities. As we chop the vegetables, let's be aware of the love we are chopping right into the sautéed dish, instead of making tomorrow's shopping list in our heads or running through the office argument. When we are aware that conscious housework makes love visible, then we can bring our whole selves to the task. When we polish the wood furniture, we can actually look at the way the wood absorbs the oil, the way its glow smiles back at us. As we do these tasks with our young children, let's tell them what we see: "See how the purple

> *In a market society, the tasks that nurture and further human life do not necessarily bear quick profits. It takes many years to see the return we get from a well-brought-up human being.*

> *As we chop the vegetables, let's be aware of the love we are chopping right into the dish.*

cabbage looks like a flower when we cut it open?" or "Here is a ladybug who rode into our kitchen on the broccoli." Our young children are very present in the moment, taking in information through their senses. We can join them there, offering them our conscious presence as we work together.

We can also put these tasks on a weekly "round," planning the work just as we have planned the meals, the shopping and so forth. When our children are young, and all the work of keeping the family lies with the adults, it is a great challenge to bring attention and joy to the work, because the load is so full. As our children become older, it is their fresh new energy and interest as they join us in the work that can help us to rediscover this for ourselves.

A Simple Plan

You will find ways to share tasks that will work for your family. Here is one way to think through the chores and accomplish them in one day. There are four major indoor jobs: 1) dusting and vacuuming, 2) laundry, 3) cleaning the kitchen, and 4) cleaning the bathroom. Let us assume there are two adults sharing these tasks, and each parent will focus on specific areas. The person who dusts and vacuums will have more flexibility, and so can be putting loads of laundry through the washer and dryer. The parent who does kitchen and bathroom is more involved with water and scrubbing, so needs more concentrated energy. When our young children are working alongside us, we will want to give attention to their "soundscape." So we can send them off to help with the kitchen, after the dusting and shining is finished, while the vacuum is being run. Usually, in the average house, these tasks can be finished in two or three hours, even with our children underfoot and helping. You can then have a good, quick lunch together, perhaps sandwiches, or leftovers. Afterward, while one parent does outdoor work and the children play in the yard, the other parent can shop for groceries. This will be easy—look at the chart of daily dinners and make the shopping list with this visual aid. Back at home, the children will go down for a nap mid-afternoon. By day's end you will have a sparkling house, a full refrigerator, clean laundry for the week, and happy children who by joining you have learned the joy of caring for life. Because you have planned well, your energy will be wisely spent, and you will be prepared for the week to come.

WEEKLY CHORE DAY PLAN

MORNING
- *One parent and child*
  Dust and vacuum
  Laundry
- *Other parent and child*
  Scrub kitchen
  Scrub bathroom

LUNCH TOGETHER IN AFTERNOON
- *One parent and children*
  Yard work
  Nap
- *Other parent*
  Grocery shop
  Errands

EVENING
- *Celebrate your day!*

To some people, all this planning may look like a form of slavery! In fact, it is through planning wisely that we actually make space for the open-ended and creative aspects of our life together. When all the necessary chores are planned into the ongoing rhythm of the day and the week, we make space available for unexpected spontaneity. We have created time to listen to the surprising insights, theories and questions our children offer, and time to imaginatively respond. We give ourselves the time to watch the butterfly with our four-year-old.

As our children grow and mature, their household tasks can evolve as well. Various chores we have shared can become their own responsibility. Of course, for many years they will not share responsibility equally, yet it is essential for their self-esteem to feel that their help and input is not only respected, but needed as well. As our children reach school age, around six or seven, we can give them daily and weekly chores. We can give the care of a family pet to our six- or seven-year-old, incorporating feeding the cat into the evening routine, perhaps as soon as dinner is finished. Or we can include setting the dinner table, or laying out his clothes the night before. The key is to attach this new responsibility onto a part of his day that is already very well incorporated. We can add a new action onto what is already a well-known habit.

The attitude we can carry, as we give our children more responsibility little by little, is, "You are a member of our family and *we need you*, in many ways, for warmth and fun, for work and play." Eventually, when our children become teenagers, we can give them various tasks to envision and accomplish on their own. Teenagers love to grocery shop, and although they may not be as thorough or economical as we are, their shopping is full of adventure and surprises. We can give them one night a week in which they are responsible for preparing the family meal. Although they may need some coaching at first, they will know many aspects of cooking, having stood on a chair beside us for so many years as we have chopped and stirred.

Playing Together

Let's return to the image of family culture as a family's container, to hold and foster the children's growth. The structured, rhythmic completion of

> *The structured completion of weekly housework can be balanced by the spaciousness of the family's play together.*

> *When we have young children, "playing together" can be as simple as going outdoors to swing them, or to weed the garden as they potter along beside us. For grade-school children, though, we can find noncompetitive, physically active games that value all players, regardless of varying ability levels. We can save competitive sports games for later.*

weekly housework can be balanced by the spaciousness and freedom of the family's play together. In the same way we considered having one day per week as a work day, we may want to choose one day for family outings. Again, you will find a rhythm of playing together that is right for your family.

For our young children, play is a way of life, and so providing opportunities to play together can be a simple matter of going outdoors together. We adults can sit and chat as we swing the children on the high seas of the hammock, or we can putter together in the garden as the children play close by. For young children, an occasional "tag" or "chase" game is fine fun with Mom and Dad. Hide and seek is sweetly poignant, as our young children call out from six feet away, "You can't find me!" Remember, though, if we enter too deeply into their magical realm with all of our adult thoughts and energy, we can actually disturb their world of play.

When our children reach grade-school age, though, they have entered a new realm, and we can join them in games that involve rules and sequencing. In the appendix you will find resource books mentioned that introduce non-competitive, physically active games that can be played by a few players or by many. Maybe you will ask another family over for an afternoon of outdoor games! Look for games that value all players, regardless of their varying ability levels. We can also choose games that call for specific qualities, such as quickness or solidity. This gives each player, regardless of capacity, his or her moment in the sun. It is marvelous for children to see their parents in a completely different role, running, hiding, falling, sliding!

We can save competitive sports games for later, when our children are near adolescence. Introduced too early, these games can restrict not only free movement, but also creative problem-solving and a sense of social inclusiveness. Sports games can also negatively affect our young children's balanced physical development, encouraging the repetitive use of specific muscle groups to the neglect of others, and encouraging specific ball-oriented eye-hand usage to the detriment of a more age-appropriate, broad-spectrum usage. At adolescence, though, when the physical development is nearly complete, competitive sports games can be introduced. Sportsman-like coaching is essential in teaching the value of the opponent and brisk competition as one avenue to further personal excellence.

Let our family's play continue to grow for a lifetime. Aspects to consider:

- *Let it be an active exploration of the child's expanding world.*

- *Let it offer opportunities to discover each other as we grow and develop.*

- *See that each person finds something to love in our joined activity.*

Another way we can bring play into our family culture is to discover what it is that we really like to do all together as a family. If we love water, we can move along a developmental waterway, so to speak, bringing to our family developmentally appropriate water activities. With our preschool children, we can take a camping trip beside a river, stopping at a spot where the water runs wide and slow. This way our little ones can potter along ankle-deep, discovering crayfish and minnows, water-skaters and salamanders. In a few years, we'll be looking for good swimming holes. Eventually canoes and boating may enter the picture, and our teenagers may vote for a whitewater rafting trip. Or, if we like to walk together, we can begin with strolls through the city park system, moving on to country hikes on trails redesigned from old railway beds, then to mountain backpacking trips. Maybe we like wheels, beginning with a tricycle ride down the sidewalk and ending many years later in a bicycle tour of France.

We will want to attend to several considerations: we need to see that our family's play is an *active* exploration of our beautiful planet, that it affords opportunities to discover each other as we grow and develop, and that each person finds something to love in our joined activities. One way our family played together was through ski vacations. All the men of the family loved to throw themselves against the elements and the mountain. I, on the other hand, loved to get them up, breakfasted, and off to the slopes. Then I had hours of solitude and silence, to read or walk in the snow, until mealtime rolled around and they arrived back, happily starving. Let's plan play into our daily, weekly, and yearly life. Our playing together is a colorful ribbon woven into the fabric of our family's culture.

LOVE'S OTHER NAME: DISCIPLINE

We have explored in depth many of the elements that combine to form family culture. Let's think about these elements as a five-pointed star whose points are Family Rhythms, Family Work and Play, Child's Play, the Child's Artistic Expression, and Discipline. In your journal, you may want to sketch the "star" of your family's culture.

The first point, Family Rhythms, encompasses our various daily and weekly rituals and routines, as well as the celebration of yearly festivals. Second, Family Work and Play incorporates the way we attend to the work-load of caring for a family, balanced by the way our family relaxes and plays. Third, Child's Play includes the creation of imaginative indoor playspaces and a variety of exploratory outdoor playspaces. Fourth, the Child's Artistic Expression includes a variety of artistic media as well as music and literature.

The first two points, Family Rhythm and Family Work and Play, act as the "legs" of the star. They are the foundation; with their strong thighs, they give support and take our family on this journey together. The next two points, Child's Play and the Child's Artistic Expression, are the "arms" of the star. They are sensitive, fine and nimble. They are the limbs whereby the child reaches toward the world.

Each of these four major areas, the legs and arms of our family, creates an embodied space for the "head," the self-reflecting aspect, which we can call Discipline. I prefer to call this last point "behavior management," because I believe that when these first four areas are balanced and functioning well, discipline is established in the subtle atmosphere of the home. This develops, eventually, into self-discipline. At the heart of the word "discipline" is the concept of discipleship, which implies "following with love." Our children *do* follow us with love, through their innate capacity of imitation. Whatever the family culture we establish, they will, in their own way, mirror it back to us in their behavior.

If we are not satisfied with their behavior, first we must look at the family culture, or these four areas of Family Rhythms, Family Work and Play, Child's Play, and the Child's Artistic Expression. We can assess bedtime, nap time and mealtimes. Look also at your child's playtime. Too much structured activity and busyness, or not enough outdoor play? Look at the balance of work and play. Also think about the stories your child has heard, or any media influence. Usually we can see where we have fallen short, and if we continue to observe, we can see patterns emerge, showing specific areas where we need to be particularly attentive. One child might be especially sensitive to the type or the timing of food. Another may need a *very* firm naptime; another may need some solitude *every* day. When we do not give the special attention to

NOT SATISFIED WITH YOUR CHILD'S BEHAVIOR?

First, look at the outer rhythm, or family culture. Adjust as necessary.

Second, look at your own inner rhythm. Too busy? Not satisfied? Adjust as necessary.

Third, work with discipline as behavior management.

specific areas of family life that each of our children needs, they will usually remind us very clearly.

Second, we must look at our own inner rhythm. The outer rhythm, or structure, needs the support of our strong inner rhythm. Who we are is more critical to our child than what we do, and the very best gift we can give our young child is a happy, well-rested, contented parent. The question each parent must keep alive as we raise our children is, "How do I care well for myself, so that I can care well for them?" Adults, too, need good solid sleep, nourishing food, enough exercise and a sense of purpose in life. Each parent has to find her own way, and create rhythms for herself, just as we create them for our children. This is not a luxury; it is a "job requirement." We know our children imitate not only everything we do, but also the very way we are human beings. They imitate us from the most concrete activities to the subtlest essence of our being. This can be a paralyzing thought! If, however, we approach ourselves with the same humor and compassion we offer our children, we will be able to appreciate our successes in finding balance, and take our failures in stride as we learn from them.

Balance and rhythm become more difficult as we proceed further into the technological era. This very difficulty asks us to continue to work consciously to find balance and inner harmony. How do we accomplish this? A golden rule toward finding this sense of inner rhythm is *SIMPLIFY*! We can simplify many areas of our lives: the toy shelf, the furniture, clothing, kitchen utensils. The less "stuff" we have to deal with, the more time we have to be at ease

Another doorway to balance your inner rhythm is to participate in some activity that truly nourishes *you*. It is easy for parents to say, "But caring for my family and enjoying the happiness this brings *is* nourishing for me." This may be true, but before you had children, there were activities that you loved, that nourished you. Find a way to keep them in your life. Or discover new ways to give yourself the satisfaction this brings. Your children need a role model who knows how to find joyful connection with himself and the world. Whether you love to play the guitar or attend the opera, whether you love to bicycle or bird watch, give yourself these moments. Eventually, sharing what you love with your children will show them how to keep this place of childlike delight open in their own hearts as they mature through

When we have adjusted our outer and inner rhythms as best we can, and she still protests and cries, what do we do?

• *First try distraction.*

• *Then bring her to join you in your work, bring her into your "heart-rhythm."*

• *Finally, enforce logical consequences, when necessary.*

Be firm and kind.

Be consistent.

life. And your enthusiasm will spill over into all the daily tasks you do with and for them.

Making these inner and outer adjustments—refining our family's rhythms and our child's experience of play and art, and refining our own inner rhythm—this is a life-time's work! It is not as though we will ever say, "Ah! Now it is all perfect." We will continue to hone these points, on a daily basis, for many years.

Firm and Kind

Now we work with the fifth point of the star, or discipline in the form of behavior management. I have discovered specific steps that, when followed, bring the result we want: a happy, harmonious child.

Let's say your six-year-old daughter is building, with the tree stump blocks you have made, an elaborate castle for her doll, the Queen. Your four-year-old son takes away the look-out block, on top. Begin with distraction; try turning his attention away from the point of contention. Draw his interest perhaps to the bird feeder at the window, or any other imaginative diversion. You can elaborate with a little story about how the bird family has already come for breakfast, and you are wondering if his felted birdie with the ribbon tail is hungry also. Sometimes this works wonders, and he will run to find the bird, and play contentedly beside his sister. The young child's consciousness is mobile enough that usually whatever is in front of it is where the attention will be drawn.

If this fails, and he keeps taking away blocks, you can bring the child into your own rhythm. Have him help with whatever task you are doing. Bringing him close to you physically helps him to re-establish his own inner rhythm by attuning to yours. There are current studies that show the human heart's electromagnetic field has a direct influence on others. This influence is called "entrainment." So when you bring your child to your side, to sweep, rake or sew with you, he comes into the electromagnetic field of your heart, and thereby his heart-rhythm becomes attuned to yours. Yes, it will take more time to complete your task, but to have him happily at your side and the conflict avoided is preferable.

What next? If you've tried the above and your child is still pushing, he is clearly asking you to create a safe boundary; he wants you to define the container for him. This is how he discovers the parameters of his world. Like the early explorers, he is pushing the envelope, finding the edges of his world's map. Understanding this can help you respond with the two watchwords of discipline: *firm* and *kind*. With firmness and kindness, you can draw the boundaries, making his world small enough to be safe and understandable, and yet large enough that he can freely walk the path of self-discovery.

Because the young child learns by doing, *action* is what is required in disciplinary situations. Explaining, reasoning, pleading, bargaining all fall on deaf ears, because he has not grown into his powers of reason just yet. What if he has his bird, the blocks have been shared fairly, and he continues to take his sister's blocks? Now comes the logical consequence. You say, "Children who can't play well with each other don't get to play at all. Come sit down. Here is the place for you to sit until you are ready to use your own blocks." Perhaps you have a child-sized rocking chair, which can be brought for him as he sits, pondering. A small rocker is grand for these "time-out" purposes, because it gives him a rhythmic activity with which to bring himself back into balance. After a short while (not longer than four minutes, one minute for each year of his age) you can let him try again to play well. Say something positive and encouraging, like "This time you'll remember to use your own blocks." Kindness will carry the day, and it is this sense of kindness that he will be left with in the end.

Be the Sun

Remember, you are the center of your child's solar system. You are the sun, bringing warmth and light. His entire world revolves around you. Your sense of peace and calm is the point upon which everything pivots. It is the axis of his world. Think of the way the sun moves tranquilly through the heavens, shining down calmly, regardless of the way we humans may curse

---

BE THE SUN!

Move slowly and compassionately, especially in disciplinary situations, bringing warmth and light—it's a tall order! You may need to practice.

Need to discipline your child? Keep your voice simple and non-emotional, as though you were saying, "The bread is on the counter."

or moan at the vagaries of the weather. The way you can remain centered, calm and even cheerful, is by knowing *very clearly* what your expectations are, what the boundaries are, and what the logical consequence of crossing the boundary is.

It is best to firmly and kindly insist. Then, if necessary, quickly and compassionately enforce small consequences. A good rule of thumb for time-out is as many minutes as the child is years old. This moves the energy very quickly beyond the "stuck" place and returns our child to harmony. We want to avoid allowing ourselves to be pushed further and further until we finally acquiesce to the child's wishes. If we capitulate, this guarantees that the cycle will repeat, since what our child is seeking is a firm boundary. We also don't want to be pushed to a point at which we become angry. Again, our inner state of being affects our child on the deepest level. He will carry within him our joy, or our anger, for a lifetime.

When it is necessary to enforce a consequence, whether the child is sent to his room or needs to sit in the rocking chair for a bit, we can remain in contact with him. If he is having a tantrum and has been sent to his room, we can tell him we hope he finishes crying soon, because we need his help filling the bird feeder (or any task). If he has refused to do what we have asked, and is having a short time-out in the rocking chair, we can tell him we miss his company, and would like him to comply so we can continue our fun together. He may say, "I hate sitting here." It's best for us to avoid a lecture, and just agree with him, "I don't like it, either. Would you like to... (do whatever he has refused)?"

We can practice keeping our tone of voice simple and unemotional, as though we were saying, "Please hand me the broom," or "The bread is on the counter." *This is a critical point, and because it is difficult, we may need much practice!* What our child needs is information about how both the inner and outer worlds function. If we give him this information in a few clear sentences, stripped of our adult emotion, what remains in his heart is the simplicity of the information. If, on the other hand, we load the information with an overlay of our own emotion, what remains is not the information but the child's experience of our emotion. If our child hits a younger sibling, and we give them the simple directive, "People who hit each other go to their rooms. In our family, we talk to each other, we don't hit." the possibility exists that

> *When disciplining a child, remember that he needs information about how the world functions. Give him a few clear sentences, not your emotional overlay.*

the next time, the child will choose to speak his needs rather than hit. If, on the other hand, we respond to his anger with our own anger, he is left with the knowledge that anger begets anger, but with no model of a positive alternative response.

Parents often ask me what to do if their child refuses a time-out and will not sit in the rocker. You can say to him, "I like having you close by and would like your time-out to be here in the rocker. But if you jump up, or hop out of the chair, you'll have to go to your room." He may have to go to his room a few times before he realizes that the problem is more quickly resolved by cooperating with your compassionate consequence.

Some fiery children simply need to up the ante, and will choose to reject the simple moments of sitting in a chair in time-out. They may often need to be sent to their room. Again, our inspiration is the sun. We want to avoid being pulled into the child's emotional heat. As the sun moves overhead, compassionately shining on everything below, we can breathe and move slowly and steadily as we walk our protesting child to her room. We can say as we go, "Okay, honey, I hope you can come back to us soon." And when she returns, greet her with, "I'm glad you're back! Next time, let's see if your time-out can be here, in the rocker." Steadying ourselves in the face of our child's strongly felt emotion is good practice for the adolescent years.

Staying in compassionate contact with our child as she is being disciplined can help both of us to sidestep power struggles. If our premise is not "You have to do it, because I said so," but rather "You need to do it, because I am here to help you learn life lessons," we will find ways to convey this to our child. When my boys were a little older, five or six and up, I would tell them, "It's my job to be the mom, and teach you many things you will need to know. It's okay with me if a time-out helps you remember." My desire was that they not feel I was "in power over them," but rather that together we had a task to do, each of us with our different roles.

Usually, this consistent, patterned, non-emotional adult response to disciplinary problems carries the day. Occasionally with children six and up, though, stronger medicine is needed. Speaking to a child with *conviction* is very different from speaking to him with *anger*. Occasionally my boys would be so busy playing or goofing around that they would simply ignore my request or demand. I would make the request in my usual ways, wanting to lead them toward the task with kindness. If this failed, I would use "The Other Voice": "COME HERE NOW." It was a voice of thunder that clearly meant business, Right Now! As soon as they complied, which was very quickly, I would return to my normal disposition. It was a "tool" I kept aside for the very rare occasion when kindness failed to get their attention. Eventually I could say to them, "Okay, boys, I've asked in my nice voice. Do you need to hear The Other Voice?"

Occasionally we *will* lose our temper; what to do then? Remember a couple of ground rules: Make "I statements," rather than blaming or judging your child. You might say something like, "Okay, I'm starting to get angry here!" rather than, "You make me so mad!" Also, you can put yourself in time-out until you gather your patience. Tell them you are feeling angry, and so will not be helpful. Then go to your room and shut the door. Your children may be so surprised that they sit quietly whispering among themselves, as mine did, until you reappear. This will not only gain for you the moments you need to breathe and re-center, it can model for them a way to deal with anger that is not destructive to relationship. So often we say things in anger that are simply passing emotion, not representative of our true feelings. Words said in anger can be lodged in our loved ones' hearts for a long time.

But what if we do respond in anger, or we finally acquiesce to their begging? There is no need to worry. Our child will give us many opportunities to try again, to do it the way we intend, with firmness and kindness. *If we establish "firm and kind" as the standard reply to discipline issues, this is what will be planted in their hearts.* The occasional flare of anger can be rectified with a heartfelt apology and a hug. Our children are generous and forgiving. They love us more than we can imagine.

Love Is the Reason

If your child asks "But *why?*" when you have made a decision he doesn't like, you can tell him, very simply, your reason. The bottom line, though, and the reason that is most understandable at a deep level, is, "Because I love you, and it is my job to choose the best for you." Sometimes, as your child develops a little reasoning ability, he will want to show you how your thoughts are faulty, or why his way is best. Sometimes, in fact, he may have a point, so make a mental note for future reference. It remains best for consistency's sake, though, to proceed with your original plan and say, "We'll think about that for next time." You can begin to practice making your replies to requests very *slowly.* You can nod and smile, saying, "Hmm, I wonder what that would be like...." This gives you time to think things through, which is tremendously helpful now and will be critical for parenting an adolescent later. To any argument that may ensue, remember that the reason at the bottom of it all is, "Because I love you." Although you may not say it every time, love's presence will be evident. *Keep love as the touchstone on the path of discipline.*

It is also important to affirm our child's emotional response to our decisions. We can say, "I can see how you would feel disappointed by my decision," or "I know this makes you sad." The end of the sentence is a reaffirmation of your decision. "I know how much you wish you could play all day. But I'll help you put away the toys for nap time." Affirming their emotional state doesn't need to affect the final decision. It simply says to your child that you recognize his process, and you empathize with him.

When we establish steady boundaries and uphold them with kind firmness, when we respond with action, when we recognize our child's emotional responses, we give him a strong foundation to grow upon. This gives him an innate sense of security. His world is stable; it is sound and founded on love. He can relax and simply be a little child in the magic and wonder of a protected world.

When, on the other hand, we are not willing to create a sturdy container, when we are indecisive and vacillate with our child's whims, we create an unstable atmosphere in which our child can easily become insecure. The world is large and complex. Our children have a short period of time to grow and mature in a protected, well-established environment. Soon enough they will need to face the work of discernment and decision-making. We can best prepare them for this future by offering them ourselves as models of steady, conscientious adults, capable of clear vision and right action. If we are willing to do the work that adulthood requires, we give him the gift of a true childhood.

> **It's Never Too Late to Begin**
>
> *Say it with a period at the end of the sentence.*
>
> *Actions speak louder than words.*
>
> *Follow through consistently.*

It's NEVER Too Late to Begin

Perhaps you have spent several years negotiating, compromising, and making deals with your child, and are now living the result of that approach. Your child may seem insecure, or may be trying her hand at tyranny; perhaps she doesn't sleep well, or has begun to whine. Don't despair; it is never too late to begin. Just begin anew, today, with the first opportunity you are given. Smile, and insist on whatever it is, with confidence and good will. "Now it's time to put our toys away, honey. Here, let me help." Say it with a cheerful period at the end of the sentence. Today, most parents make a statement, and then negate it with the typical question mark, "okay?" Declarative sentences are the best approach. Actions speak louder than words, so follow through with action. If you are asking your child to do something, do it yourself as well, so she has someone to imitate. If she cannot join you through imitation, then a consequence may be necessary. Usually you will need to enforce small consequences only a few times. Your child will learn quickly that your word is good, that whatever you say will happen. She may need to push the boundary a little at first, just to be sure. Once certainty is established, though, she can relax into her natural innocence and trust.

If your child is older, seven and up, you may need to work at this a little more. He may push the boundary harder, in order to really experience how this new method works. He may question you about your changed approach. Even for a grade-school child, long theoretical explanations are unnecessary and can confuse the issue. Simple affirmations that yes, his perceptions are correct, and yes, we are doing things differently now, because we love you, will usually suffice until the new way becomes old. Especially with an older child, remember to recognize your child's emotional reactions. "I know you'd rather negotiate with Mom and me, but we've already talked about this and have decided." He may reply, "Well, I didn't get to tell you all the reasons! Besides, Billy gets to go!" Now is the moment to say, "This must make you mad." Who knows what his response may be? A nod of the head? Or maybe the real emotion will arise—for example, maybe he doesn't care so much to go, but is afraid that Billy will laugh at him if he misses the event.

Remember that it is better, during these early years, to be consistent than perfect. If you have decided something, and midway you realize it

> ### THREE ESSENTIALS IN NEGOTIATING CHILDREN'S QUARRELS
>
> *1) Use the same tone of voice you use for "Here's the towel."*
>
> *2) Rarely is there a true "victim" or "aggressor," it takes two to tango.*
>
> *3) Use few words with great skill.*

could have been improved upon, just slowly and consistently proceed as planned, until you are finished. Keep your new insight for the next time. In this way you can relax and enjoy, knowing that there is plenty of time for all the fine-tuning parenting requires. Acting with confidence gives our children not only a model of competence, but also the palpable experience that they are in capable and loving hands. *Our* uncertainty and insecurity creates the same in them. When we grow confident in our role as the decision maker, our child will know that whatever comes, we will, with love and kindness, make the best choice possible, and that we will listen to her disagreement without being swayed by it. You *can* do this! And in the end your young child will thank you by growing into her natural trusting, willing and innocent self.

Children's Quarrels

Parents are often advised to stay out of children's quarrels. I believe this advice has emerged because it is difficult for parents to remain neutral when their children are fighting. When our children's emotions run high, it is typical for us to respond with emotion, also. Indeed, if we cannot come to emotional neutrality, this is sound advice.

But I would offer an alternative. It will require us to take our own emotions in hand and work with ourselves, not only to model justice, but also to shed light on human dynamics and creative problem-solving at an early age. Our young children lack the skills necessary to come to equitable resolutions, and we can, with simplicity and clarity, *show them*, not tell them, the way. We can begin to work this way with our children when they are as young as three years old, depending on maturity and verbal skills.

There are three essential elements to remember. 1) Use the same tone of voice you use for "Here's the towel"—simple, informative, clear. 2) Rarely is there a true "victim" and an "aggressor." There are two sides to every disagreement, and you need to know both. 3) Keep it simple. A few words used skillfully are far more effective than the best lecture on justice and equity.

When one of your children comes to you with a complaint about the other, take a long breath, breathe out, and then call the other child to you. With both of them standing in front of you, ask the complainer to repeat the complaint. The complainee will probably interrupt midway with his perspective. Stop him, and tell him it will be his turn in a minute. When the complainer is finished, ask the complainee what happened, and listen. This teaches both of them to *listen*, and when they are older, they will know by experience that there really *is* a valid perspective other than their own. When you have heard both, then you will have a clearer idea of how to proceed. A conversation may look something like this:

Molly: "Daddy! Sean pushed me!"

Daddy: "Sean, come here."

Sean comes.

Daddy: "Say it again, Molly."

Molly: "Sean pushed me."

Daddy: "Sean, why does Molly say you pushed her?"

Sean: "Yeah, well, she knocked over my castle!"

Daddy: "What happened, Molly?"

Molly: "I was just going to use the ladder for my fire truck."

Daddy: "So you took the ladder without asking?"

Molly: "I *did* ask!"

Daddy: "What did Sean say?"

Molly: "He said NO! So I had to grab it."

Sean: "Then she fell on top of my castle!"

Daddy: "And you pushed her?"

Sean nods.

Daddy: "Molly, Sean pushed you because you took his ladder even when he said you couldn't. We need to listen to what people say. We get in trouble when we don't. Next time, ask Sean when it will be your turn.

"Sean, we don't push people in this family, no matter what. Use your words. Ask Molly to help you build your castle again. If that doesn't work, you can come to me for help.

"Molly, say 'sorry' for grabbing Sean's ladder. Sean, say 'sorry' for pushing."

When we went through this process at our home, usually by the "sorries" my boys were twinkling at each other, ready to run off and play again. Sometimes if they returned to their play and still could not play well together, I would ask them to play alone in their rooms for a while. This usually did the trick. After a few minutes of regrouping and collecting themselves alone, they were begging to play together again.

> WHEN THEY COME TO US FOR HELP WITH PROBLEM-SOLVING
>
> *First listen carefully to both sides of the story.*
>
> *Help them see how the problem arose, step by step.*
>
> *Show them a positive alternative.*
>
> *Repeat this pattern each time.*
>
> *Soon they will incorporate it.*

This brings up the question of saying "sorry." I believe that, even if there is a residue of anger, saying a conciliatory word to each other actually helps the energy move more quickly toward resolution. Sometimes one of my boys would not be able to say "sorry," and I would tell the other, "He can't say 'sorry' now, because he's still mad, but he'll feel better later." I know this is a controversial subject, and each family needs to find its own way toward conciliation when sibling quarrels occur. "Sorry" is simple, direct, short, easy, and follows societal norms. If we don't demand it, but ask for it and model it, it can become a stepping-stone on the road toward mutual conciliation.

Sometimes children quarrel in the middle of a terrific game, and come to us to help resolve the problem. They are looking for resolution so the game can continue. This is not the time to probe deeply into our child's emotions. More often than not, for a young child feelings are like squalls at sea. They come quickly, their fury is intense, and then they pass, leaving a blue horizon. Naming the feeling is a healthy response. "Do you wish you had a doll just like Annie's?" It gives permission for her to feel it, and allows it to pass in its natural short duration. Later, when our children are grade-school age, a deeper exploration becomes important. For now, though, naming it is usually sufficient. If a little more is called for, we can simply *be* with our child until the energy of the emotion is spent and the child is ready to jump back into play. Although her emotions may be variable, the great ocean of play is eternal!

The predicament of Molly and Sean, above, is an example of a simple problem. First we listen. Then we lay the problem out, step by step, so they can see how the problem arose and can see where their behavior brought about a negative result. Then we show them what a positive alternative would have been. If we repeat this process each time they ask for help, in time they will incorporate the more positive actions.

Another way we can help is to offer new perspectives for sticky dilemmas. When our children cannot decide together the way a game should proceed, and are squabbling, we can offer new ideas: "Tommy wants to be a dog, and I want to fly the spaceship!" they say. Our reply can be something like, "The spaceship really needs a guard dog!" Usually when we offer a solution one of two things happens: either the idea is adopted wholesale, and off they go, or it is rejected wholesale because a new, better idea has occurred to one

Usually a young child's emotions are like squalls at sea. They come quickly, their fury is intense, and then they pass, leaving a blue horizon.

of them. The incredibly rich creative force of imaginative play is usually compelling enough that our children are very committed to move through difficulties quickly, in order that the play may go on.

What about Hitting?

If hitting persists after we have repeatedly affirmed to our child that under no circumstance is hitting allowed in our family, then we need to enforce stronger measures. We can put a rule into place, across the board, that "If we hit, we go to our rooms." We have to be prepared to follow through every time, but we first need to go through the whole process above, listening to both sides of the whole story. Usually there is a very good reason why the "victim" got hit. Then we verbally state, *every* time, "People who hit others go to their rooms." We say it in the same tone of voice as though we were saying, "People who touch the stove get burned." This is just a reaffirmation of information. We need to send the little instigator, the victim, to his room, too. This shows the children that we have heard the whole story and are not just siding with the apparent underdog. Very, very rarely will a child get hit with absolutely no collaboration with the hitter. If you think this is the case, you probably have not gotten to the bottom of the story just yet. Usually the internal drive to play will soon override any residual anger, and they will be begging to play together again. And remember, no more minutes in time-out than years of their age.

If you listen carefully, remain unemotional, and consistently offer reasonable consequences to both parties, you can probably avoid the trap of being lied to, either by the "victim" or by the "aggressor." If you come to a situation in which the sides of the story don't match up, and you really can't tell what happened, then they can both go off to their rooms with the statement, "I can't tell what happened, so both of you need some time alone." Because you consistently remain unswayed by their emotion, and with fairness to all parties, offer good alternatives as well as small consequences, your children will trust you. Eventually, "the truth will out."

As with the arbitration of all children's quarrels, the success of this method stands on your own inner quiet. Although much more difficult, this is not different from teaching your child how to set the table. You say

---

Is Hitting a Problem?

Enforce a rule, across the board: "If we hit, we go to our room!" Follow through every time.

Find out what preceded the blow. Most often, the "victim" has done something that justifies time alone in her room, too. Remember the "minutes to years" ratio.

The internal drive to play is strong. Soon, they will be begging to play together again!

each time, "Put the cup above the plate, honey." And you continue to show her how, until it becomes internalized. When we consistently model open listening and fair, compassionate justice, our children will internalize this as well.

BLENDED FAMILIES

As with all structures in our society, the shape of the family is changing rapidly. This is a tremendously challenging time for families, as we struggle to keep the ties of love intact. As we know, there is little support from the larger culture. With all of the difficulties these times present to us, *love can and will prevail* if we give ourselves unstintingly to the task, every day, in all the small and large ventures that family life entails.

When we put together the lives of two full, complete adult people, and then we add several children, all with varying temperaments, needs, strengths and weaknesses, we have a complex system to operate within. When we double the ingredients—add two households, two sets of values, either a smaller or greater amount of emotional stress, and different places in the sibling order depending on the day of the week—we have a *very* complex system! How can we manage such complexity, in a life filled with ever greater career demands, financial intricacy and generalized pressure? This is a huge question, and we can only accomplish the task piece by piece, *with love as our guide, our strength and our respite.*

It is a piece of ancient wisdom that the child grows within the subtle atmosphere that exists between the parents. No matter what the new shape of our twenty-first-century families, this basic tenet remains true. Even if we do not live our lives with our child's other parent, the atmosphere that exists between us will affect the well-being of our child. Knowing this gives us a very big incentive to process through our own emotions, to work toward clarity, and to keep the channels of communication open.

In the best of all possible worlds, when two families raise the same children, we would be able, as adults, to sit down and discuss the various elements of family life and come to some general agreements on basic principles, like bedtimes, types of food, age-appropriate activities and so

---

BLENDED FAMILY RULES TO LIVE BY

Never talk badly about your child's other parent, if the child is close by—no matter what!

Talk to your ex-spouse directly; do not send messages through your child.

Arrange the weekly schedule in large blocks of time, to minimize transition times.

Keep this schedule absolutely firm, barring emergencies.

Seek professional family counseling, if necessary.

forth. This is always a goal to strive toward, and sometimes we can manage it. The heartfelt intention toward agreement, whether we achieve it or not, will benefit our children on a subtle level. What if we can't agree, and there is great difficulty between us? This is the moment to get help! There are professionals whose lives are given to helping families of every persuasion find peace together.

My own children were raised in a blended family, and I have talked with many, many parents raising children in a blended family. There are several fundamental rules of life in the blended family that lay a foundation for everything you do. 1) Do not talk badly about your child's other parent while your child is anywhere in the house, maybe even the yard—no matter what. 2) Talk to your ex-spouse directly; do not send messages through your child. 3) When arranging their weekly schedule, create large blocks of time, such as Sunday through Wednesday morning with Dad, and Wednesday afternoon through Saturday with Mom. 4) Keep this schedule absolutely firm, barring emergencies. 5) Get professional family counseling if dynamics become more challenging than you can manage.

As with the creation of all of family culture, we are working with both inner conviction and outer manifestation. The bedrock of love upon which we stand, is the inner foundation. And the outer principle is how we manifest this love.

One way we can manifest our love is by looking carefully at our children's schedules. Within the blended family, we will want to keep the time spent in transition to a minimum. Transitions are always a time filled with challenge and promise, and the time our children spend adjusting and re-adjusting to the different "family climates" is a reality that must be dealt with. Again, giving our children large blocks of the week with each parent will reduce the amount of time lost to transition. We can learn our child's pattern as she moves through the transition, and can perhaps find small release valves to help keep the energy flowing. A good transition for nearly any child is to plan a walk, a time in the park, or some other nature activity as soon as possible, when she has returned home to us. Time in nature helps to harmonize emotions and to sharpen mental acuity, and positively affects overall health. So when your child arrives back home cranky or mad, put on your coats, or sunblock and sun hats, and go outside!

EXPECT A MIRACLE

And work unstintingly toward it.

You will also want to keep the weekly schedule as sacrosanct. Not only does your child's emotional stability depend on a regular, predictable schedule, but even cognitive functioning is dependent on predictability. Especially for your young child, in whom the cognitive function of sequencing is just forming, a regular, fixed weekly schedule is critical. Sequencing underlies nearly all language and reading capacity. So save schedule changes for emergencies.

Sibling relationships are richly textured palettes filled with possibility. The quality of these relationships is determined to a large degree by our parenting abilities. Step-sibling relationships are even more complex, filled with more emotional material, but also bright with possibility. We may well need help learning how to find the way into the complex dynamics of parenting a stepchild. Never be shy to ask for professional help; never feel like a failure, or that this is something you should already know. We are just navigating these waters *consciously* for the first time in our society. So know when you need help, ask for it, and keep an open attitude.

Expect miracles! Our family was a miracle of tremendous love, emotional openness, and adult willingness to slog through all the discomfort of staying in communication with an ex-spouse, our partner's ex-spouse, our children, stepchildren, siblings, step siblings, our own spouses, counselors and ourselves. Amazingly, in the midst of all the complexity, our children remained innocent, carefree and filled with curiosity and delight. Yours can, too. Love carries the day. *Miracles happen!*

WHAT WILL YOUR FAMILY CULTURE BECOME?

This is an exciting question, one that you will carry all the many years you weave together the threads of your lives into the tapestry of Our Family. Although the question remains the same, the answer is an ever-changing, growing, dynamic living organism. Most of all, we want to *relax and enjoy* the answer as it unfolds day by day.

ENDNOTES

CHAPTER 1

1. Carla Hannaford, *Smart Moves: Why Learning Is Not All in Your Head* (Arlington, VA: Great Ocean Publishers, 1995), p. 54.

2. Ibid., p. 48.

3. Joseph Chilton Pearce, *The Biology of Transcendence: A Blueprint of the Human Spirit* (Rochester, VT: Park Street Press, 2002), p. 101.

4. Ibid., p. 100.

5. Ibid., p. 102.

6. Carla Hannaford, op. cit., p. 52.

7. Joseph Chilton Pearce, lecture given March 26, 2004 at the Nova Institute, Washington D.C. (from the research of Alan Shore).

8. Ibid.

9. Carla Hannaford, op. cit., p.167.

10. Pearce, *The Biology of Transcendence*, op. cit., p. 41.

11. Ibid.

12. Ibid., p. 43.

13. Joseph Chilton Pearce, *The Biology of Transcendence*, op. cit., pp. 102–103.

14. Carol Stock Kranowitz, *The Out-of-Sync Child: Recognizing and Coping with Sensory Integration Dysfunction* (New York: Perigree Book, 1998), p. 48.

15. Ibid., p. 12.

16. Carla Hannaford, op. cit., pp. 80–81.

17. Ibid., p. 100.

18. Ibid., p. 163.

19. Ibid.

20. Ibid., p. 104.

21. Brain Gym is a Registered Trademark of the Educational Kinesiology Foundation.

22. Carla Hannaford, op. cit., p. 160.

23. Brian Greene, *The Elegant Universe* (New York: Norton, 1999), p. 146.

24. Carla Hannaford, op. cit., p. 162.

25. Ibid., p. 162.

26. Ibid., p. 160.

27. Ibid., p. 160.

28. Carol Stock Kranowitz, op. cit., pp. 8–11.

29. Carla Hannaford, op. cit., p. 138.

30. Ibid., p. 151.

31. Ibid., p. 152.

32. Ibid., p. 27.

33. Ibid., p. 92.

34. Huston, Dunnerstein, Fairchild, et al., *Big World, Small Screen: The Role of Television in American Society* (Lincoln, NE: University of Nebraska Press, 1992).

35. Bushman and Anderson, "Media Violence and the American Public: Scientific Fact Versus Media Misinformation." *American Psychologist* 2001: 56(6/7): 477–489.

36. Jordan A. and E. Woodard, "Electronic Childhood: The Availability and Use of Household Media by 2- to 3-Year-Olds." *Zero to Three* 2001; 22(2): 4–9.

37. Carol Stock Kranowitz, op. cit., p. 227.

38. L. Rowell Huesmann and Leonard D. Eron, *Television and the Aggressive Child* (Hillsdale, NJ: Erlbaum, 1986), p. 65.

39. Mary G. Burke, "The Influence of Television and Visual Electronic Media on Brain Development." *Brown University Child and Adolescent Behavior Letter*, July 2003; 19(7). "Reviewing the Literature," point 3.

40. Ibid. "Reviewing the Literature," point 4.

41. Carla Hannaford, op. cit., p. 172.

42. Committee on Public Education, "Media Violence." *Journal of the American Academy of Pediatrics* Nov. 2001: 108 (5): 1222–1226.

43. National Association for the Education of the Young Child's position statement on media violence and children (1990).

44. Ibid.

45. L. Rowell Huesmann and Leonard D. Eron, op. cit., p. 65.

46. NAEYC, op. cit.

47. Mary G. Burke, op. cit.

48. Ibid.

CHAPTER 2

1   Darcy Thompson and Dimitri Christakis, "The Association between Television Viewing and Irregular Sleep Schedules among Children Less Than Three Years of Age." *Journal of the American Academy of Pediatrics* 116 (4): 851–856.

CHAPTER 4

1   Carla Hannaford, *Smart Moves: Why Learning Is Not All in Your Head* (Arlington, VA: Great Ocean Publishers, 1995), p. 30.

2   Ibid., p. 95.

CHAPTER 6

1   Bruno Bettelheim, *The Uses of Enchantment: The Meaning and Importance of Fairy Tales* (New York: Knopf, 1989), p. 7.

CHAPTER NOTES

CHAPTER ONE: HOW CHILDREN LEARN

BRAIN GYM INTERNATIONAL
  1575 Spinnaker Dr., Suite 204B
  Ventura, CA 93001 / (800) 356-2109 or (805) 658-7942
  www.braingymn.org / edukfd@earthlink.net

LA LECHE LEAGUE
  1400 Meacham Rd.
  Schaumburg, IL 60173-4808
  (847) 519-7730 / www.lalecheleague.org

INFORMED HOMEBIRTH / INFORMED BIRTH & PARENTING
  Founded by Rahima Baldwin Dancy
  PO Box 3675
  Ann Arbor, MI 48106-3675 / (313) 662-6851

CHAPTER TWO: THE WORLD OF RHYTHM

FOR NON-ELECTRIC TOOLS AND APPLIANCES:
  Lehman Hardware and Appliances
  888-438-5346 / www.lehmans.com / info@lehmans.com
  Serves the Mennonite community with non-electric household tools and
  appliances.

FOR NURSERY RHYMES FROM AROUND THE WORLD:
  Anne Scott. *The Laughing Baby: Remembering Nursery Rhymes and Reasons* (Bergin
  and Garvey, 1987).

STORIES FOR NAP TIME:
  Jill Barklem, *The Complete Brambly Hedge* (Picture Lions, 1999)
  Thornton Burgess, *Old Mother West Wind* (Henry Holt & Co., 2003)
  Laura Ingalls Wilder, The Little House on the Prairie Series (Harper Trophy,
  1994). Check the Bibliography for many more!

CHAPTER THREE: CELEBRATING FESTIVALS TOGETHER

APPLE CORER, PEELER, SLICER:
Williams Sonoma
(877) 812-6235

STORY OF TRANSFORMATION:
John Steptoe, *The Story of Jumping Mouse* (Harper Trophy, 1989)

SEASONAL CRAFTS FOR PARTIES:
Diana Carey, *Festivals, Family and Foods* (Floris Books, 1986)

MORE CRAFTS:
Stephanie Cooper, *The Children's Year* (Hawthorn Press, 1986)

Noncompetitive party games:
Jody Blosser, *Everybody Wins: Noncompetitive Party Games* (Sterling Publishing, 1997)

CHAPTER FOUR: INDOOR PLAY

INFORMATION ON HOW SOUND SHAPES US:
Spectrum Center, Inc.
4715 Cordell Avenue, 4th Floor
Bethesda, MD 20814
(301) 657-0988 / info@spectrumcenter.com

Spectrum Center
307 E. 53rd St., 4th floor
New York, NY 10022
(212) 223-2928 / info@spectrumcommunicationcenter.com
www.spectrumcenter.com

TOY MAKING:
Petra Berger, *Feltcraft* (Floris Books, 1994)

MOSQUITO NETTING ON A HOOP:
Bed, Bath and Beyond stores
Amazon.com: Pagoda Gazebo

CHAPTER FIVE: OUTDOOR PLAY

Check the Environment section of the Bibliography for inspiration about the great outdoors.

SMITH AND HAWKEN
(415) 383-2000 / www.smithandhawken.com
Carries composters, seeds, garden tools, children's tools.

BROOKSTONE HARD-TO-FIND TOOLS
(603) 924-9541 / www.brookstone.com/world.asp
Carries all kinds of tools and gadgets.

PLOW AND HEARTH
(800) 627-1712 / www.plowhearth.com
Carries garden tools, birdbaths, bird feeders, etc.

CHAPTER SIX: THE WONDER OF STORIES

Check the bibliography to find a great selection of picture books for small fry, and chapter books for five- to eight-year-olds.

FOR LANGUAGE DEVELOPMENT:
Kundry Willwerth, *Let's Dance and Sing: Story Games for Children* (Mercury Press, 1996)

CHAPTER SEVEN: ARTISTIC EXPERIENCE

Frank Wilson, *The Hand and How It Shapes the Brain, Language and Culture* (Pantheon Books, 1998)

FOR ALL ARTISTIC SUPPLIES:
Waldorf Market
916-863-7400 / www.waldorfmarket.com
Carries painting supplies, pottery, wooden toys, organic foods, clothing, etc.

WATERCOLOR PAINTING
Mercurius
4321 Anthony Ct. #5
Rocklin, CA 95677
916-625-9696 / www.mercurius-usa.com

Check the website for distributors.
> Paper: item #10310100 / 150 double-sized sheets
> Order with several friends, and paint together!
> Paints: 85043001 / carmine red
> 85043005 / lemon yellow
> 85043019 / cobalt blue; order the smallest jar.
> Paint brush: item #25528022 / called the "Kindergarten brush"
> Paint board: item #25920003 / fits large paper

Paper, Scissors, Stone
PO Box 428
Viroqua, WI 54665
608-675-3858 / www.waldorfsupplies.com
Carries all painting supplies, yarn, felt, flannel, craft supplies.

Beeswax Crayoning
Drawing Paper:
J.L. Hammett / 800-955-2200
item # 12002

Crayons:
Mercurius (above); check online for distributors
Item # 85034001 / A rainbow-hued mix of block crayons.
Item #85031000 / A good mix of stick crayons.
Item # 85035061 / A combination of stick and block.

Beeswax Modeling
Mercurius (above)
Item # 85052200 / A mix of twelve luminous colors.

Wool for Felting
West Earl Woolen Mill
130 Cocalico Creek Rd.
Ephrata, PA 17522
717-859-2241
Already cleaned and carded. Gather several friends, and order one bat together—it's a lot of wool!

Handheld Awl
Lehman Hardware and Appliance
PO Box 41
Kidron, OH 44636
888-438-5346 / 888-780-4975 (fax)

info@lehmans.com / www.lehmans.com
Serves the Mennonite community with non-electric household tools and
appliances for simple, self-sufficient living.

A very big thank you to Chery Sackett for the great play dough recipe!

CHAPTER EIGHT: OTHER TOPICS PARENTS WONDER ABOUT

ITCH-FREE WOOL CLOTHING:
Woolykids
866-966-5954 / www.woolykids.com

NON-IRRITATING SEAMS, ORGANIC COTTONS, AND LAYERS FOR GIRLS' PLAY:
Hanna Andersson
1010 NW Flanders
Portland, OR 97209
800-222-0544 / www.hannaandersson.com

HELPFUL BOOKS ON THE DEATH OF A PET:
Cynthia Rylant, *Dog Heaven* (Blue Sky Press, 1995) and *Cat Heaven* (Blue Sky
Press, 1997)

CHAPTER NINE: CREATING YOUR FAMILY CULTURE

For information about the intelligence of the heart:
HeartMath Institute
14700 West Park Ave.
Boulder Creek, CA 95006
831-338-8500 / www.heartmath.org / info@heartmath.org

Thanks to Joan Almon, friend, mentor, and former president of the
Waldorf Kindergarten Association, for her image of the young child's emotions as "squalls at sea!"

For further reading about creating family, check the bibliography's
Practical and Inspiring section.

ONLINE LIBRARY: www.waldorflibrary.org

Appendix

Crafts & Handwork

Acorn's Journey
4 Glenwood Avenue, Guelph, ON, NIH 4L2, Canada
(519) 837-0322 / (519) 837-2758 (fax) / acornsjrny@golden.net
Mail order catalog geared to meeting the needs of Waldorf-inspired home-schoolers. Books (curriculum, parenting resources, children's picture books), art and craft supplies, toys, instruments.

Aetna Felt Corporation
2401 W. Emaus Ave., Allentown, PA 18103
(610) 791-0900 / (610) 791-5791 (fax)
snyderk@aetnafelt.com / www.aetnafelt.com
Wool and wool blend felts, synthetic felts.

Bartlettyarns, Inc.
PO Box 36, Harmony, ME 04942-0036
(207) 683-2251 / www.bartlettyarns.com
100% wool knitting yarns and rovings, including four all-natural, undyed colors, and heathers, solids, tweeds, and Fisherman bulky.

Central Shippee, Inc.
46 Star Lake Road, Bloomingdale, NJ 07403
(800) 631-8968 / (973) 838-8273 (fax)
1felt@optonline.net / www.thefeltpeople.com
Felt in 100% wool and wool blends.

Chasselle, Inc.
9645 Gerwig Lane, Columbia, MD 21046
(301) 381-9611
Colored tissue paper and art supplies.

Del Mar, Knorr Beeswax Products, Inc.
14906 Via de la Valle, Del Mar, CA 95014
(800) 807-BEES / sprickett@knorrbeeswax.com
Sheets of colored beeswax, beeswax candles and ornaments from molds.

Dharma Trading Co.
PO Box 916, San Rafael, CA 94915
(800) 542-5227
Wools, roving, also cotton clothing for dyeing and textile supplies.

Earth Guild
37 Haywood Street, Asheville, NC 28801
(800) 327-8448
Supplies for spinning, weaving and dyeing, including natural dyes.

Fairmont Farm
Thomas Road #148, Rindge, NH 03461
(603) 899-5445
Fleece in lovely natural colors—white, gray, brown, black—from spinner's flock, for felting.

Mercurius
4321 Anthony Ct. #5, Rocklin, CA 95677
(919) 652-9696 / (919) 652-5221
info@mercurius-usa.com / www.mercurius-usa.com
Full range of supplies for Waldorf Schools.

Mountain Sunrise
279 Swanzey Lake Rd., West Swanzey, NH 03469
(603) 357-9622
Plant-dyed wool in the form of fleece, 100% wool felt and yarn.

Naturally Creative
PO Box 163, Sandpoint, ID 83864
Felt sewing and weaving kits.

Paper, Scissors, Stone
c/o Annette Park, PO Box 428, Viroqua, WI 54665
(608) 675-3858 / (608) 675-3868 (fax)
www.waldorfsupplies.com
Watercolor paints and paper, boards, colored pencils, yarns, wool/rayon felt, flannel, roving, craft supplies.

Sarah's Silks
131 Third Street, Windsor, CA 95492
(707) 836-0679
Silk in natural and low-impact dyes, rainbow silks. Wholesale to schools and stores.

Strauss and Company
> 1701 Inverness Avenue, Baltimore, MD 21230
> (800) 638-5555
> Cheesecloth wholesale.

Sureway Trading Enterprises
> 826 Pine Ave., Suites 5, Niagara Falls, NY 14301
> (716) 282-4887 / (716) 282-8211 (fax) / Surewaytdg@aol.com
> Variety of silks in white and colors.

The Arts and Crafts Materials Institute
> 100 Boylston Street, Suite 1050, Boston, MA 02116
> (617) 426-6400
> Information on nontoxic art supplies.

West Earl Woolen Mill
> 110 Cocalico Creek Road, Ephrata, PA 17522
> (717) 859-2241
> 100% Peruvian wool batting, wool roving.

Babies, Bodies, and Clothing

Babies in Balance
> www.BabiesinBalance.com / Gentle, natural and organic products for mama
> and child, including natural fiber dolls, toys, clothing, bedding and much
> more.

Comfy Bummy
> www.ComfyBummy.com / For all your cloth diapering needs, low prices and
> terrific customer service. Bummies, Kushies, Little Forest and more.

Danish Import Family Wear
> Tine Kejser, N. 1509 Wildwood Road, Lake Geneva, WI 53147
> (262) 249-0719 / (262) 249-0981 (fax)
> kejser@charter.net / www.elknet.net/kejser
> 100% Demeter wool, 100% mulberry silk, 100% bioRe cotton, undergar-
> ments for the entire family.

Diaper Safari
    www.diapersafari.com / Cloth diapering made easy. Huge selection of cloth
    diapers and accessories, nursing bras and natural skin care products.

Ecobaby Organics
    332 Coogan Way, El Cajon, CA 92020
    (800) 596-7450 / dottie@ecobaby.com / www.ecobaby.com
    Offers beds, bedding and sheets for adults and babies, as well as baby-specific
    items such as diapers, clothing, organic formula and more.

Mira
    43 Bradford Street, Concord, MA 01742
    (978) 369-8222 / www.miraorganics.com
    Distributor of Natura by Sidema of Switzerland. Demeter wool, biodynamic
    cotton, untreated silk for the whole family. Long johns, undershirts, sleep-
    wear, camisoles, briefs.

Morning Rose
    1628 Lawrence Street, Eugene, OR 97401
    (877) 686-8200 / www.childrenswoolens.com
    Woolen undergarments and other clothing for adults and children.

Natural Resources
    1307 Castro Street, San Francisco, CA 94114
    (415) 550-2611 / www.naturalresourcesonline.com
    Books and baby products, health-care products (Weleda).

Nordic Natural Woollens
    201 Price Rd., Salt Spring Island, BC, V8K 2E9, Canada
    (877) 858-9665 / www.nordicwoollens.com
    Ultrasoft 100% merino wool and silk undergarments for babies, children
    and adults. Completely natural. No additives, chemicals or dyes.

Nova Natural Toys and Crafts
    Ordering: 140 Webster Rd., Shelburne, VT 05482
    Store: 817 Chestnut Ridge Rd., Chestnut Ridge, NY 10977
    (877) 668-2111 / ted@novanatural.com / www.novanatural.com
    Products formerly available from Lilling—soft, all-natural woolens from
    organic merino wool for the whole family. Also cotton diapers and Eucalan
    woolwash.

Padraig Cottage Industries
> 1035 Shakespeare Avenue, North Vancouver, BC, V7K 1E9 Canada
> (800) 881-2848 / (604) 980-0557 (fax)
> Clothing from hand-dyed, hand-spun wool, handmade slippers for children and adults.

Saffron Rouge
> 1-866-FACE-CARE / www.SaffronRouge.com
> Organic and biodynamic skin care, cosmetics, and body care.

Steiner Storehouse
> 5915 SE Division Street, #2, Portland, OR 97206
> 503-777-1251 / www.steinerstorehouse.com
> Featuring anthroposophically inspired products: books, biodynamic food, Dr. Hauschka cosmetics, body care products, medicines.

The Apothecary
> 6 Red Schoolhouse Rd., Chestnut Ridge, NY 10977
> (845) 352-6156 / (845) 425 1088 (fax)
> Anthroposophical medicine and beauty products. Complete Weleda line, Dr. Hauschka products, books and gift items.

The Weston A. Price Foundation
> PMB 106-380, 4200 Wisconsin Ave., Washington, DC 20016
> (202) 333-HEAL / westonaprice@msn.com / www.westonaprice.org
> Provides vital nutrition information that helps children achieve optimum health. Free brochure containing *Dietary Guidelines* and *Truths about Nutrition.*

Vidar Goods
> PO Box 41, Faber, VA 22938
> (434) 263-8895 / (434) 263-8895 (fax) / vidargoods@earthlink.net
> Holistic and anthroposophic body care, art cards and prints, Ostheimer toys.

WALA Raphael Pharmacy
> 4003 Bridge St., Fair Oaks, CA 95628
> (916) 962-1099 / (916) 967-0510 (fax)
> Dr. Haushka skin care products and decorative cosmetics, high-quality herbal teas, anthroposophic books on medicine, WALA remedies.

Wee Bees Essential Baby Products
PO Box 712, Littleton, CO 80160-0712
(303) 794-0966
Diapers, diaper covers, training pants, etc.

Weleda, Inc.
175 Route 9W, Congers, NY 10920
(800) 241-1030 / www.weleda.com
Pharmacy for anthroposophic remedies and health-care products.

Woolykids
(866) 966-5954 / www.woolykids.com
Machine wash and tumble dry naturally cozy merino wool adventure and
playwear, shirts, pants, leggings, pullovers, hand-knits and baby clothes.

WOODWORKS

Catino and Co.
611 Mountain View Rd., Petaluma, CA 94952
Chairs, dollhouses, tables, hutches, cubbies made to order.

Community Playthings
359 Gibson Hill Rd., Chester, NY 10918
(800) 777-4244 / (800) 336-5948 (fax) / www.communityplaythings.com
Wooden furniture and toys and trikes for children, blocks, playstations.

Elves and Angels
PO Box 70, Wytopitlock, ME 04497-0070
(207) 456-7575 / (207) 456-7164 (fax) / elves@gwi.net
Beautifully handcrafted wooden toys, including kitchens, refrigerators, washing machine/dishwashers, playstands, castles, dollhouses, cribs, doll beds,
high chairs.

Scott Crumpton
6506 NW 136th Street, Gainesville, FL 32653
(352) 331-7993 / scc@naturetables.com / www.naturetables.com
Handmade nature tables, cradles, playstands, painting boards and drying
racks, one-legged stools, ornaments and painting supplies.

HOUSEHOLD AND ENVIRONMENT

Coop America
> 2100 Main Street, NW, Suite 403, Washington, DC 20036
> (202) 223-1881 / Ecologically sound and socially responsible products of all
> kinds, including composters.

Eco Design Co.
> 1365 Rufina Circle, Santa Fe, MN 87501
> (505) 438-3448 / Natural art supplies and household products.

Eco Source
> 9051 Mill Station Rd., Bldg. E, Sebastopol, CA 95472
> (707) 829-7957 / Housekeeping and other environmental supplies.

Edible Landscaping
> 361 Spirit Ridge Lane, Afton, VA 22920
> (434) 361-9134 / (434) 361-1916 (fax)
> el@estone.net / www.ediblelandscaping.com
> Potted, less-care fruiting plants sent year round. Mail order catalog available.

Lehman Hardware and Appliance
> PO Box 41, Kidron, OH 44636
> (888) 438-5346 / (888) 780-4975 (fax)
> info@lehmans.com / www.lehmans.com
> Serves the Mennonite community with non-electric household tools and
> appliances for simple, self-sufficient living.

Real Goods
> 966 Mazzoni St., Ukiah, CA 95482
> (800) 762-7325 / An interesting catalog with all kinds of products to pro-
> mote energy independence in one way or another, including composters.

Tomten Beeworks
> 46 Town Farm Rd., Ipswich, MA 01938
> (978) 356-5657 / tomten@prodigy.net / www.tomtenbeeworks.com
> 100% beeswax honey pots, candles, figurines, ornaments, window hangings.

Vermont Country Store
> PO Box 6999, Rutland, VT 05702
> (802) 362-2400 / Old fashioned, good quality household goods and clothing.

TOYS

A Real Doll
> PO Box 1044, Sebastopol, CA 95473
> Doll and toy kits, cotton knits, supplies.

Apple Garden
> PO Box 2666, Napa, CA 94558
> (800) 600-8291 / Handmade toys, books, kits, etc.

Back to Basics Toys
> (800) 353-5360
> Large selection of toys including craft supplies, dollhouses, games.

Creative Hands
> PO Box 2217, Eugene, OR 97402
> (541) 343-1562 / Natural fiber dolls, crafts, kits, books and materials.

Dollies & Co.
> 860 Inca Pkwy., Boulder, CO 80303
> (303) 499-2611 / Dolls, doll-making and supplies.

Elves and Angels
> PO Box 70. Wytopitlock, ME 04497-0070
> (207) 456-7575 / (207) 456-7164 (fax) / elves@gwi.net
> Beautifully handcrafted wooden toys, kitchens, refrigerators, washing machine/
> dishwashers, playstands, castles, dollhouses, cribs, doll beds, high chairs.

Family Pastimes
> RR4, Pert, ON, K7H 3C6, Canada
> (613) 267-4819 / (613) 264-0696 (fax)
> fp@superaje.com / www.familypastimes.com
> Cooperative board games for all ages and all situations.

Magic Cabin Doll
> PO Box 64, Viroqua, WI 54665
> (608) 637-2735 / Dolls, toys, props for play.

Marvelous Toy Works
> RR1, Box 124A, Stillwater, PA 17878
> (707) 925-5708 / Wooden cars, wagons, rocking horses, toys and games.

Nova Natural Toys and Crafts
Ordering: 140 Webster Rd, Shelburne, VT 05482
Store: 817 Chestnut Ridge Rd., Chestnut Ridge, NY 10977
(877) 668-2111 / ted@novanatural.com / www.novanatural.com
Dolls, toys, games, art supplies and wholesale supplies for kindergartens.

Sarah's Silks
8591 Trenton Rd., Forestville, CA 95436
(707) 887-1295 / mlee@sonic.net
Silk playcloths, silk dress-ups, silk baby blankets. Wholesale only to school stores. $100 minimum.

The Ark
4413 Marble Way, Carmichael, CA 95608
(800) 743-7007 / Sets of natural building blocks, art supplies, beeswax, crayons, quality wooden toys and books

Waldorf Market
(916) 863-7400 / www.waldorfmarket.com
First online marketplace dedicated to supporting the international Waldorf education community. Paintings, pottery, wooden toys, organic foods, musical instruments, clothing, etc.

Weir Dolls
2909 Pakridge Dr., Ann Arbor, MI 48103
(734) 668-6992 / (734) 668-9320 (fax)
info@weirdolls.com / www.weirdolls.com
Waldorf dolls, doll-making kits, patterns, handworking supplies, knitted gnomes and kits.

GINGERBREAD DOLL PATTERN

MATERIALS YOU WILL NEED:

Felt *(sizes are approximate)*
One 9x9 for doll body
One 8x4 for tunic or 4x4 for apron
One 5x4 for hat
One long strip for boy's belt
Small scraps for flower appliqué
Sewing thread
Embroidery thread
Embroidery needle
Scissors
Square of cotton knit (6x6) for head
Wool batting

PATTERN PIECES: SEE FOLLOWING PAGES

DIRECTIONS

Cut out the pattern pieces and pin them to the appropriate felt pieces. Then cut the felt pieces, noting where necessary to cut two.

Doll body: Pin the two pieces of the body together and stitch around the edges of the doll body with the embroidery thread, leaving one edge open where indicated. You may want to use a decorative edging stitch for this process. Stuff the body with the wool batting, making sure to get the batting down into the legs and arms. When you've stuffed as much as possible, and the body is rounded and not lumpy, then continue stitching up to the neck. Finish stuffing to the neck opening.

Head: Take a handful of batting and wad it up into a *very tight* ball. Lay the cotton knit in your open hand and place the wool "ball" into the center. Pull the corners of the knit together *very tightly*, making a "sack." Then turn the sack upside down and measure it against the doll body. *(Please note that the finished head should measure one-third the size of the doll body, or twenty-five percent of the completed doll.)* Add or subtract batting as necessary.

You want a very hard, tightly stuffed head. When you've acquired the correct head size, then wrap sewing thread tightly around the cotton knit, at the "neck." Tie a knot in the thread. Trim the excess fabric and stuff the raw edges of the knit fabric inside the opening at the top of the doll body.

Stitch the head onto the felt body at the very top of the neck, using embroidery thread. Make sure to stitch **above** the area where the thread is wrapped around the cotton knit to avoid having the head droop. Stitch **through** the neck, front to back, rather than around in a circle. This technique will also keep the finished head from drooping.

Boy's tunic: Slip the tunic over the head and stitch it onto the body of the doll. If it's tight, you can cut a small slit in the front of the neckline. Align the tunic so that the front and back are even.

Boy's belt: Cut a long narrow strip of felt, and wrap around doll's body and tunic, pulling them in to create a *slight* tension, and overlap the ends in the front. With regular sewing thread, stitch several passes through the doll, front to back, attaching the belt securely in place.

Boy's hat: With embroidery thread, stitch two sides of the hat as indicated on the pattern piece, using the same edging stitch that was used on the doll body. Position the hat over the head so that the back rests on the neck. Tack the hat in place with a few hidden stitches at the back of the neck and again at the side or front where necessary to keep it from flopping. Tuck carded wool under cap, to create hair, and stitch in place.

Girl's apron: *Appliqué*—from felt scraps, cut the flower & leaf pattern, or exercise your creativity and come up with your own design! Adorn the front of the apron with this design, either tacking with a hidden stitch from beneath or using a decorative stitch on the front side and edges of your design. *Apron*—then stitch the apron to the doll body, again by tacking with a hidden stitch from beneath or using a decorative stitch around the edge.

Girl's hat: Sew a running stitch about 1" inside the edge of the hat. Pull to slightly gather, making the hat three-dimensional. Then knot the ends of the thread. This forms the dome of the hat and gives a ruffled effect to the brim. Position the hat over the doll's head and stitch it in place from underneath, following the line of the running stitch.

Hair: Tuck small tufts of the raw wool up against the inside of the hat where it meets the doll's head. Tack in place with a few hidden stitches.

Congratulations! Your gingerbread doll is complete. Enjoy the fruits of your creativity.

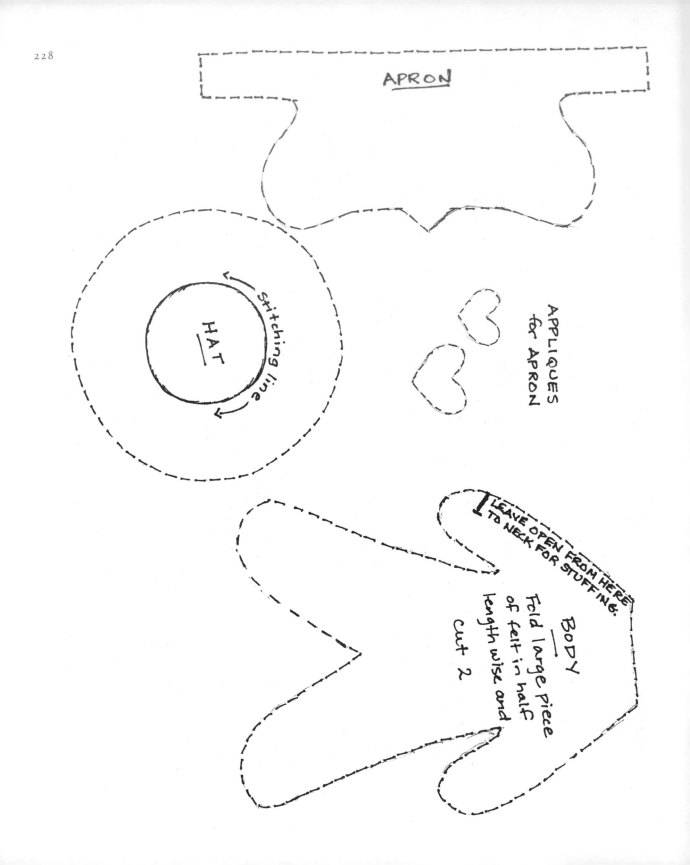

APRON

Stitching line

HAT

APPLIQUES
for APRON

LEAVE OPEN FROM HERE
TO NECK FOR STUFFING.

BODY
Fold large piece
of felt in half
lengthwise and
cut 2

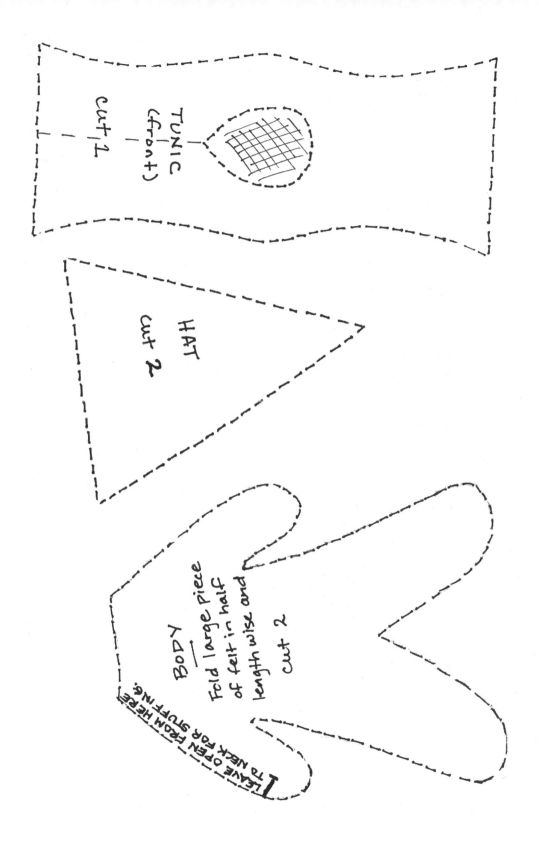

229

TUNIC
(front)

Cut 1

HAT
cut 2

Body
Fold large piece
of felt in half
lengthwise and
cut 2

LEAVE OPEN FROM HERE
TO NECK FOR STUFFING.

1. BOOKS FOR CHILDREN

3–6 YEARS (PICTURE BOOKS)

Aardeman, Verna. *Bringing the Rain to Kapiti Plain*. Dial Press.

Beskow, Elsa. *Around the Year*. Floris Books.

———. *Children of the Harvest*. Floris Books.

———. *Christopher's Harvest Time*. Floris Books.

———. *Flowers' Festival*. Floris Books.

———. *Pelle's New Suit*. Floris Books.

Capek, Jindra. *A Child Is Born*. Floris Books.

———. *The Star-Child. A Fable by Oscar Wilde*. Floris Books.

Carlstrom, Nancy White. *Wild Sunflower Child Anna*. Macmillan Publishing Co.

Ets, Marie Hall. *Gilberto and the Wind*. Viking Press.

Frost, Robert. *Stopping by Woods on a Snowy Evening*. Holt, Rinehart & Winston.

Gibbons, Gail. *The Seasons of Arnold's Apple Tree*. Harcourt Brace.

Hasler, Eveline. *Winter Magic*. William Morrow & Co.

Koopmans, Loek. *Any Room for Me?* Floris Books.

Kroll, Linda. *Winter, Awake!* Bell Pond Books.

Lindberg, Reeve. *Johnny Appleseed*. Little, Brown & Co.

———. *The Midnight Farm*. Dial Books.

Lindgren, Astrid. *The Tomten*. Coward-McMann, Inc.

———. *The Tomten and the Fox*. Floris Books.

Locker, Thomas. *Where the River Begins*. Dial Books.

Müller, Gerda. Board book series: *Spring. Summer. Autumn. Winter*. Floris Books.

Müller, Marina. *Pico the Gnome*. Floris Books.

Pearson, Susan. *My Favorite Time of Year*. Harper & Row.

Provensen, Alice and Martin. *The Year at Maple Hill Farm*. Atheneum.

Rockwell, Anne. *Apples and Pumpkins*. Macmillan Publishing Co.

———. *My Spring Robin*. Macmillan Publishing Co.

Rockwell, Anne and Harlow. *The First Snowfall*. Macmillan Publishing Co.

Romanova, Natalia. *Once There Was a Tree*. Dial Books.

Rosenstein, Richard. *Little Boy and Little Cat*. Floris Books.

Ryder, Joanne. *Chipmunk Song*. E.P. Dutton.

Rylant, Cynthia. *The Year's Garden*. Macmillan Publishing Co.

Serfazo, Mary. *Rain Talk*. Margaret K. McElderry Books.

Showers, Paul. *The Listening Walk*. HarperCollins Publishers.

Soya, Kiyoshi. *A House of Leaves*. Philomel Books.

Streit, Jakob. *Liputto. Stories of Gnomes and Trolls*. AWSNA.

Titherington, Jeanne. *Pumpkin Pumpkin*. Scholastic Inc.

Turner, Charles. *The Turtle and the Moon*. Dutton Children's Books.

Udry, Janice May. *A Tree Is Nice.* HarperCollins.

Van Dort, Evelien. *The Chicken Who Wanted to Fly.* Floris Books.

Van Hichtum, Nienke. *The Apple Creek.* Floris Books.

Visconti, Guido. *The Scarecrow Who Wanted a Hug.* Floris Books.

Von Olfers, Sibylle. *The Princess in the Forest.* Floris Books.

———. Sibylle. *The Story of the Root Children.* Floris Books.

Wagner-Koch, Elisabeth. *Snow White & the Seven Dwarfs.* Temple Lodge.

Wildsmith, Brian. *Squirrels.* Oxford University Press.

Yolen, Jane. *Owl Moon.* Philomel Books.

Zagwyn, Deborah Turney. *The Pumpkin Blanket.* Celestial Arts.

5–9 YEARS

Alexander, Sibylle. *Told by the Peat Fire.* Hawthorn Press.

Archipova, Anastasiya. *Favourite Grimm's Tales.* Floris Books.

———. *Favourite Tales from Hans Christian Andersen.* Floris Books.

Berger, Thomas. *The Little Troll.* Floris Books.

Cohn, Diana. *Mr. Goethe's Garden.* Bell Pond Books.

Colum, Padraic. *Myths of the World.* Floris Books.

———. *The King of Ireland's Son. An Irish Folk Tale.* Floris Books.

Copple, Rudolf. *To Grow and Become. Stories for Children.* Association of Waldorf Schools of North America.

Dunlop, Eileen. *A Royal Ring of Gold. Stories from the Life of Mungo.* Floris Books.

Lagerlöf, Selma. *The Emperor's Vision & Other Christ Legends.* Floris Books.

———. *The Wonderful Adventures of Nils.* Floris Books.

Large, Judy. *Troll of Tree Hill.* Hawthorn Press.

Lobato, Arcadio. *The Valley of Mist.* Floris Books.

Locker, Thomas. *In Blue Mountains. An Artist's Return to America's First Wilderness.* Bell Pond Books.

Masters, Brien. *Patter-Paws the Fox.* Temple Lodge.

———. *Trumpets of Happiness & Other Stories.* Temple Lodge.

Moore, C.J. *Peter William Butterblow and Other Little Folk.* Floris Books.

Müller, Martina. *Sleeping Beauty.* Floris Books.

Sehlin, Gunhild. *Mary's Little Donkey.* Floris Books.

Streit, Jakob. *Liputto. Stories of Gnomes and Trolls.* Association of Waldorf Schools of North America.

Verschuren, I., ed. *The Christmas Story Book.* Floris Books.

Visconti, Guido. *The Enchanted Kingdom.* Floris Books.

Wilde, Oscar. *The Selfish Giant.* Floris Books.

Wilkeshuis, Cornelius. *The Gift for the Child.* Floris Books.

Wyatt, Isabel. *The Book of Fairy Princes.* Floris Books.

———. *King Beetle-Tamer and Other Lighthearted Wonder Tales.* Floris Books.

———. *The Seven-Year-Old Wonder Book.* Floris Books.

———. *Thorkill of Iceland. Viking Hero Tales.* Floris Books.

Young, Ella. *Celtic Wonder Tales & Other Stories.* Floris Books.

2. SING WITH YOUNG CHILDREN

Songbooks from Mary Thienes-Schunemann and Naturally You Can Sing Productions:

Lavender Blue, Dilly, Dilly

Sing a Song of Seasons

Sing a Song with Baby

The Christmas Star

The Wonder of Lullabies

This is the Way We Wash-a-Day

3. PRACTICAL AND INSPIRING BOOKS FOR PARENTS

PUBLISHERS AND DISTRIBUTORS:

AWSNA = Association of Waldorf Schools of North America, (916) 961-0927, email: awsna@awsn.org, web site: www.awsna.org

SB = SteinerBooks, (703) 661-1594, email: service@steinerbooks.org, web site: www.steinerbooks.org

HP = Hawthorne Press, I Lansdown Lane, Lansdown, Stroud, Gios, GL5 IBJ, England

MP = Mercury Press, (845) 425-9357

RSC = Rudolf Steiner College Bookstore, (916) 961-8729, email: Bookstore@steinercollege.edu, web site: www.steinercollege.edu

WECAN = Waldorf Early Childhood Association, (845) 352-1690, email: info@waldorfearlychildhood.org, web site: www.waldorfearlychildhood.org

~

Baldwin, Rahima. *You Are Your Child's First Teacher.* SB and RSC.

Barz, Brigitte. *Festivals with Children.* Gryphon House.

Berger, Thomas. *The Christmas Craft Book.* RSC.

———. *The Harvest Craft Book.* SB and RSC.

Berger, Thomas and Petra. *The Easter Craft Book.* SB and RSC.

Blythe, Sally Goodward. *The Well Balanced Child: Movement and Early Learning.* Hawthorn Press, Early Years Series.

Britz-Crecelius, Heidi. *Children at Play: A Preparation for Life.* Park St. Press.

Burton, Michael. *In the Light of a Child.* SB.

Carey, Diana and Judy Large. *Festivals, Family and Food.* SB and RSC.

———. *Celebrating Festivals Around the World.* SB.

Cooper, Stephanie et al. *The Children's Year.* SB and RSC.

Davy, Gudrun, and Bons Voors, eds. *Lifeways: Working with Family Questions,* SB and RSC.

Day, Christopher. *A Haven for Childhood: The Building of a Steiner Kindergarten.* SteinerBooks, 1998.

Druitt, Ann. *All Year Round.* SB.

Ellersiek, Wilma. *Giving Love-Bringing Joy.* WECAN.

Fallon, Sally. *Nourishing Traditions.* New Trends.

Finger Plays. (Fifty-two finger plays.) MP.

Fitzjohn, Sue, Weston, Minda, and Judy Large. *Festivals Together*, HP.

Foster, Nancy. The Acorn Hill anthologies. *Dancing as We Sing* and *Let Us Form a Ring*. Acorn Hill.

Glöckler, Michaela. *The Dignity of the Young Child: Care and Training for the First Three Years*, The Goetheanum.

————. *A Healing Education*. RSC.

Grahl, Ursula. *The Wisdom in Fairy Tales*.

Green, Marian. *A Calendar of Festivals, Traditional Celebrations, Songs, and Seasonal Recipes*. RSC.

Grunelius, Elizabeth. *Early Childhood Education and the Waldorf School Plan*. RSC.

Haller, I. *How Children Play*. SB.

Heckmann, Helle. *Nøkken: A Danish Waldorf Child Care*. WECAN.

Jaffke, Freya. *Feste im Kindergarten Elternhaus, Work and Play in Early Childhood*. SB.

————. *Toymaking with Children*. SB and RSC.

Kenison, Katrina. *Mitten Strings for God*. Warner Books.

Knierim, Julius. *Quintenlieder: Music for Young Children in the Mood of the Fifth*. RSC.

Köhler, Henning. *Working with Anxious, Nervous and Depressed Children*. AWSNA.

Lebret, Elisabeth. *Pentatonic Songs*. Waldorf School Association of Ontario.

Leenwen, M. van and J. Moeskops. *The Nature Corner*. SB and RSC.

Lenz, Friedel. *Celebrating the Festivals with Young Children*. SB.

Mellon, Nancy. *Storytelling and the Art of Imagination*. RSC.

Mitchell, David, ed. *Developmental Insights: Discussions between Doctors and Teachers*. AWSNA.

Müller, Rudolf. *Painting with Children*. SB and RSC.

Neuschutz, Karin. *The Doll Book: Soft Dolls and Creative Play*. Larson Publications.

Odent, Michel. *Rediscovering the Needs of Women during Pregnancy and Childbirth*. Clairview Books.

Oldfield, Lynne. *Free to Learn: Introducing Steiner Waldorf Early Childhood Education*. Hawthorne Press.

Patterson, Barbara and Bradley. *Beyond the Rainbow Bridge*. Michaelmas Press.

Peckham, Margaret. *Fairy Tales and Nature Stories*. RSC and MP.

Petrash, Carol. *Earthways: Simple Environmental Activities for Young Children*. Gryphon House.

Reinckens, Sunnhild. *Making Dolls*. SB.

Russ, Johanne. *Clump-a-Dump and Snickle-Snack: Pentatonic Children's Songs*. MP.

Scott, Ann. *The Laughing Baby: Remembering Nursery Rhymes and Reasons*. Bergin & Garrey.

Smith, Susan. *Echoes of a Dream: Artistic Activities for Young Children*. RSC.

Spock, Marjorie. *Fairy Worlds and Workers*. OP.

Strauss, Michaela. *Understanding Children's Drawings*. SB.

Tudor, Tasha. *A Time to Keep*. Simon and Schuster.

Waldorf Early Childhood Association. *Gateways*, the newsletter of the Waldorf Early Childhood Association.
Vol. 1: *An Overview of the Waldorf Kindergarten*.
Vol. 2: *A Deeper Understanding of the Waldorf Kindergarten*.

Willwerth, Kundry. *Let's Dance and Sing: Story Games for Children*, MP.

Wynstones Kindergarten. Collection of songs, stories and verses from the British kindergartens: *Summer, Autumn, Winter, Spring, Spindrift, Gateways*. Wynstones Press.

Zahligen, Bronja. *Plays for Puppets and Marionettes*. WECAN.

4. DEEPER READING

Aeppli, Willi. *The Care and Development of the Human Senses*. SB.

Buzzell, Keith. *The Children of Cyclops: Influences of Television Viewing on the Developing Human Brain*. AWSNA.

Complete Grimm's Fairy Tales, with introduction by Padraic Colum. Pantheon.

Elium, Don and Jeanne. *Raising a Son, Raising a Daughter*. SB.

———. *Raising a Family*. SB.

Elkind, David. *The Hurried Child: Growing Up Too Fast Too Soon*. Perseus Books.

———. *Miseducation: Preschoolers at Risk*. Knopf.

Gatto, John Taylor. *Dumbing Us Down: The Hidden Curriculum of Compulsory Schooling*. SB.

Gerber, Magda. *Your Self-Confident Baby*. Wiley.

———. *Dear Parent: Caring for Infants with Respect*. Resources for Infant Educarers.

Glas, Norbert. *Conception, Birth and Early Childhood*. SB.

Harwood, A.C. *The Recovery of Man in Childhood*. SB and RSC.

———. *The Way of the Child*. SB.

Healy, Jane. *Endangered Minds: Why Our Children Don't Think*. Simon and Schuster.

———. *Failure to Connect*. Simon and Schuster.

———. *Your Child's Growing Mind, A Guide to Learning*. Doubleday.

Heydebrand, Caroline von. *Childhood: A Study of the Growing Soul*. SB and RSC.

Hogan, Pat. *Alison's Gift*. Nosila Publishing.

Large, Martin. *Who's Bringing Them Up? Television and Child Development*. SB and RSC.

Mander, Jerry. *Four Arguments for the Elimination of Television*. RSC.

Murphy, Christine, ed. *The Vaccination Dilemma*. Lantern Books.

Pearce, Joseph Chilton. *The Bond of Power*. Dutton.

———. *The Crack in the Cosmic Egg*. Julian Press.

———. *Evolution's End: Claiming the Potential of Our Intelligence*. Harper Plough.

———. *The Magical Child*. Bantam.

———. *The Magical Child Matures*. Dutton.

Postman, Neal. *Amusing Ourselves to Death*. Viking Penguin.

Prokofieff, Sergei. *The Cycle of the Year as a Path of Initiation*. Temple Lodge.

Sanders, Barry. *A is for Ox: Violence, Electronic Media, and the Silencing of the Written Word*. Pantheon Books.

Schmidt-Brabant, Manfred. *The Spiritual Tasks of the Homemaker*. Temple Lodge.

Sing Through the Day and *Sing Through the Seasons* (800-521-8011).

Steiner, Rudolf. *The Calendar of the Soul*. SB.

———. *The Cycle of the Year as a Breathing Process of the Earth*. SB.

Talbott, Stephen. *The Future Does Not Compute*. RSC.

Uphoff, James et al. *Summer Children: Ready or Not for School.* J&J Publishing.

Winn, Marie. *Children Without Childhood.* Pantheon.

———. *The Plug-In Drug.* Penguin.

———. *Unplugging the Plug-In Drug.* Penguin.

5. THE ENVIRONMENT

The Art of Composting. Available free of charge from The Metropolitan Service District, 2000 S.W. 1st Ave., Portland, OR 97201.

Campbell, Student. *Let it Rot! The Home Gardener's Guide to Composting.* Garden Way Publishing.

Cornell, Joseph. *Sharing Nature with Children.* Dawn Publications.

Dadd, Debra L. *Nontoxic and Natural: How to Avoid Dangerous Everyday Products and Buy or Make Safe Ones.* Tarcher.

———. *The Nontoxic Home: Protecting Yourself and Your Family from Everyday Toxins and Health Hazards.* Tarcher.

———. *Nontoxic, Natural and Earthwise: How to Protect Yourself and Your Family from Harmful Products and Live in Harmony with the Earth.* Tarcher.

The Earth Works Group. *50 Simple Things Kids Can Do to Save the Earth.* Earthworks Press.

———. *50 Simple Things You Can Do to Save the Earth.* Earthworks Press.

Elkington, John, Hailes, Julia, and Joel Malkow. *The Green Consumer.* Penguin Books.

Foster, Catharine Osgood. *The Organic Gardener.* Random House.

MacEachern, Diane. *Save Our Planet: 750 Everyday Ways You Can Help Clean Up the Earth.* Dell Publishing.

Makower, Joel. *The Green Consumer Supermarket Guide: Brand Name Products that Don't Cost the Earth.* Penguin Books.

Minnick, Jerry and Marjorie Hunt et al. *The Rodale Guide to Composting.* Rodale Press.

Proctor, Nobel. *Garden Books: How to Attract Birds to Your Garden.* Rodale Press.

Rifkin, Jeremy. *The Green Lifestyle Handbook.* Henry Holt & Co.

Seymour, John and Herbert Girardet. *Blueprint for a Green Planet: Your Practical Guide to Restoring the World's Environment.* Prentice-Hall.

The Rodale Press, Inc., 33 East Minor Street, Emmanus, Pennsylvania 18049, is an excellent source for myriad books on all aspects of gardening organically, composting, etc.

About the Author

Sharifa Oppenheimer was the founding teacher of the Charlottesville Waldorf School, Virginia, where she taught kindergarten for twenty-one years and served as day care director of the early-childhood program. She has helped develop new teachers through teacher-training programs at Sunbridge College in New York State and at Rudolf Steiner College near Sacramento as a master teacher offering practicum and internship opportunities. She has written many articles on Waldorf education, helping the parents of her students create supportive home environments. Recently she initiated a home-based kindergarten program, The Rose Garden. Sharifa is the mother of three grown sons, who received Waldorf educations. She lives in an enchanted forest in Virginia.

PO Box 84
Batesville, VA 22924
(434) 823-7026
sharifao@cstone.net

About the Photographer

Stephanie Gross has viewed the world through a camera lens for nearly twenty-five years. A freelance photographer, she holds a bachelor's degree in fine arts from the Rhode Island School of Design. She lives on a farm in the foothills of Virginia's Blue Ridge Mountains with her husband Charles and her son Emmet, who spent two wonderful years in Sharifa's magical Rose Garden.